Evaluating Transition to School Programs

Transition to school represents a time of great change for all involved. Many transition to school programs have been developed to support positive transitions to school. While these programs have involved complex planning and implementation, often they have not been evaluated in rigorous or systematic ways. This book brings together Australian and international perspectives on research and practice to explore approaches to evaluating transition to school programs.

For children, school is quite different from anything else they have experienced. For families and educators, there are considerable changes as they interact with new people and take on new roles. Developing effective transition to school programs is a key policy initiative around the world, based on recognition of the importance of a positive start to school and the impact of this for future school engagement and outcomes. Throughout the chapters of this book, authors from Australia, Germany, Sweden, Ireland and Jamaica share examples of evaluation practice, with the aim of encouraging educators to reflect on their own contexts and adopt evaluation practices that are relevant and appropriate for them. The book brings together the fields of evaluation research and transition to school. A wide range of examples and figures is used to relate research and practice and to illustrate possible applications of evaluation strategies.

Evaluating Transition to School Programs highlights the importance of multiple perspectives of the transition to school and offers suggestions about how the perspectives of children, families, educators and community members might be included and analysed in evaluation strategies. Other themes throughout the book include the importance of collaboration, respectful and trusting relationships, practitioner-driven inquiry, strengths-based approaches and developing programs that are responsive to context. This book is written for educators and leaders in early years and primary school settings and will also be of interest to researchers, students and policy makers in the field.

Sue Dockett, Emeritus Professor, Charles Sturt University and Director, Peridot Education Pty Ltd.

Bob Perry, Emeritus Professor, Charles Sturt University and Director, Peridot Education Pty Ltd.

Evaluating Transition to School Programs
Learning from Research and Practice

Sue Dockett and Bob Perry

*with contributions from Helena Ackesjö,
Tess Boyle, Petra Büker, Mary Daly,
Derek Grant, Julia Höke, Mirja Kekeritz,
Anna Kilderry, Zoyah Kinkead-Clark,
Andrea Nolan, Jana Ogrodowski
and Sven Persson*

First published 2022
by Routledge
2 Park Square, Milton Park, Abingdon, Oxon OX14 4RN

and by Routledge
605 Third Avenue, New York, NY 10158

Routledge is an imprint of the Taylor & Francis Group, an informa business

© 2022 Sue Dockett and Bob Perry

The right of Sue Dockett and Bob Perry to be identified as authors of this work has been asserted by them in accordance with sections 77 and 78 of the Copyright, Designs and Patents Act 1988.

All rights reserved. No part of this book may be reprinted or reproduced or utilised in any form or by any electronic, mechanical, or other means, now known or hereafter invented, including photocopying and recording, or in any information storage or retrieval system, without permission in writing from the publishers.

Trademark notice: Product or corporate names may be trademarks or registered trademarks, and are used only for identification and explanation without intent to infringe.

British Library Cataloguing-in-Publication Data
A catalogue record for this book is available from the British Library

Library of Congress Cataloging-in-Publication Data
A catalog record for this book has been requested

ISBN: 978-0-367-51765-6 (hbk)
ISBN: 978-0-367-51767-0 (pbk)
ISBN: 978-1-003-05511-2 (ebk)

DOI: 10.4324/9781003055112

Typeset in Galliard
by Apex CoVantage, LLC

Sue Dockett and Bob Perry wish to dedicate this book to the memory of Professor Don Williams (1935–2020), former Dean of Education, University of Western Sydney.

Don was an inspiration to both Sue and Bob: professionally, personally and ethically.

He is remembered fondly for his leadership, mentorship and humility.

Don's untimely death occurred during the period of writing this book, and his memory is an integral part of it.

Thanks for everything, Don.

Contents

List of figures   xiv
List of tables   xvi
List of contributors   xvii

1 **Setting the scene**   1
   SUE DOCKETT AND BOB PERRY

  Introduction 1
  Evaluating and monitoring transition 1
  For whom is the book written? 3
  Transition to school as a field of research, practice, and policy making 4
  Authors 6
  Structure of the book 6
  Outcomes of engaging with the book 10
  How to use the book 10
  References 11

2 **Defining transition**   15
   SUE DOCKETT AND BOB PERRY

  Introduction 15
  Transition and change 15
  Transition and continuity 18
  Transition as a time of continuity and change 19
  Key transitions research 19
  Transition and readiness 21
  Transition activities, practices, and programs 22
  Conclusion 26

2A **To be or not to be (a school child) – from national to global discourses about the child in the school start age**   27
   HELENA ACKESJÖ AND SVEN PERSSON

  A conceptual frame for analysis 27
  To be or not to be a school child 27

Schoolarisation – discourses of the six-year-old legitimise a position shift in the education system *29*
References 30

3 What is meant by a successful or effective transition to school program?   37
SUE DOCKETT AND BOB PERRY

Introduction 37
What are the aims of the transition to school program? 38
Frameworks for evaluating effective transitions 40
Belonging as a marker of effective transition 42
Belonging and the transition to school 44
Effectiveness for whom? 48
What makes an effective transition to school program? 50
Conclusion 51

3A Paderborner Qualitätsstern (PQ³): Self-evaluation of transition to school programs for educators and teachers   52
PETRA BÜKER, JULIA HÖKE, AND JANA OGRODOWSKI

Introduction 52
Development context of the self-evaluation instrument 52
The Paderborner Qualitätsstern (PQ³) 54
   A: Pedagogical activities with the children *55*
   B: Structures within the individual institutions *55*
   C: Working in cooperation networks *56*
Evaluation 58
Conclusion 58
References 58

4 Evaluation of transition to school programs – an introduction   64
SUE DOCKETT AND BOB PERRY

Introduction 64
What is meant by evaluation? 64
Evaluating transition to school programs 65
Purposes of evaluation 65
Types of evaluation 66
   Needs analysis *66*
   Process evaluation *67*
   Outcome evaluation *69*
   Process, outcome, or both? *72*
Evaluation frameworks 73

An evaluation model 75
Evaluating promising practices 76
Participatory evaluation 78
Practitioner inquiry 79
Participatory action research 79
The project approach 81
Conclusion 82

4A Support for children and families at risk of experiencing vulnerability in early years transitions 83
ANDREA NOLAN AND ANNA KILDERRY

Introduction 83
Aims of the practice review 83
Designing the evaluation: respectful, ethical, and fit-for-purpose 84
Practice review outcomes 85
    Collaboration 86
    Evaluation 86
    Staff capacity building 86
    Designated leader 86
    Communication and confidentiality protocols 87
    A nominated "key" transition person in primary schools 87
    Resource funding 87
Conclusion 87
References 87

5 Planning an evaluation of transition to school programs 91
SUE DOCKETT AND BOB PERRY

Introduction 91
Planning the evaluation 91
Purpose of the evaluation 92
Focus of the evaluation 93
Planning evaluation activities 94
Evaluation implementation 95
Data analysis and synthesis 95
Reporting the results of the evaluation 97
Ethical considerations 98
Conclusion 100

5A Putting it into practice: Planning and implementing an evaluation 101
SUE DOCKETT

Purpose of the evaluation 101
    What is the context for the program? 101
    Purpose of the program 102

Why evaluate the program? 102
What was the outcome of the evaluation expected to be? 102
What resources were available for the evaluation? 103
Did the evaluation draw on external expertise? 103
Focus of the evaluation 103
What was evaluated? 103
Which stakeholders were involved in the evaluation? 103
What constraints were there? 103
What evaluation questions were asked? 104
What model of evaluation was used? 104
What were the criteria for the program to be described as successful or effective? 104
Evaluation planning 104
What were the ethical issues invoked by the evaluation? 104
How were data generated? 105
Timing of the evaluation 106
Data analysis 107
Reporting the results of the evaluation 107
What was learned from the evaluation? 107
What changed as a result of the evaluation? 108
References 108

6 Generating and analysing data for the evaluation of transition to school programs – perspectives of children   110
SUE DOCKETT AND BOB PERRY

Introduction 110
Why involve children in evaluation of transition programs? 111
Participatory evaluation 112
Involving children in evaluations 114
Children's perspectives of school visits 115
Building familiarity and belonging 117
How do we know if children are familiar with the school and feel like they belong? 118
Data analysis 126
The impact of children's perspectives 129
Ethical challenges and children's perspectives 130
Conclusion 131

6A Listening to the voices of Jamaican children about their transitional experiences   132
ZOYAH KINKEAD-CLARK

Introduction 132
Overview of extant literature on Jamaican children's transitions 132
Methodology 133

Findings 133
  Feeding off adult expectations 134
  What about play? 134
  Am I ready? 135
Discussion and conclusion 136
References 136

7 **Generating and analysing data for the evaluation of transition to school programs – perspectives of adults**   141
  SUE DOCKETT AND BOB PERRY

Introduction 141
Stakeholders and their involvement in evaluation of transition programs 141
Engaging with adults 143
  Consultation 143
  Participatory evaluation 146
Generating data for the evaluation of transition programs 147
Ethical considerations 158
Conclusion 159

7A **Professional relationships and spaces as children start school**   160
  TESS BOYLE

Introduction 160
Site 160
Theoretical framework 161
Evidence and analysis 161
Changing practices 163
Conclusion 164
References 164

8 **Development and use of a rubric framework for the evaluation of transition to school programs**   169
  SUE DOCKETT AND BOB PERRY

Introduction 169
History of the Peridot Education Transition Reflection Instrument 170
  Indicators of Progress 171
  The Transition to School: Position Statement 173
Developments in Queensland 173
The Peridot Education Transition Reflection Instrument 176
  Documenting progress – an example 181
  Use of the Peridot Education Transition Reflection Instrument 183
Conclusion 185

xii Contents

8A *Mo Scéal* (My Story): Evaluation of the transition to school initiative in Ireland   186
MARY DALY AND DEREK GRANT

Introduction 186
Literature review 186
The preschool to primary school transition initiative 187
   Implementation of the transition initiative 187
   Analysis of the transition initiative 188
Findings from the transition initiative 188
   Benefits 188
   Challenges 189
Conclusion 189
Notes 190
References 190

9 Using evaluation to plan future transition to school programs   194
SUE DOCKETT AND BOB PERRY

Introduction 194
Communicating findings 194
   With whom are the findings to be shared? 195
   What is the purpose of sharing the findings? 203
Using findings to inform future programs 204
Changes to transition programs 206
Conclusion 207

9A Challenges of and strategies within interprofessional cooperation between ECEC institutions and primary schools   209
MIRJA KEKERITZ

Introduction 209
Levels of cooperation 209
   What factors influence the level of cooperation? 210
Case study about a co-constructional cooperation 212
Challenges and strategies of interprofessional cooperation 213
   Curricular orientation 213
   Didactic approach 214
   Negotiations of a cooperative pedagogy 215
Successful transition in cooperative settings 215
   Shared aims of the cooperation partners (integration) 216
   Reciprocal interactions between the cooperation partners (interprofessional interaction) 216

Confidence among the cooperation partners (cooperation
   climate) 216
Autonomy of the cooperation partners (differentiation) 216
References 216

10 Looking forward — 220
SUE DOCKETT AND BOB PERRY

Introduction 220
Evaluation and transition to school programs 221
   Invisible transitions 221
   The importance of program theory 222
   Building evaluation into program design and
      implementation 223
   Involving a range of stakeholders 224
   Leadership in evaluating transition to school programs 224
   Learning from success and failure 225
   Potential benefits of evaluation 226
References 226

Index — 230

Figures

2.1	Phases of transition (after van Gennep, 1960)	17
3A.1	A duly completed Paderborner Qualitätsstern	57
5.1	Reporting to different audiences	97
5.2	Example of an information booklet for children	99
5A.1	Child permission	105
5A.2	*Transition to School: Position Statement* image	106
6.1	Brainstorm: Is preschool different to school? What is different? (Dockett & Perry, 2014, p. 74)	116
6.2	Jonah: We went to assembly. There's no babies at assembly	117
6.3	Tristan: ". . . have a door to the toilets and you shut the door to the toilets. No one told me where the toilets are . . . I think about the toilets. Now I know where the toilets are."	118
6.4	Gillian: "I'm drawing my school and everything in my school. I'm drawing me . . . the toilets. This is a map so the kids know where to go. First stop, toilets."	119
6.5	What might the children at preschool ask me about big school?	120
6.6	What if I need to go to the toilet in class time?	120
6.7	What do new children need to know? They need to know how to buy food at the canteen	121
6.8	They need to know what to do in assembly. Now I know that I have to be quiet at assembly	121
6.9	They need to know where to go to get a drink – at the bubblers	122
6.10	They need to know they're not allowed to 'out of bounds' because you're not allowed to go there	122
6.11	That's me not crying at school	123
6.12	Reflection	123
6.13	This is me next to my classroom	124
6.14	This is basketball at my school	124
6.15	This is my teacher	125
6.16	Rating scale for children (Dockett & Perry, 2019)	126
7.1	Consultation noticeboard	145
7.2	ECEC educators' brainstorming	152
7.3	Comparison of educator responses over time	155

7.4	Communication Diary Log (Hopps, 2014, p. 395)	156
7.5	*Transition to School: Position Statement* image	157
7A.1	Collated response to Q2 of the Cycle 1 survey questionnaire	162
8.1	Profile for expectations for children over time	182
8.2	Complete profile across the four constructs for families	182
8.3	Complete profiles of two schools using the *Peridot Education Transition Reflection Instrument*	184
9.1	Important information from first-year-of-school children to children starting school. (Darling Heights State School, 2020; reproduced with permission)	196
9.2	Important information from older primary school children to children starting school. (Darling Heights State School, 2020; reproduced with permission)	196
9.3	Reporting about the buddy program	197
9.4	Mind map	198
9.5	Information brochures for families available in different languages	199
9.6	Summary information for parents	200
9A.1	Dimensions of cooperation (after Rathmer, 2012)	211
9A.2	Dimensions of an evaluative approach to interprofessional cooperation (after Rathmer, 2012)	212

Tables

2.1	Transition practices and examples	24
3.1	Belonging during the transition to school	45
3A.1	Pedagogical and didactical aims	55
3A.2	Role of the heads of educational institutions within the cooperation	56
3A.3	Roles of collaboration	57
4.1	Mechanism for change	75
4.2	Evidence of impact model applied to transition programs	76
6.1	Ranking of response categories across groups – highest to lowest	127
7.1	Questionnaire on the usefulness of transition practices (ECEC educators)	149
7.2	Sorting data into codes and categories	154
7.3	Contact log	156
7A.1	Evidence gathered	162
8.1	Framework for the first key element for the Guideline *Effective transition programs establish positive relationships between children, parents and educators* (Level 4 highest)	172
8.2	Action area *reciprocal relationships* from the *School Decision-Making* matrix	175
8.3	*Peridot Education Transition Reflection Instrument*: Opportunities	177
8.4	*Peridot Education Transition Reflection Instrument*: Aspirations	178
8.5	*Peridot Education Transition Reflection Instrument*: Expectations	179
8.6	*Peridot Education Transition Reflection Instrument*: Entitlements	180

Contributors

Helena Ackesjö is Associate Professor at Linnæus University in Sweden. Helena has a special interest in the Swedish preschool class, which is central to children's transition from preschool to school. In her research, Helena is focused on teachers' professional perspectives and didactic perspectives on transitions as well as children's perspectives on transitions. Central to her research is the concept of continuity. Helena publishes both nationally and internationally in these areas. Besides researching and teaching at the teacher education level, Helena is often engaged in work together with the Swedish National Agency for Education and the National School Inspectorate with issues concerning children's transitions between school forms as well as the education in the preschool class. On commission from the Swedish Ministry of Education, Helena has written research reviews about the preschool class, children's transition from preschool to school and children's school start together with Sven Persson. Helena is a co-chair of the Special Interest Group on Transitions at the European Early Childhood Education Research Association.

Tess Boyle has recently retired after 40 years of school and university teaching and research. She is currently an Adjunct Lecturer in the Centre for Children and Young People at Southern Cross University, Australia, and Director, Tess Boyle Consulting. Through these roles Tess continues to maintain her research and publication interests in early childhood education; educational transitions; ethical practices involving children; practice theories; praxis; middle leading; assessment, pedagogy, and curriculum. Tess has an impressive list of publications in high-ranking peer-reviewed journals, and she has presented at esteemed national and international conferences. Recently, she has worked with the Department of Education, Queensland, Australia, on a number of practice-orientated early childhood education projects.

Petra Büker is Professor at the Institute of Education at University of Paderborn, Germany. She is working in the field of early childhood education and primary school pedagogy. The main focus of Petra's research work is on child-centred pedagogy and researching with children. Her interests are rights-based participation of children, transition processes, heterogeneity, intersectionality, interculturality, and inclusion in kindergarten and primary school. She is editor of a book series about children's biographies and is also involved in various projects in the fields of inclusion and digital education with a focus on the professionalisation of emerging teachers.

Mary Daly is an Education Officer with the National Council for Curriculum and Assessment (NCCA) in the Republic of Ireland. Mary has worked in the area of early childhood over the past 20 years. She has been with the NCCA for the last 15 years. Her work there involved the development of *Aistear, the Early Childhood Curriculum Framework* (NCCA, 2009) along with the Aistear Síolta Practice Guide (www.aistearsiolta.ie), an online resource to help improve the quality of curriculum practice in Ireland. She has also worked on supporting children's transition from preschool to primary school over a number of years. Mary has a BA in early childhood studies from University College Cork (UCC) and a PhD from UCC (1999–2002). A book based on her PhD called *Developing the Whole Child: The Importance of the Emotional, Social, Moral and Spiritual in Early Years Education and Care* was published in 2004.

Sue Dockett is Emeritus Professor, Charles Sturt University, Australia, and Director, Peridot Education Pty Ltd. While recently retired from university life, Sue remains an active researcher in the field of early childhood education. Sue has been a long-time advocate for the importance of recognising and responding to young children's perspectives. She maintains this position in her current work with children, families and educators in explorations of transitions to school, children's play and learning. Sue has published extensively both nationally and internationally in these areas. She is a co-chair of the Special Interest Group on Transitions at the European Early Childhood Education Research Association.

Derek Grant is a Director, Curriculum and Assessment at the National Council for Curriculum and Assessment (NCCA) in the Republic of Ireland. A graduate of Trinity College Dublin, Derek began his career as a primary school teacher in 2001. He was appointed as deputy principal (2002–2005) and then as principal in another school (2005–2016), where he led curriculum and assessment developments. Having completed a Master of Science in education management in the University of Ulster and a Doctorate of Education in the University of Lincoln, UK, Derek joined the NCCA in 2016. Through his roles as education officer (2016–2019) and now as director, he has worked on areas such as supporting children's transition from preschool to primary school, the STEM Education Policy (Department of Education) and the ongoing primary curriculum review and redevelopment.

Julia Höke is Professor of Didactics and Methodology of Childhood Education and Social Work at the Catholic University of Applied Sciences of North-Rhine-Westphalia, Germany. In addition to transitions, her teaching includes children's play, research-based learning, and documentation of learning processes. She is interested in educational quality and professionalisation of the staff in kindergarten and primary school. In her current research, she is focused on children's perspectives on participation and ethical reflections about interviews with children.

Mirja Kekeritz is currently a temporary professor of primary school education at the University of Koblenz-Landau, Germany. In her doctoral thesis she examined cooperation projects between kindergarten and elementary school and particularly researched the inter-institutional interactions between children and professionals. In her international research project *Children's Voices in Transition – Starting School in Sri Lanka* and her work at the Lower Saxony Institute for Early Childhood Education and Development (nifbe), she addressed the transition between kindergarten and elementary school and ways of cooperation. Currently, she is working on a research project on *Learning in Times of the Covid 19 Pandemic*, examining the challenges and strategies of primary schoolchildren as they transition between home schooling and the classroom. Other research areas and focal points include: pedagogue–child interactions; individualised (primary school) teaching; qualitative methods of childhood research – especially children's drawings; and aesthetic forms of learning in childhood.

Anna Kilderry is Associate Professor in Education (Early Childhood) at Deakin University in Melbourne and has worked as an academic for more than 20 years in Australia and England. Anna is an experienced lecturer, PhD supervisor, and qualitative researcher. Researching from critical perspectives, Anna has led projects investigating early childhood education, policy, professional practice, and early years transitions. Anna has conducted research with children, teachers, and families in diverse communities, and her work is published and cited internationally. Realising the need for an interdisciplinary evidence-informed approach in early childhood education, recently Anna co-edited a book with Professor Bridie Raban titled *Strong Foundations: Evidence Informing Practice in Early Childhood Education and Care*.

Zoyah Kinkead-Clark is a Senior Lecturer and coordinator of early childhood programs at The University of the West Indies, Mona. As a researcher, she is particularly interested in understanding how young children are shaped by their ecological experiences within the home and wider community with the view to explore how educators can build on these in early years settings.

Zoyah currently serves as an external examiner in Early Childhood Education for the Joint Board of Teacher Education. She is also a member of Jamaica's Early Childhood Development Oversight Committee, the body tasked with overseeing the development of a comprehensive strategy to revitalise the vision for Jamaican children.

Andrea Nolan is Professor of Early Childhood Education in the School of Education, Deakin University, Australia. She is a member of Deakin University's Education Strategic Research Centre – Research for Educational Impact (REDI) and a deputy leader of the Children, Young People and their Communities research strand. Andrea is the founder and chair of the Victorian Early Childhood Research Consortium, a group of 83 cross-disciplinary researchers across Victorian universities who come together to support research capacity building. Since 2007, she has produced a significant body of research focusing on the capabilities of the early childhood workforce with a specific interest in the professional learning of teachers. Educator practice is a complementary theme to her research, where she has focused on young children's language learning, transition to school practices and equity provision. Andrea has attracted more than $7 million in research funding throughout her career, and her research has been cited in 44 countries.

Jana Ogrodowski is a doctoral student and research assistant in the field of early childhood education and primary school pedagogy at University of Paderborn, Germany, since 2017. She is interested in the design of transition processes in the context of primary school, research with children, and documentation of learning processes. In her doctoral thesis, she uses a longitudinal design to investigate the perspectives of children in the transition from primary to secondary school to derive individual coping strategies and conditions for a successful transition. Moreover, she is involved in various projects in the fields of inclusion and digital education with a focus on the professionalisation processes of teachers.

Bob Perry has recently retired after 45 years of university teaching and research. He is Emeritus Professor at Charles Sturt University, Australia, and Director, Peridot Education Pty Ltd. In conjunction with Sue Dockett, he continues research, consultancy, and publication in early childhood mathematics education; educational transitions, with particular emphasis on transition to primary school; researching with children; and evaluation of educational programs. Bob continues to publish extensively both nationally and internationally in these areas. Currently, he is revising materials for a preschool mathematics intervention run by Australia's leading educational charity and co-editing a book on Latin American research in educational transitions. He is a co-chair of the Special Interest Group on Mathematics 0–8 Years at the European Early Childhood Education Research Association.

Sven Persson is a Senior Professor at Malmö University in Sweden. Sven has an interest in the development of early childhood education and care (ECEC) institutions, which he has analysed from a macro and a micro perspective. From a macro perspective, the development of ECEC institutions in Sweden in relation to societal changes and professionalization is a special interest. From a micro perspective, he has developed the concept of pedagogical relations. Sven has written several research reviews about quality aspects in ECEC institutions and the potential of ECEC to promote equal conditions for children. In conjunction with Helena Ackesjö he conducts research on the Swedish preschool class. On commission from the Swedish Ministry of Education, they have written research reviews about preschool class, children's transition from preschool to school and children's school start.

1 Setting the scene

Sue Dockett and Bob Perry

Introduction

Welcome to *Evaluating Transition to School Programs: Learning from Research and Practice*, an innovative text which takes the authors and the readers on a learning adventure. This adventure builds on and contextualises the large amount of national and international research, policy, and practice around the development, implementation and evaluation of effective programs which link families, children, early childhood and school educators, and many others, as children begin their school education journey.

Evaluating Transition to School Programs: Learning from Research and Practice synthesises research, policy, and practice from around the world to assist local transition to school communities as they determine whether the programs and practices they have created, adopted, and implemented are the most effective possible. While this is not a book about the construction of transition practices and programs, per se, it does build on more than 20 years of work by the authors and many national and international colleagues aimed at ensuring that children, their families, and all other participants in the transition journey experience the best possible start to school.

Evaluating and monitoring transition

The book addresses a gap in the evaluation of transition programs. Little has been written with a specific focus on the evaluation of transition to school programs and individual transitions for children, families, and educators. Anecdotal responses to the question "How do you know that your transition program was effective?" are often along the lines of "There were fewer tears this year than last", "I didn't hear any complaints", and "The children have settled well and are straight into the curriculum". Given the amount of effort and resources dedicated to transition to school programs across the world each year, there need to be better ways of evaluating the effectiveness of these programs. *Evaluating Transition to School Programs: Learning from Research and Practice* utilises extant national and international research and practice to fill this gap.

DOI: 10.4324/9781003055112-1

Internationally, efforts to monitor and evaluate transition practices often have focused on assessing the readiness of individual children (Ahtola et al., 2011; Dockett & Perry, 2013; Petriwskyj, Thorpe, & Tayler, 2005). Meisels (2007, p. 44) has cautioned that such assessments of individual children are not sufficient measures to "render a valid decision about whether a program is realising its promise or achieving its goals". Rather, more comprehensive measures that incorporate a range of perspectives (including those of children, families, educators, and other stakeholders), are required to consider the context in which programs operate, the purposes and aims of programs, as well as how well the programs achieve these. Specifically, we need strategies that provide a holistic approach to understanding the effectiveness of programs in supporting children and families as well as the work of educators.

These views are supported by the Organisation for Economic Cooperation and Development (OECD) (2017) focus in *Starting Strong V*, which advocates for a broad view of transitions moving away from the traditional focus on individual children's readiness, supporting instead the contemporary view that effective transitions involve many people and attend to the ways in which schools and communities respond to children and families, as well as what children bring with them to school (Centre for Community Child Health, 2008; Dockett & Perry, 2014; Margetts & Kienig, 2013). While a great deal of national and international research exists on the topic of transition to school (see, for example, Brooker, 2008; Dunlop & Fabian, 2007; Kagan & Tarrant, 2010; Lillejord et al., 2017; O'Kane, 2016; Perry, Dockett, & Petriwskyj, 2014; Peters, 2010), there is limited research about the evaluation of transitions and the ways in which this can be used to identify effective practices within specific contexts, promote equity of provision and access to effective transition practices, and provide feedback about the relative effectiveness and impact of transition practice (OECD, 2017). Equity issues have been recognised as significant at the time of transition, with families and children experiencing disadvantage or marginalisation identified as less likely than their more-advantaged counterparts to access transition programs (Dockett, Perry, & Kearney, 2010, 2011; OECD, 2017; Smart et al., 2008).

The country background reports for *Starting Strong V* indicate that most monitoring of transition programs and/or practices is done at the local level, often using informal means, although, for example, national surveys in Norway seek limited information about transition practices (Norwegian Directorate for Education and Training, 2017). While there are no common measures to monitor transition practices, Sweden has developed a self-evaluation form for educators responsible for the preschool class and the first year of school, with the aim of identifying effective practices as well as areas for improvement (Ministry of Education and Research, 2016). Finnish, Danish, and Austrian transition practices are also monitored at the local level (Charlotte Bühler Institut, 2016; Ministry for Children and Social Affairs, 2017; Ministry of Education and Culture, Finland, 2017). The aims of monitoring transition programs seem to be twofold: supporting individual children's transitions and also considering the overall impact of the transition program. The latter may involve surveys for families as well as educators.

A recent New Zealand report indicated that schools and early childhood settings considered responsive to their children, families, and communities undertook regular review of their transition programs:

> . . . in schools with only informal review processes, teachers were reactive. They monitored children's progress and made adjustments to their programme to suit the child or group of children in the new entrants' class. Teachers and senior leaders' discussions about transition practices were based on anecdotal evidence, including feedback from parents, rather than analysis of sound data. Senior leaders rarely reported to the board about the effectiveness of transition practices.
>
> Most of the 'very responsive' schools had robust, formal self review practices, and their responses were proactive. They analysed data and looked for how they could improve the whole process of transition. Senior leaders considered children's wellbeing as well as assessment data and sought parents' and children's views. Their focus was on providing a smooth transition to ensure minimal disruption to each child's learning.
>
> (Education Review Office, 2015, p. 49)

It is challenging to identify comprehensive measures that address both program and individual components at the point of transition to school, as early childhood education and care (ECEC) and school sectors "work in different worlds in terms of the dominant methods and metrics for assessing their work" (Schultz, 2010, p. 274). However, differences in expectations, understandings, and perspectives can be bridged in a number of ways – including the sharing of information and participation in professional networks (Boyle & Petriwskyj, 2014; Dockett & Perry, 2006, 2014; Edwards, 2011; Karila & Rantavuori, 2014). In addition, some specific evaluation tools have been developed to promote connection between ECEC and school experiences. These include the sharing of documentation, such as transition statements. While these statements have become a feature of many Australian transition programs supported by various state and territory departments of education, they have also been used internationally (O'Kane & Murphy, 2016a, 2016b). The use of transition statements is not without critique (Hopps, 2014; Hopps-Wallis & Perry, 2017). While transition statements are recognised as a potentially important element of transition programs, they are not sufficient to monitor or evaluate such programs overall.

For whom is the book written?

Ultimately, *Evaluating Transition to School Programs: Learning from Research and Practice* is written for all of the children starting primary school in any particular year. Its prime purpose is to help these children experience as effective a transition to school as possible. It is unlikely, however, that (m)any of these children will read this book so, perhaps it is better to think of them as the motivation for the book but not the readership.

The book is aimed towards educators in ECEC and primary school settings and those preparing for such roles. Leaders in both settings will delve into the book to assist them in making relevant decisions around the evaluation of transition practices in their contexts. Some family members, particularly those working with educators in transition networks, may wish to consult parts of the book. Researchers, research students, and policy makers in the early childhood field will also find much in the book which will be helpful to them.

While *Evaluating Transition to School Programs: Learning from Research and Practice* is based on the extensive body of research in transition to primary school, it is, first and foremost, a practical book which provides a sound basis of national and international research and practice. Using this information, transition to school programs can be evaluated at the local level with the aim of ensuring their effectiveness for all participants. However, the book does not provide *recipes for success*, as all processes and practices need to be judged against their appropriateness and fit with the local contexts. The book does provide systems, guidelines, and suggested experiences which can complement the local expertise of adults and children to plan, implement, and evaluate the most effective transition to school programs possible.

Transition to school as a field of research, practice, and policy making

Over the last 25 years, transition to school has been the subject of very active research agendas in many areas of the world. Initial emphasis, particularly in the USA, was on children's school readiness; that is, how well children are prepared for the academic and structural requirements of school – what literacy and numeracy skills do the children have, and how well do they fit into the school classroom? Notions of transition to school have broadened conceptions of school readiness over the ensuing years, although there is still emphasis in many jurisdictions on what children know and can do as they enter school.

A key impetus for reconceptualising transition to school came from the work of Uri Bronfenbrenner and his colleagues, whose ecological systems theory was applied to starting school. A definitive article by Rimm-Kaufman and Pianta (2000) provided a framework for research into ecological and dynamic models of transition and became one of the critical foundation stones for our (and many others') work in the field (see, for example, Dunlop, 2014). The critical importance in the ecological model of systems of processes and interactions across contexts reflected the reality of transition to school, where there are many participants – not only the children starting school but their families and communities, educators in ECEC and schools, and many others – interacting within the specific contexts surrounding the children. The importance of the relationships which are formed during processes of interaction among the participants began to be emphasised, and the establishment of such relationships became one of the key aspects of what were seen to be effective transition to school programs. In 2001, we published a set of ten guidelines for effective transition to school programs with the first being "effective transition programs establish positive relationships between children, parents and educators" (Dockett & Perry, 2001b, p. v). This commitment has stayed with us ever since. While the language of effective transitions now incorporates the pillars of opportunities, expectations, aspirations and entitlements (Educational Transitions and Change (ETC) Research Group, 2011), the belief that the critical outcomes of effective transition programs are trusting and respectful relationships among all the participants is still foundational to our work and to this book.

There have been many developments in research and practice in the field of educational transitions. A range of theoretical frameworks has been applied, including Bronfenbrenner and Morris's (2006) bioecological model of human development and the consequent exposure to proximal processes, context, and time and their implications for transitions (Dockett, Griebel, & Perry, 2017). An overview of this and other theoretical frameworks is provided in Chapter 2. The impact of the United Nations *Convention on the Rights of the Child* (United Nations (UN), 1989) and Childhood Studies (James, Jenks, & Prout, 1998) have meant that children's voices are now seen as an essential component of the planning and implementing of transition to school programs. This book also positions these voices as essential elements of the evaluation of such programs.

Transition to school practice has evolved in direct response to the changed directions in research. Transition to school programs are now much more than traditional short-term orientation programs run by the receiving school and designed to have the children and, sometimes, their families, get to know what is required of them by the school and, to a lesser extent, allow the school to learn something about the children. Many programs are designed to encourage the development of relationships among children and between children and their potential first-year-of-school teachers. As well, relationships may be built between ECEC and school educators and among families, although these are not universal features of transition to school programs. Evaluation of transition to school programs at the local community or school level is just beginning to feature in current programs, although, in general, such evaluation processes are often ad hoc, not rigorous, and not necessarily aimed at the evaluation of program outcomes. However, several statewide education systems have made progress in attempting to fill this gap (Department for Education and Child Development, South Australia, 2014; Department of Education, NSW, 2020; Department of Education and Early Childhood Development, Victoria, 2017; Queensland Department of Education, 2020; West et al., 2012). While progress is being made in evaluating transition programs, it remains the case that there is often "no reliable information about the outcomes of particular approaches, strategies or methods" (Victorian Auditor-General, 2015, p. xiii), making it difficult for those involved to "understand whether their actions have been effective" (p. xiv). The aim of this book is to assist those involved in transition as they redress this.

Authors

This book has many *authors*. There are those whose names appear on the title page and the opening pages of chapters. There are many colleagues of these people who are researchers, educators, and policy makers vitally interested and active in the field of transition to school. Then, there are very large numbers of children, family members, and both ECEC and school educators who have assisted and participated in research projects; professional learning opportunities; and the development, trialling, and evaluation of materials; and have engaged in very many conversations about transition to school. All of these people have influenced this book.

The content of this book has been written by two groups of people. The first group – Sue Dockett and Bob Perry – have each been researching and publishing in the transition to school field for almost 25 years and have a national and international reputation for their expertise. It was their idea to approach Routledge and establish the publisher's interest in a book designed to fill a particular gap in the field. Sue and Bob are also responsible for the thinking behind the slightly unusual structure of the book, involving chapters that they have written supplemented with contributed chapters from the second group of authors. This second group comprises another 12 authors from five different countries who have provided examples of research, practice, and policy illustrative of the key points made in the relevant substantive chapters. Each of these contributing authors has substantial expertise in the transitions to school field, and all are connected to the Transitions Special Interest Group of the European Early Childhood Education Research Association (EECERA).

Structure of the book

The aim of this research-based and educator-oriented book is to celebrate the most up-to-date research and practice in the evaluation of transition to school programs and, hence, provide means for educators and researchers to evaluate such programs in their own contexts in ethical, rigorous, and valid ways which consider the perspectives of all stakeholders.

The substantive chapters introduce current research and practice in the field of transition to school, followed by a more detailed treatment of research and practice specifically targeted to the evaluation of transition to primary school programs. These chapters consider what is meant by effective transition to school programs and develop and outline strategies for evaluation that can be adopted by local transition to school groups and networks. They also consider ways in which all of the stakeholders in transition to school programs can be involved and have their voices heard in the evaluation of these programs. The contributed chapters attached to Chapters 2–9 provide national and international perspectives on the opportunities and challenges raised in these chapters.

Chapter 2 provides an overview of current definitions of transition and how these impact on the nature of transition to school programs. It explores recent transitions research and practice and reflects on debates about transition and readiness. The chapter concludes with consideration of key stakeholders in transition and an outline of transition practices and programs. The theme of tensions between representations of transition and readiness is exemplified in Chapter 2A, where Ackesjö and Persson reflect on the image of the child and implications of this for transition, as evident in Swedish national policy documents over a period of 80 years. They conclude by emphasising that the construction of the *school child* is a reflection of broader social expectations and caution that increased focus on international comparisons, competition, and calls for knowledge efficiency contribute to the downward push of academic expectations for children as they experience the transition to school.

Having defined transition to school, Chapter 3 moves to consideration of what constitutes a successful or effective transition for the various stakeholders involved. While there is no consensus about what makes a program effective, this chapter highlights the importance of establishing the aims of the transition program and ensuring that these are the focus of any evaluation. In this chapter we introduce the *Guidelines for Effective Transition to School Programs* first published 20 years ago (Dockett & Perry, 2001b), and the refinement of these in the *Transition to School Position Statement* (ETC Research Group, 2011). Across much of our work we have argued that a sense of belonging is the marker of an effective transition. In this chapter, we utilise the cartography developed by Sumsion and Wong (2011) to unpack what this sense of belonging might look like for those involved in the transition. One of the potential markers of belonging for educators from both ECEC and school sectors working to support transitions involves cooperation based on mutually respectful relationships. In Chapter 3A, Büker, Höke, and Ogrodowski describe a self-evaluation tool to support educators as they reflect on the development and implementation of transition programs and the cooperation that supports these. The tool is designed to promote process evaluation, that is to consider how cooperation among ECEC and school educators provides the basis for the design and implementation of programs and for the ongoing recognition of professional practice in the transition space. The tool supports both broad criterion-based and locally based participant evaluation of the effectiveness of programs. As such, it links also with Chapter 4, which explores concepts of evaluation and their application to transition to school programs.

Chapter 4 also addresses the purpose of evaluation and shares examples of different types of evaluation: needs analysis; process evaluation; and outcome or impact evaluation. Evaluation frameworks are discussed, and the importance of a logic model or program theory in setting out the plans for a transition program and its evaluation are emphasised. The identification of the proposed mechanism for change to be engaged during the program is highlighted and maintained as a theme that continues throughout the book. One of the purposes of Chapter 4 is to help readers outline what is to be evaluated, establishing a clear focus to guide the evaluation. Forms of participatory evaluation – practitioner inquiry, participatory action research, and the project approach – are introduced. In Chapter 4A, Nolan and Kilderry provide an overview of a needs analysis conducted in the Australian state of Victoria which identified and mapped existing supports and effective practices relevant for children experiencing vulnerability. A statewide survey generated the data to map both existing supports and practices and identify transition networks for follow-up focus group and individual interviews. The review generated recommendations for policy and practice, including several aimed at enhancing the involvement of ECEC professionals in transdisciplinary teams to support children and families. As in Chapter 3A, this chapter notes the importance of collaboration across sectors.

Planning an evaluation of transition to school programs is the focus of Chapter 5. As well as identifying the specific purpose(s) of the evaluation, the chapter discusses potential participants in the evaluation, approaches to data generation and analysis, and some strategies for sharing the outcomes of the evaluation. While not in any way providing a recipe, this chapter does provide guidance through prompt questions, with the aim that responses can be used to frame the evaluation. These questions are also used as organisers in Chapter 5A (Dockett), which documents the processes involved in a recent evaluation of a transition to school program. The context, purposes, and plans for the evaluation are described, as are ethical issues, data generation, and data analysis. Though impacted by restrictions and challenges associated with COVID-19, the evaluation created an atmosphere that supported change as well as some directions for immediate, as well as future, improvements to the transition to school program.

Children's perspectives of transition and their potential to contribute to the evaluation of transition programs are the focus of Chapter 6. This chapter recognises the increased awareness (from adults) of seeking and valuing children's perspectives of their experiences in contexts that affect them. Drawing on the bases of children's rights and competence, this chapter argues that children's insights make a valuable contribution to the evaluation of transition programs. While the chapter provides examples of several potential methods for accessing children's perspectives, it emphasises the importance of the interpretive frameworks in which these exist and the ways that these guide adult interpretations of children's rights and competence. Kinkead-Clark (Chapter 6A) provides an example of how Jamaican children's perspectives contributed to understandings of the nature and importance of transition. Through interviews, preschool children shared their insights about transition, mainly gleaned from the comments of adults. One major concern for these children was the potential loss of time for play – with school associated much more with work than with play. Kinkead-Clark's conclusions highlight not only the importance of listening to children's perspectives but also realising that while they take on the comments of adults, they often give these their own meaning.

Chapter 7 addresses strategies for involving various adult stakeholders in the evaluation of transition to school programs. Recognising that there are many different groups of adult stakeholders, this chapter draws on a range of examples to consider approaches to consultation and participatory evaluation. Examples of different methods, including questionnaires, rating scales, and conversational interviews, are included, as is an example of data analysis through thematic coding. The chapter also highlights several ethical considerations. In Chapter 7A, Boyle reports an investigation of transition to school practices within a professional learning community. The importance of professional relationships is at the core of this chapter, as these provide a sound basis for both generating and analysing data. Boyle describes how utilising the processes of participatory action research created a context to build and support professional relationships, facilitating spaces to discuss and change practice. In particular, these spaces were needed to engage in conversations about the purposes and aims of the transition program, particularly in the light of the different perspectives of different stakeholders.

Chapter 8 considers several instruments developed to assist in the evaluation of transition to school programs. While the main focus is on instruments developed in Australia, Daly and Grant (Chapter 8A) describe an international example from Ireland, and reference is made to Chapter 3A, which outlined an example from Germany of systemwide consideration of what makes transition to school programs effective and how such programs can be evaluated. Each of the measures outlined utilises a rubric, or matrix, to plot progress along a set of criteria or dimensions that have been identified as contributing to effective transition to school programs. The chapter introduces the *Peridot Education Transition Reflection Instrument*, which has been built on the *Guidelines for Effective Transition to School* (Dockett & Perry, 2001a) and the *Transition to School: Position Statement* (ETC Research Group, 2011). Each of these instruments outlines the processes used to support educators in helping children and their families experience a positive, effective transition.

The importance of communicating the evaluation findings is the subject of Chapter 9. Preparing and sharing the findings of the evaluation process can influence the impact of the evaluation and guide the future development and implementation of the program. This chapter considers how and to whom the results of the evaluation could be communicated, noting the importance of reporting in different ways to different audiences and the different stakeholders who have been involved. Kekeritz (Chapter 9A) picks up the discussion of multiple stakeholders and multiple perspectives by highlighting the importance of cooperation across ECEC and school contexts and considering how this might be assessed and reported. Linking back to discussions in Chapter 3 about what makes a successful transition and to Chapter 7A, which highlights the value of cooperation across ECEC and school settings, Chapter 9A challenges readers to consider the benefits of cooperation and how it could be measured and reported.

The final chapter looks to the future, drawing some general conclusions and overall thoughts that have emerged as we have compiled the chapters in this book. It identifies some of the gaps and challenges in exploring the evaluation of transition to school programs, including the recognition of invisible transitions and the involvement of a range of stakeholders. This chapter reiterates the value of including evaluation in overall approaches to planning and concludes with a reminder of some of the benefits to be gained from evaluating transition to school programs.

Outcomes of engaging with the book

What readers get out of this book will depend a great deal on what their roles are and how they are involved in transition to school endeavours. Educators with responsibilities in transition to school programs will find a great deal of information about how they might go about evaluating their local efforts, including ways to reflect on current programs, gather evidence on the effectiveness of the programs, analyse these data, report and communicate findings, and use the findings to assist in planning future transition to school programs.

Ethical processes are highlighted throughout the book, as is the involvement of all participants, especially children and families. Emerging ECEC and school educators will learn about all of these aspects of evaluation of transition to school programs and access foundational material about the nature of transition to school, the importance of listening to the voices of all involved, and what makes an effective transition to school program. Researchers in the field will find a useful resource of current research-based material and a model for how such material might be communicated to practising and preservice educators. Teacher educators will find a great deal of material about transition to school and its evaluation which will be pertinent to their classes and study materials. Policy makers with responsibilities for creation and dissemination of policy documents and support materials will find in this book many research- and practice-based ideas relevant to their policies.

How to use the book

While we would like to think that many people will read *Evaluating Transition to School Programs: Learning from Research and Practice* from cover to cover and allow the gradual buildup of knowledge and skills relevant to the evaluation of transition to school programs, it is unlikely that this is the way the book will be used by most people. Rather, this is a book to be *dipped into* to find input on specific matters: perhaps you will want some suggestions about involving children's perspectives in the evaluation of your local program – Chapters 6 and 6A will be your first step; perhaps you need some information about analysing data – Chapters 6, 7, and 8 and the associated contributed chapters will be your reading destinations. If the local transition network wants to reflect on and revise the evaluation of transition to school programs in their community or seek confirmation of current practices, various members can be assigned different chapters and report on their reading at the next network meeting. You may want to find very specific information about a particular item and use the index rather than searching through a chapter.

There are many ways in which the authors can see the book being used. No doubt, there are many other ways in which groups and individuals will find the book helpful. However it is used, the authors will be encouraged and satisfied to hear that *Evaluating Transition to School Programs: Learning from Research and Practice* has been read and utilised to develop and implement ethical, rigorous, and valid evaluations of the effectiveness of transition to school programs.

References

Ahtola, A., Silinskas, G., Poikonen, P.-L., Kontoniemi, M., Niemi, P., & Nurmi, J.-E. (2011). Transition to formal schooling: Do transition practices matter for academic performance? *Early Childhood Research Quarterly*, 26(3), 295–302. https://doi.org/10.1016/j.ecresq.2010.12.002

Boyle, T., & Petriwskyj, A. (2014). Transitions to school: Reframing professional relationships. *Early Years: An International Research Journal*, 34(4), 392–404. https://doi.org/10.1080/09575146.2014.953042

Bronfenbrenner, U., & Morris, P. A. (2006). The bioecological model of human development. In W. Damon & R. M. Lerner (Eds.), *Handbook of child psychology, Vol. 1: Theoretical models of human development* (6th ed., pp. 793–828). New York: Wiley. https://doi.org/10.1002/9780470147658.chpsy0114

Brooker, L. (2008). *Supporting transitions in the early years*. Maidenhead, Berkshire: Open University.

Centre for Community Child Health. (2008). *Rethinking school readiness: CCCH Policy Brief 10*. www.rch.org.au/emplibrary/ccch/PB10_SchoolReadiness.pdf.

Charlotte Bühler Institut. (2016). *OECD Thematic review of policies on transitions between ECEC and primary education: Country background report for Austria*. www.oecd.org/edu/school/SS5-country-background-report-austria.pdf

Department for Education and Child Development, South Australia. (2014). *Transition to school rubric*. www.beachroadpartnership.sa.edu.au/wp-content/uploads/2013/03/Transition-to-school-rubric.pdf

Department of Education, NSW. (2020). *Transition assessment and planning tool*. https://education.nsw.gov.au/teaching-and-learning/curriculum/early-learning/transition/transition-guidelines#Transition1

Department of Education and Early Childhood Development, Victoria (DEECD). (2017). *Transition: A positive start to school. Resource kit*. www.education.vic.gov.au/Documents/childhood/professionals/learning/Transition%20to%20School%20Resource%20Kit%202017%20FINAL.pdf

Dockett, S., Griebel, W., & Perry, B. (Eds.). (2017). *Families and the transition to school*. Cham, Switzerland: Springer. https://doi.org/10.1007/978-3-319-58329-7

Dockett, S., & Perry, B. (2001a). Starting school: Effective transitions. *Early Childhood Research and Practice*, 3(2). http://ecrp.uiuc.edu/v3n2/dockett.html

Dockett, S., & Perry, B. (Eds.). (2001b). *Beginning school together: Sharing strengths*. Watson, ACT: Australian Early Childhood Association.

Dockett, S., & Perry, B. (2006). *Starting school: A handbook for early childhood educators*. Sydney: Pademelon Press.

Dockett, S., & Perry, B. (2013). Trends and tensions: Australian and international research about starting school. *International Journal of Early Years Education*, 21(2–3), 163–177. https://doi.org/10.1080/09669760.2013.832943

Dockett, S., & Perry, B. (2014). *Continuity of learning: A resource to support effective transition to school and school age care*. Canberra, ACT: Australian Government Department of Education. https://docs.education.gov.au/system/files/doc/other/pdf_with_bookmarking_-_continuity_of_learning-_30_october_2014_1_0.pdf

Dockett, S., Perry, B., & Kearney, E. (2010). *School readiness: What does it mean for Indigenous children, families, schools and communities?* Canberra: Closing the Gap Clearinghouse. www.aihw.gov.au/reports/indigenous-australians/school-readiness-what-does-it-mean-for-indigenous/contents/table-of-contents

Dockett, S., Perry, B., & Kearney, E. (2011). Starting school with special needs: Issues for families with complex support needs as their children start school. *Exceptionality Education International*, 21(2), 45–61. https://doi.org/10.5206/eei.v21i2.7675

Dunlop, A.-W. (2014). Thinking about transitions – One framework or many? Populating the theoretical model over time. In B. Perry, S. Dockett, & A. Petriwskyj (Eds.), *Transitions to school: International research policy and practice* (pp. 31–46). Dordrecht: Springer. https://doi.org/10.1007/978-94-007-7350-9_3

Dunlop, A.-W., & Fabian, H. (Eds.). (2007). *Informing transitions in the early years. Research, policy and practice*. London: Open University Press.

Education Review Office. (2015). *Continuity of learning: Transitions from early childhood services to schools*. www.ero.govt.nz/assets/Uploads/ERO-Continuity-of-Learning-FINAL.pdf

Educational Transitions and Change (ETC) Research Group. (2011). *Transition to school: Position statement*. https://arts-ed.csu.edu.au/education/transitions/publications/Position-Statement.pdf

Edwards, A. (2011). Building common knowledge at the boundaries between professional practices: Relational agency and relational expertise in system of distributed expertise. *International Journal of Educational Research*, 50(1), 33–39. https://doi.org/10.1016/j.ijer.2011.04.007

Hopps, K. (2014). Preschool + school + communication = What for educator relationships? *Early Years*, 34(4), 405–419. https://doi.org/10.1080/09575146.2014.963032

Hopps-Wallis, K., & Perry, B. (2017). "You can't write that": The challenges of written communication between preschools and schools. *Australasian Journal of Early Childhood*, 42(3), 22–30. https://doi.org/10.23965/AJEC.42.3.03

James, A., Jenks, C., & Prout, A. (1998). *Theorizing childhood*. New York: Teachers College Press.

Kagan, S., & Tarrant, K. (Eds.). (2010). *Transitions for young children: Creating connections across early childhood systems*. Baltimore, MD: Paul H Brookes.

Karila, K., & Rantavuori, L. (2014). Discourses at the boundary spaces: Developing a fluent transition from preschool to school. *Early Years*, 34(4), 377–391. https://doi.org/10.1080/09575146.2014.967663

Lillejord, S., Børte, K., Halvorsrud, K., Ruud, E., & Freyr, T. (2017). *Transition from kindergarten to school: A systematic review*. Oslo: Knowledge Centre for Education. www.kunnskapssenter.no

Margetts, K., & Kienig, A. (Eds.). (2013). *International perspectives on transitions to school: Reconceptualising beliefs, policy and practice*. Abingdon, OX: Routledge.

Meisels, S. (2007). Accountability in early childhood: No easy answers. In R. Pianta, M. Cox, & K. Snow (Eds.), *School readiness and the transition to kindergarten in the era of* accountability (pp. 31–47). Baltimore, MD: Paul H Brookes.

Ministry for Children and Social Affairs. (2017). *Country background report Denmark – Transitions from ECEC to school*. www.oecd.org/edu/school/SS5-country-background-report-denmark.pdf

Ministry of Education and Culture, Finland. (2017). *Finnish country note on transitions in ECEC*. www.oecd.org/edu/school/SS5-country-background-report-finland.pdf

Ministry of Education and Research. (2016). *Country note on transitions: Sweden*. www.oecd.org/edu/school/SS5-country-background-report-sweden.pdf

Norwegian Directorate for Education and Training. (2017). *Norway country background report on transitions from ECEC to primary education*. www.oecd.org/edu/school/SS5-country-background-report-norway.pdf

O'Kane, M. (2016). *Transition from preschool to primary school*. Research Report No. 19. Dublin: National Council for Curriculum and Assessment. www.ncca.ie/media/2471/transition-research-report-no-19.pdf

O'Kane, M., & Murphy, R. (2016a). *Transition from preschool to primary school: Audit of policy in 14 jurisdictions*. Dublin: National Council for Curriculum and Assessment. www.ncca.ie/media/2468/transition-from-preschool-to-primary-school-audit-of-policy-in-14-jurisdictions.pdf

O'Kane, M., & Murphy, R. (2016b). *Supporting the transition from preschool to primary School: Audit of transfer documentation in Ireland*. Dublin: National Council for Curriculum and Assessment. www.ncca.ie/media/2469/transition-from-preschool-to-primary-school-audit-of-transfer-documentation-in-ireland.pdf

Organisation for Economic Cooperation and Development (OECD). (2017). *Starting strong V. Transitions from early childhood education and care to primary education*. Paris: OECD Publishing. https://doi.org/10.1787/9789264276253-en

Perry, B., Dockett, S., & Petriwskyj, A. (Eds.). (2014). *Transitions to school – International research, policy and practice*. Dordrecht: Springer. https://doi.org/10.1007/978-94-007-7350-9

Peters, S. (2010). *Literature review: Transition from early childhood education to school*. Waikato: New Zealand Ministry of Education. http://ece.manukau.ac.nz/__data/assets/pdf_file/0008/85841/956_ECELitReview.pdf

Petriwskyj, A., Thorpe, K., & Tayler, C. (2005). Trends in construction of transition to school in three western regions, 1990–2004. *International Journal of Early Years Education*, 13(1), 55–69. https://doi.org/10.1080/09669760500048360

Queensland Department of Education. (2020). *Supporting successful transitions: School decision-making tool*. https://earlychildhood.qld.gov.au/earlyYears/Documents/transition-to-school-decision-making-tool.pdf

Rimm-Kaufman, S. E., & Pianta, R. C. (2000). An ecological perspective on the transition to kindergarten: A theoretical framework to guide empirical research. *Journal of Applied Developmental Psychology*, 21(5), 491–511. https://doi.org/10.1016/S0193-3973(00)00051-4

Schultz, T. (2010). Accountability policies and transition. In S. Kagan & K. Tarrant (Eds.), *Transitions for young children: Creating connections across early childhood systems* (pp. 267–278). Baltimore, MD: Paul H Brookes.

Smart, D., Sanson, A., Baxter, J., Edwards, B., & Hayes, A. (2008). *Home-to-school transitions for financially disadvantaged children. Final report.* Sydney. The Smith Family and Australian Institute of Family Studies. www.thesmithfamily.com.au/-/media/files/research/reports/home-school-full-2008.pdf?la=en&hash=732D9B6AF03B74A4A20BAED828E09588

Sumsion, J., & Wong, S. (2011). Interrogating "belonging" in belonging, being and becoming: The early years learning framework for Australia. *Contemporary Issues in Early Childhood, 12*(1), 28–45. https://doi.org/10.2304/ciec.2011.12.1.28

United Nations. (1989). *The United Nations convention on the rights of the child.* New York, United Nations. www.ohchr.org/EN/ProfessionalInterest/Pages/CRC.aspx.

Victorian Auditor-General. (2015). *Education transitions.* www.audit.vic.gov.au/sites/default/files/20150318-Education-transitions.pdf

West, S., et al. (2012). *Outcomes and indicators of a positive start to school: Development of framework and tools.* www.education.vic.gov.au/Documents/about/research/outcomesandindicators.pdf

2 Defining transition

Sue Dockett and Bob Perry

Introduction

In recent years, transition and transition to school have been the focus of a great deal of research, policy, and practice. Key transition to school research highlights the potential benefits of transition programs but also indicates differences in conceptualisations of readiness and transition. In the following discussion we highlight the processes of continuity and change in transition in definitions of transition.

Transition and change

Several theoretical frameworks can be used to explore transitions (Dunlop, 2014). Modern approaches have shied away from developmental frameworks emphasising a fixed sequence of child development and have instead embraced frameworks that explore transitions as interactions among ecologies and systems, based on ecological and bioecological theory (Bronfenbrenner, 1979; Bronfenbrenner & Morris, 2006); highlight the influence of social and cultural contexts (Corsaro, 2011; Rogoff, 2003); promote the rights and competence of children (James, Jenks, & Prout, 1998; United Nations (UN), 1989); and question normative or expected patterns of interactions and/or outcomes (Dockett, 2014; Petriwskyj, 2014). In our ongoing work, we draw on each of these bioecological, socio-cultural, sociology of childhood, and critical frameworks to explore transitions to school. We also draw on perspectives from anthropology (van Gennep, 1960) and psychology (Cowan, 1991; Zittoun, 2016).

We start with the position that transitions are times when "individuals change their role in their community's structure" (Rogoff, 2003, p. 150). This definition highlights both individual change and the importance of social and cultural contexts as we experience transitions throughout life. For example, as we leave school and enter the workforce, we change our role in our community structure; when we become partners or parents, we experience role change. When children start school, they too experience role change as they cease to be *preschoolers* and become *school students*. For all of us, major life events provide impetus to change our sense of who we are and where we belong in the world.

Role changes are important. They signal to the individual, as well as to those around them, that things are different. Role changes involve both internal and external changes. The first day of school can signal change, as children don their school uniform and backpack and leave their parents at the classroom door or the school gate. At the same time as this external change, an internal change is likely to occur – where children start to think of themselves as a school child and start to construct their school identity – their sense of *who I am at school*. Changes in the ways children think about themselves contribute to changes in identity. So too do the ways in which others think about and interact with children. As children start school, they tell us that they feel different, look different, are expected to do different things, and are treated differently by others.

However, such changes are not only evident for children. Families also experience changes in role, identity, status, and agency. For example, as the parent of a school student there are expectations about what ought to be done to support children and how parents ought to engage with the ethos and requirements of school. These include clear expectations about attendance, drop off and pick-up times, school uniforms, and homework.

Educators can also experience changes in roles and identities. Teachers of the first year of school can have a specific identity as the Prep teacher, Kindergarten teacher, Reception teacher, Pre-Primary teacher, or Transition teacher. Each of these titles conveys a range of expectations about roles and identities – often bringing together elements of nurture as well as education. Educators in early childhood education and care (ECEC) settings also experience changes in roles and identity as one group of children leaves ECEC and another is formed.

The work of Griebel and Niesel (2009) has highlighted the transformational nature of the transition to school for families as well as individual family members. They describe changes at the individual, interactional, and contextual levels. For example, there are changes for individuals and families as they assume different roles and identities and respond to different expectations. At the interactional level, some relationships are lost, some are maintained and/or changed, and others need to be built. Within families and other social contexts, it is also possible to see changes in interactions. For example, parental interactions with children may change, and interactions among peers and between children and educators change as contexts change. At the contextual level, all experience change in routines and responsibilities in efforts to integrate home, school, and work lives.

Change is an integral element of transition. Indeed, without change, there is no need for transition. The changes in roles and identities that occur during times of transition are qualitative shifts – changes in the ways people see and think about themselves that incorporate changes in the relationships and roles that make up their everyday lives. While events to mark these changes are important, the events themselves are only part of transition experiences. Perhaps more important than events (such as the first day of school) are the internal

Defining transition 17

changes that come from how individuals perceive themselves and how others perceive them. Importantly, Cowan (1991, p. 5) notes that "passing a life marker (e.g. entering school) . . . does not in itself signify that a transition has been completed".

Nevertheless, the first day of school is an important event and constitutes one element of the transition to school. Ackesjö's (2013) research reminds us that while children and their families often look forward to this first day, another important marker of the transition to school involves detachment from their previous educational setting – in other words, saying goodbye to their ECEC settings (Dockett & Perry, 2014a) and creating the identity of a *former kindergarten child* (Ackesjö, 2013). In other words, the transition to school is not only about looking forward; it is also about looking back.

The importance of exiting one context and moving on to another is at the heart of van Gennep's (1960) anthropological studies of transition. van Gennep focused on significant life events and the rituals associated with these. If we position the transition to school as a significant life event, we can relate it to the three phases outlined by van Gennep: the preliminal phase where individuals separate from their present status; the liminal or in-between phase where the individual is between states; and the post-liminal phase where the new status is incorporated. In relation to transition to school, these phases of separation, transition, and incorporation can be represented as shown in Figure 2.1.

Thinking of transition across these phases reminds us that the transition to school is much more than a one-off event; it is a process involving individual and social change, influenced by communities and contexts and, within these, the relationships, identities, agency and power of all involved (Dockett & Perry, 2014a). Further, it is a process that begins well before the first day of school and extends well after.

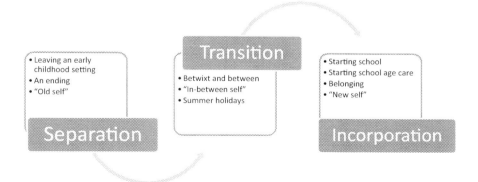

Figure 2.1 Phases of transition (after van Gennep, 1960).

Bronfenbrenner's (Bronfenbrenner & Morris, 2006) bioecological theory also attends to the importance of social and cultural contexts as well as the patterns of interaction between and among those within different contexts, across time. Bronfenbrenner's (1979) ecological model of nested concentric circles highlights the range of contexts relevant for young children. This model is at the heart of Rimm-Kaufman and Pianta's (2000) *Ecological and Dynamic Model of Transition*, which positions transition

> in terms of the influence of contexts (e.g., family, classroom, community), and the connections among these contexts (e.g. family–school relationships) at any given time and across time.
> (Pianta, Rimm-Kaufman, & Cox, 1999, p. 4)

Change can leave people feeling anxious and uncertain. Change can also be exciting. Children, families, and educators have described transitions to school in each of these ways. Recognising and responding to this time of potentially mixed emotions are key elements in managing change and supporting effective transitions. Developing strategies to manage change is one of the features encompassed by Dunlop's (2014) description of transitions capital, where experiences of effective transitions help to build the skills, knowledge, confidence, and resources that support future effective transitions experiences.

Transition and continuity

Some transitions – such as the transition to school – usually happen only once as children move to the next educational phase. This vertical transition is in contrast to the horizontal transitions children make every day as they move between contexts such as home and school and school and school age care. Horizontal transitions occur as individuals are simultaneously members of more than one context (Dockett, Griebel, & Perry, 2017).

While change is an essential element, most transitions also involve continuity. For many children, families provide continuity as they maintain a range of routines, interactions, and expectations. Continuity also can be seen as children's interests and favourite pastimes are maintained over the transition to school. It can be tempting to focus on the changes during the transition and challenges associated with these. However, it is important to recognise the significance of continuity in the lives of children and families – as well as educators – and the ways in which this can support transitions and help people manage change (Dockett & Einarsdóttir, 2017).

Continuity has become a major focus for transitions policy, with calls to promote continuity – particularly in children's learning – and reduce discontinuity as children start school. These calls do not seek to create prior-to-school and school settings as *mirror images* of each other. Nor do they necessarily promote notions of a *seamless* transition between settings (Boyle, Petriwskjy, & Grieshaber, 2018). Rather, they advocate for strategies that support the continuation of children's learning as they progress from ECEC to school settings, promoting "experiences and learning that build on what has gone before" (Dockett & Einarsdóttir, 2017, p. 133). Meaningful collaboration among ECEC and school educators is promoted as the prime means to achieve this continuity (Lillejord et al., 2017). However, it is important to consider how continuity is enacted and experienced by those involved rather than how continuity is planned for or outlined in curriculum documents. Of the many forms of continuity that have been described, Boyle et al. (2018) have proposed relational, practical, and policy continuity as areas for building innovative approaches to transitions and transitions research. Though using different terms, there is some overlap in these areas with the focus on professional, pedagogical, and developmental continuity outlined by the Organisation for Economic Co-operation and Development (OECD) (2017).

Transition as a time of continuity and change

Definitions of transition involve processes of both continuity and change. They recognise the significance of special events, such as the first day of school and last day of ECEC, and highlight the subtle and complex processes of identity construction associated with *becoming* a school student, school parent, ECEC educator for a new group, or first-year-of-school teacher. For most involved in the transition to school, some things remain the same. Family and community provide some of this continuity. Dunlop (2015, p. 148) highlights the role of both continuity and change in her characterisation of transitions as "intersections between prior and new experiences" where "points of similarity and difference become clearer and as a result spaces for action are opened up".

Definitions of transition also position it as a process that involves a wide range of people: the children themselves, family members, community connections, educators, support staff, professionals, and professional organisations all can be contributors to the transition to school. Transition processes occur over time rather than in a specifically designated transition program. We have argued that transition begins when children and families start to think and talk about starting school and only concludes when all involved feel a sense of belonging within the new school context (Dockett & Perry, 2014a). Zittoun (2016, p. 8) describes transition as the "processes by which a new sphere of experience is elaborated, until it feels like a taken-for-granted". In the case of starting school, these processes continue until school and the classroom feel like *natural* places to be. This means that some children and families may experience extended periods of transition. Educators have key roles in recognising and responding to individual differences in transition while also being aware of the social and cultural contexts that influence these.

Key transitions research

The transition to school is identified as a significant life event for children and for their families. Entering the school environment brings a great deal of change as individuals and groups encounter changed social, academic, behavioural, and physical contexts. There is a range of research evidence that indicates that children's early school experiences can impact their ongoing engagement and educational outcomes (Ahtola et al., 2011; LoCasale-Crouch et al., 2012). Given this, it is not surprising that families and educators are eager to ensure that the transition to school is as effective as possible. The ways in which this can be achieved are the subject of ongoing research.

While the majority of children starting school are reported to manage this effectively, this is not necessarily the case for all children (Lillejord et al., 2017). It is tempting to categorise those experiencing challenges as having *disadvantaged* backgrounds. Disrupting assumptions that all members of specific groups will experience *problematic* transitions and recognising that some situations may generate challenges for any child and/or family (Peters, 2010) is important if we are to question normative expectations and promote socially just and equitable approaches to transition (Lago, 2017; Lehrer, Bigras, & Laurin, 2017; Perry, 2014). So too is adopting strengths-based approaches that acknowledge the existing knowledge, skills, and understandings of individuals and groups (Hopps-Wallis, Fenton, & Dockett, 2016).

A substantial body of research explores the perspectives and experiences of stakeholders across the transition process. In summarising recent research of children's perspectives of the transition to school, Dockett, Einarsdóttir, and Perry (2019) conclude that most children look forward to starting school, regarding it as a progression. They are active participants in their transition (Huf, 2013; Jadue-Roa, 2019) and expect both change and continuity. Children may take on a brokerage role as they move between different settings (Pálsdóttir, 2019), connecting different communities of practice (Wenger, 1998). Recognising this brokerage role and listening to children's perspectives affords educators the opportunity to build connections across settings and to plan transition programs that are relevant and meaningful for the children involved (Büker & Höke, 2019).

Investigations of family engagement in the transition to school often highlight the role of the family in preparing children for school, generating a supportive home environment, and promoting the school's educational agenda at home (Dockett et al., 2017). While each of these areas is important, recent research problematises assumptions that the key role of families is to prepare children for school and reminds us that families also experience transitions as children start school (Griebel et al., 2017).

The importance of relationships between families and those in educational settings is noted, both as a means of promoting collaboration and for addressing concerns and/or anxieties family members may experience (Ackesjö, 2017; Wilder & Lillvist, 2017). Family–educator relationships that are characterised as respectful, reciprocal, and regular (Ahtola et al., 2015; Miller, 2015; Peters, 2014) provide support for effective transitions experiences. In most instances, families are willing to engage in a range of experiences to support the transition to school. However, not all transition practices and their rationales are labelled as such. Ackesjö (2013) and Turunen (2012) have urged educators to be explicit in describing transition practices and in providing relevant information about these to both children and families as well as to other educators.

Relationships between educators in ECEC and school settings contribute to the effectiveness of transition practices. Collaboration among educators can go a long way to promoting continuity (Dockett & Perry, 2014a). Professional relationships can be challenging when there are clear asymmetries across ECEC and school systems, status, curriculum, pedagogies, histories, and traditions (Boyle & Petriwskyj, 2014; Karila & Rantavuori, 2014; Lillejord et al., 2017). Nevertheless, collaboration can be both productive and worthwhile when educators know and respect each other's expertise (Hopps, 2014), build a common knowledge base (Edwards, 2011), and have the time and resources to work from this to construct a set of common goals as well as strategies to work towards achieving these (Educational Transitions and Change (ETC) Research Group, 2011).

Transition and readiness

One of the challenges to professional relationships can be the pressure felt by ECEC educators to prepare children for school. While ECEC educators draw on many experiences to help children build the necessary skills and understandings to support transitions, they also report pressure to ensure that children are made *ready* for school through preparatory activities (Dockett & Perry, 2014b). Typically, the focus on readiness emphasises children's academic skills, particularly their literacy and numeracy skills (Dockett & Perry, 2009), with the rationale that *ready* children can start learning as soon as they start school. The pushing down of academic curriculum has been termed *schoolification* (Moss, 2013) and *schoolarisation* (Ackesjö & Persson, 2019; see also Chapter 2A), with the result that some researchers have questioned whether kindergarten [preschool] has become the new first year of school (Bassok, Latham, & Rorem, 2016). Critique of this focus reminds us that readiness is a broad concept that incorporates not only children's readiness but also the readiness of schools for children and of families and communities to support children (Dockett & Perry, 2009); identifies the influence of social and cultural contexts on perceptions of readiness (Petriwskyj, 2014); recognises that play-based experiences support the development of a wide range of skills and understandings (Broström, 2013); and positions transition as a much broader concept than readiness (Ahtola et al., 2011; Dockett & Perry, 2013).

Approaches to transition and readiness are guided by how we conceptualise children, their development, and the role of education. Chapter 2A explores changes in these conceptualisations in Sweden since the 1940s, tracking changes in how prevailing images of children have influenced educational provision. In Sweden and other contexts around the world, different theoretical bases have influenced these beliefs. For example, maturational theory emphasises biological determinants of development and argues that children develop according to their own schedule. This perspective proposes that readiness cannot be hurried but rather relies on the *gift of time* (Graue, 2006). Transition programs adopting this theoretical base aim to provide time for children's knowledge and skills to emerge. Environmental theories focus on the ways the environment shapes learning and development and how children demonstrate their learning and skills. Related transition programs create environments to teach the specific set of knowledge and skills considered necessary to engage with school education (Meisels, 1999).

In contrast, the importance of social and cultural contexts is emphasised in theories that situate readiness and transition within local communities (Corsaro, 2011; Graue & Reineke, 2014). These theories highlight interactions between children, families, educators, and communities, the importance of relationships, and the contexts in which these interactions and relationships occur. Approaches to readiness and transition adopting socio-cultural theories regard children as competent contributors to transitions, draw on strengths-based strategies, and are shaped to local contexts. The ecological model described by Rimm-Kaufman and Pianta (2000) is an example of this theoretical framing. In recent years, these approaches have been complemented by researchers adopting critical perspectives, questioning normative assumptions, and examining issues related to power and equity (Petriwskyj, 2014). The combination of focus on social and cultural contexts, the importance of relationships, strengths-based approaches, recognised competence of children, and the importance of challenging assumptions underpins the work we report in this book.

Different conceptualisations of readiness and transition generate different transition programs and practices. Differences are also reflected as social expectations and attitudes change. Chapter 2A provides an example of changing trends in Sweden, noting the move towards global discourses of readiness and readying the child for school – referred to as schoolarisation. Similar trends worldwide contribute to tensions around conceptualisations of transition and readiness (Moss, 2013). However, they also open up spaces where various meanings and interpretations, the many guises of readiness, as well as the possibilities of transition can be debated.

Transition activities, practices, and programs

Transition activities and practices contribute to transition programs. In this discussion we consider a range of transition activities – defined as procedures or actions that are designed to promote learning about, and engagement with, the transition to school. Transition activities may be spontaneous as well as planned; designed specifically for individuals or targeted towards a group; one-off orientation events or part of a sequence. Those who plan, implement and/or participate in transition activities may be any or all of the stakeholders: children, families, educators, community members, professionals, and others involved in the transition to school. Activities become practices when they occur regularly. Transition programs consist of a plan or schedule of activities and practices that aim to promote positive transition to school experiences for all involved.

A range of transitions activities can be identified. Many of these are described as preparatory or orientating (Boyle et al., 2018), with the aim of assisting children and families to adjust to the school environment. Other practices aim to prepare schools for the children and families entering their setting. Some practices focus on building relationships among stakeholders; others aim to share information; still others seek to promote the broad notions of readiness that incorporate ready children, families, schools, and communities (Dockett & Perry, 2014a).

Example: Practices to support transition

A research–practice partnership in Madison, Wisconsin identified a range of transitions practices used to "help children and families move smoothly into kindergarten" (Lauter et al., 2020, p. 6). Teachers working in settings equivalent to Australian preschools identified much of their preschool program as supporting children's move into school, including the teaching of social-emotional and academic skills. They also noted the importance of program changes, such as reducing rest time, to align with school schedules. Teachers also communicated with families about the forthcoming transition. Visits to school classrooms were made by some, but not all, preschool groups.

At the school level, typical transition practices included opportunities for children enrolled at the school and their families to visit the school; organised play dates where families and teachers met at a local park; and 15-minute school-based conferences with each family prior to the start of school.

(Woo et al., 2019)

Many transition practices have been used in different contexts. The most appropriate practices in any context can be identified through interactions with stakeholders. Where transition teams or networks exist, it is possible to brainstorm a working list of possible practices that reflect the strengths and challenges within the local community. Children and families can also make valuable contributions to this list (see, for example, Dockett et al., 2019; Perry & Dockett, 2011 for some suggestions from children). Pianta and Kraft-Sayre (2003) and Dockett and Perry (2006) refer to a menu of possible practices. Examples of many possible practices gleaned from a national study are detailed in Dockett and Perry (2014a). Some general practices and examples are listed in Table 2.1.

The *Transition: A Positive Start to School* initiative in Victoria has promoted several promising practices including the creation of local transition networks, reciprocal visits to ECEC and school settings, buddy programs for children, and the use of social story boards (Victorian Department of Education and Training, 2020).

Table 2.1 Transition practices and examples (Derived from Dockett & Perry, 2014a, pp. 5–6).

General practices	Examples
Connecting with children	Buddy programs Personal communication School and school age care visits
Connecting with families	Meeting families before school starts Information sharing Regular communication with families
Connecting with professionals	Collaboration among educators Communicating with other professionals Establishing professional networks
Connecting with communities	Sharing information Engaging the community in transition Being seen in the community
Flexible and responsive transition programs	Involving a range of stakeholders Providing resources in a range of languages Accessing appropriate support for children and families
Recognising strengths	Documentation to celebrate children's achievements Family-centred practice Sharing aspirations and expectations
Reflective practice	Regular meetings of educators Joint professional learning Monitoring transition practices and outcomes
Building relationships	Promoting positive relationships among children, families, and educators Developing community partnerships

Example: Supporting Aboriginal and Torres Strait Islander children's transition to primary school

SNAICC reports a range of practices to support transition as Aboriginal and Torres Strait Islander children and families move to primary school. Drawing on practices from multiple settings, they note the importance of practices that help children and families become familiar with the school environment; promote relationships between ECEC settings and schools; promote information sharing and exchange visits between settings; the creation of transition books to record children's visits to school and help to prompt ongoing conversations; and the provision of ongoing support that continues into the school year.

(Mason-White, 2014)

While there are many possible transition practices, it is important to note that the most appropriate practices depend on the contexts and the people involved.

In our work, we resist reference to *best* practice or *universal* practice, as these terms suggest that there is one common set of practices that will be effective and relevant in any context. Rather, we established very early in our research agenda that "effective transition programs take into account contextual aspects of community, and of individual families and children within that community" (Dockett & Perry, 2001).

Transition practices can be described in terms of the intensity of contact. Some transition practices involve generic contact and are described as low-intensity. Examples include newsletters and posters about starting school. Personal contact is characteristic of high-intensity practices such as meetings with children, families, and other educators and visits to different settings (Einarsdóttir, Perry, & Dockett, 2008; Pianta & Kraft-Sayre, 2003). High-intensity practices promote the building of relationships that are positively connected to children's school outcomes (Cook & Coley, 2017; Schulting, Malone, & Dodge, 2005). They are also the practices that require the greatest time commitment. The sharing of written information – transition to school statements – is increasingly common across Australia and in some other countries (O'Kane & Murphy, 2016). The level of intensity involved with sharing this information will depend on the strategies for generating, sharing, and interpreting the information. In determining appropriate transition practices, many transition teams aim for a balance of low- and high-intensity activities.

Example: Comparing transitions practices

A comparison of common transitions practices in Iceland and Australia revealed some differences as well as commonalities. Both Icelandic and Australian teachers were likely to support school visits by preschool children, and most of those teachers surveyed in each setting were willing to share records about individual children as they moved onto school. Relatively few teachers in each context promoted visits back to the preschool by those children who had recently started school. However, more Australian than Icelandic teachers reported visits by primary school teachers to preschools, and more Icelandic primary school teachers reported sending a letter to children before they started school than their Australian counterparts.

(Einarsdóttir et al., 2008)

The timing of transition practices is important. Some practices may occur before or after the start of school; others may be ongoing. The reach of transition practices also varies. Some activities reach out to families and build home–school and/or ECEC–school connections. Others are specific to home, ECEC, or school contexts.

While much of the focus on transition considers the readiness of children to start school, in their ecological model, Pianta et al. (1999) consider transition practices that support the notion of ready schools – schools ready to adapt to and work with their communities. They promote transition practices that:

- reach out – build links with families and ECEC settings to build relationships and connections that support collaborative transition practices;
- reach back in time – linking with families and ECEC settings well before the first day of school; and
- reach with appropriate intensity – recognising that a range of practices will be appropriate for different people at different times.

How many activities and practices are needed to make a program? There are many possible answers to this question. Some research has suggested positive outcomes when children and their families engage in six or more transition activities (Margetts, 2003). While access to transition activities has been shown to be important (LoCasale-Crouch et al., 2008), a recent US study (Little, 2017) has reported no relationship between the number of transition practices offered and student outcomes during the first year of school.

These studies highlight some subtle differences. The first is the difference between what activities are offered and actual participation. Regardless of how many activities are planned and implemented, they will be ineffective if they do not engage key stakeholders. Differences in the intensity, timing, and reach of activities also need to be considered, as does the location of these activities. Further, there may be many elements to transition programs but with no expectation that everyone will engage in every element. In other words, the nature, quality, timing, location, and relevance for potential participants will be important factors in determining their effectiveness. Considering these factors reminds us that transition occurs within social and cultural contexts, as children, families, and educators participate in different ecologies and communities of practice.

Conclusion

In recent decades we have witnessed increasing global interest in the transition to school. While recognising this as a *big step for children* (OECD, 2017), the significance of the transition for families and educators as well as systems and communities has also been recognised (ETC Research Group, 2011). To set the scene for what follows, this chapter has defined the transition to school as a process incorporating both continuity and change, involving multiple stakeholders, and occurring over time. We have positioned children as active participants in their own transitions but also reliant on those around them to build the relationships and participate in the interactions that promote the effective engagement with school that, in turn, generate a sense of belonging. Key transition to school research highlights the potential benefits of transition programs, but also indicates differences in conceptualisations of readiness and transition, as well as continuing trends towards the schoolarisation of ECEC as outlined in Chapter 2A. The ways in which transition practices and programs may contribute to effective transitions – and how we might evaluate these – are the focus of following chapters.

2A To be or not to be (a school child) – from national to global discourses about the child in the school start age

Helena Ackesjö and Sven Persson

A conceptual frame for analysis

Policy mobilises and formulates truths rather than reflecting the social reality. Policy discourses play a major role in how problems and solutions are defined and how the effects of reforms in education systems are measured over time (Ball, 2017). Policy discourses formulate assertions about a subject, namely, the child/pupil who will be educated. To promote change, policies must lay claim to the education system as a whole; that is, what the child should be qualified for.

Swedish policy documents from the 1940s to 2017 have been analysed using the concepts of *subjectification* and *qualification*. According to Biesta (2009), policy expresses discourses about subjectification, the individual to be educated. This means that there will be (truth) claims in the policy texts about the child's nature and what the child will become through education. The discourse on qualification relates to the preparation for the next educational level. In the following we apply the aspects of subjectification and qualification to the discussion of children's transitions to school.

To be or not to be a school child

We begin our analysis with Swedish state policy documents from the 1940s. During this time, many women were employed outside the home, resulting in the need to expand education and care for very young children. The transition to school, either from home or from preschool, was conditioned by maturity requirements, and this is the dominant discourse across documents.

In policy, the six-year-old is re-presented as *a problematic child*, and the children at home in the big cities need to be taken care of while parents worked (SOU, 1948:27). The purpose of the preschool program for five- to seven-year-olds was social fostering in a protected environment while complementing the home. The focus for qualifying children was character formation, to nurture social relations, and make children become responsible individuals (SOU, 1951:15).

From the 1960s to the '70s, preschool pedagogy gained societal recognition as well as a more scientific, professional approach, and the state articulated

DOI: 10.4324/9781003055112-3

growing responsibility for a preschool program (Hammarström-Lewenhagen, 2016). More children attended preschool, and preschool activities that complemented the home appear highly prioritised as well as children's own activities and play (SOU, 1972:26). During this time, the six-year-old is described as an *anxious, energetic, and enterprising child*. The discussion continues about the school-(im)mature child.

In order to start school, it was required that the child (both six- and seven-year-old) had to reach a certain level of maturity, and a school maturity test (pedagogical test and medical examination) was introduced to determine this (SOU, 1948:27). The concept of school maturity was introduced in the Education Act for the first time in 1946. The aim of the school maturity test was to enable the school to create "desirable homogeneity in terms of the age of intelligence in the classes" (SOU, 1948:27, p. 10). If the child was not considered sufficiently mature for starting school, they were directed to wait another year at home or preschool (SOU, 1951:15).

The School Law (1962:319, chapter 6, section 32) stated that children who had not yet reached the school start age but who were considered mature may start school at six years old. Further, each child should be supported and stimulated based on their special prerequisites (SOU, 1972:27).

During the 1970s, the transition to school became prioritised in policy texts. The school maturity tests were criticised and replaced with emphasis on the importance of differentiating the instructions "so that every child can continue in the school framework from where he [sic] left off in preschool" (SOU, 1974:53, pp. 93–95). For this to be possible, the preschool and school were encouraged to come closer together in terms of goals, content, and methodology; only then could the compulsory school continue on the foundation laid in the preschool (SOU, 1974:53).

In the 1980s and 1990s, the image of the six-year-old changed. *The child who needs to be prepared and adapted* to school is re-presented in the policy documents, based on the idea that a relatively passive pupil role is required in primary education compared to preschool (SOU, 1985:22). Discussion about school maturity continued at the beginning of this period. It is pointed out that qualifying (preparing) the six-year-olds for school should be a joint collaboration between preschool and school in order to construct a smooth transition for the child. However, it is also stated that six-year-olds need to be prepared before their school start: "To learn to sit still and work at one's place, quietly and on one's own, carry out prescribed usually individual tasks, wait for one's turn, raise one's hand . . ." are examples of desirable behaviours (SOU, 1985:22, p. 106) and skills that the six-year-old needed to develop before starting school.

Several educational policy initiatives were undertaken during this time in Sweden and in the following decades in order to strengthen both the preschool and school and children's transition between them. At this time, the government gave parents the right to decide if their child should start school at six or seven years of age, suggesting that state policy recognised that parents had the knowledge to judge their child's maturity level and their needs and abilities for participating in school (Government proposition, 1990/91:115).

A discursive break occurs during the period of 1997–2012. This is the period when the child emerges with a face in the policy document descriptions. When the preschool class was implemented in 1998, it was again stated that education should be adapted to the pupils' different knowledge levels and conditions and not vice versa. During this time, the six-year-old is described as a *playful, explorative child* (SOU, 1997:21). The emphasis in the policy texts is placed on what the child *is* rather than on what the child should *become*. Unlike descriptions of the child as incomplete and immature and as individuals who must be formed in society and school (*becomings*), which commonly appeared in the earlier texts, the child during this time period is described as competent and having important individual abilities (*beings*). Qualification was to be based on the individual child's interests and curiosity, portraying the child as an active agent in their education rather than as a passive recipient (Lee, 2001). As the responsibility for judging school maturity and starting school shifted from the state to parents, the school start was made flexible (at six or seven years) based on the child's (and parents') necessities and wishes (SOU, 1997:21, 2010:67).

Starting in 2010, the language used for the education of the six-year-olds changed to focus on adapting the preschool class instruction and the six-year-olds to the culture and organization of the school. From 2010 onwards, these descriptions focus on knowledge outcomes and increased societal differences. Discussion departs from descriptions of the essential child and now emphasises the conditions in which Swedish children are growing up. Policy documents recognise that children have different prerequisites and abilities and specifically stress the support of children in need of special education. In the compulsory school report (SOU, 2015:91), the formulations change from what the child *is* to what the child should *become*. The term *child* is replaced by *pupil*, and the six-year-old is re-presented as a *performing school pupil*. During the intensive reform period of 2012–2017, the school start age is lowered, and a ten-year compulsory school is established, with a compulsory preschool class including obligatory school attendance (Government proposition, 2017/18:9) together with a clarified instructional mission aimed at the school knowledge requirements (SOU, 2015:91; Government proposition, 2017/18:9). Later, a compulsory assessment of the six-year-olds' linguistic awareness and mathematical thinking was introduced (SOU, 2016:59), which could appear as an *inverse school maturity test*. This implies that children's transition to school demands a major change of role, from the playing preschool child to the performing and obligated pupil in school.

Schoolarisation – discourses of the six-year-old legitimise a position shift in the education system

Since 1940, many educational policy initiatives have been undertaken to strengthen both the preschool and school in Sweden. However, the six-year-old has often ended up in the shadow of, or the border between, preschool and school. The six-year-old has been portrayed as too mature to be in preschool and not mature enough to be in school. In this final section, we place the results in a global educational policy context.

At the beginning of the studied period, there is a clear relation to the national circumstances. Sweden is in the post-war era and is on the way to building a welfare state through investments in public institutions. The six-year-old is re-presented as an immature child, not expected to be mature enough to pass through the eye of the needle to school. At the end of the period, the global discourses on the child and the qualifications for school are both implicitly and explicitly present. The discursive break that occurs in the period of 1997–2012, when the six-year-old is described as a playful, explorative child, is exceptional in that it is assumed that school should adapt to the child's abilities instead of the other way around. However, the ongoing shift in policy descriptions over time, from the *immature, problematic child* in the 1940s and '50s to the *performing (obligated) pupil* in the 2010s, is a national adaptation to a global discourse on knowledge efficiency competition where the qualification of very young children in the education system is essential.

Educational policy reforms in the last decade have mainly been about finding success factors for increased learning as well as qualifying children for further schooling. Swedish school pupils' results in global knowledge assessments motivate the investment in reforms to increase the level of knowledge of very young children, in our study exemplified through discourses about the six-year-old. We call this shift *schoolarisation* (Ackesjö & Persson, 2019); a concept which describes a position shift of two processes: one is getting closer to the school content, goals, and teaching, while simultaneously the other is distancing from the content, goals, and teaching in the preschool. The re-presentation of the six-year-old as a performing and obligated school pupil in policy documents is coherent with a global context that holds up competition, knowledge efficiency, and economic incentives for schoolarisation. Accompanying this has been the increased emphasis on transition to school as a time of qualifying (preparing) the child for the next educational level.

We noted in the introduction that education is basically about *producing* a person, based on ideas about the child to be educated and a vision of the educated person. Our analysis indicates that this discursive representation of the six-year-old legitimises an ongoing schoolarisation of the Swedish education system.

Acknowledgement: This study is part of the project *The preschool class in transition*, financed by the Swedish Research Council (Ackesjö, dnr. 2017–03592), 2018–2021.

References

Ackesjö, H. (2013). Children crossing borders: School visits as initial incorporation rites in transition to preschool class. *International Journal of Early Childhood*, 45(3), 387–410. https://doi.org/10.1007/s13158-013-0080-7

Ackesjö, H. (2017). Parents' emotional and academic attitudes towards children's transition to preschool class – Dimensions of school readiness and continuity. In S. Dockett, W. Griebel, & B. Perry (Eds.), *Families and the transition to school* (pp. 147–161). Cham, Switzerland: Springer. https://doi.org/10.1007/978-3-319-58329-7_10

Ackesjö, H., & Persson, S. (2019). The schoolarization of the preschool class – Policy discourses and educational restructuring in Sweden. *Nordic Journal of Studies in Educational Policy, 5*(2), 127–136. https://doi.org/10.1080/20020317.2019.1642082

Ahtola, A., Silinskas, G., Poikonen, P. L., Kontoniemi, M., Niemi, P., & Nurmi, J. E. (2011). Transition to formal schooling: Do transition practices matter for academic performance? *Early Childhood Research Quarterly, 26*(3), 295–302. https://doi.org/10.1016/j.ecresq.2010.12.002

Ahtola, A., Björn, M., Turunen, T., Poikonen, P.-L., Kontoniemi, M., Lerkkanen, M.-K., & Nurmi, J.-E. (2015). The concordance between teachers' and parents' perceptions of school transition practices: A solid base for the future. *Scandinavian Journal of Educational Research, 60*(2), 168–181. https://doi.org/10.1080/00313831.2014.996598

Ball, S. J. (2017). *The education debate* (3rd ed.). Bristol: Policy Press.

Bassok, D., Latham, S., & Rorem, A. (2016). Is kindergarten the new first grade? *AERA Open, 2*(1). https://doi.org/10.1177/2332858415616358

Biesta, G. (2009). Good education in an age of measurement: On the need to reconnect with the question of purpose in education. *Educational Assessment Evaluation and Accountability, 21*(1), 33–46. https://doi.org/10.1007/s11092-008-9064-9

Boyle, T., & Petriwskyj, A. (2014). Transitions to school: Reframing professional relationships. *Early Years: An International Research Journal, 34*(4), 392–404. https://doi.org/10.1080/09575146.2014.953042

Boyle, T., Petriwskyj, A., & Grieshaber, S. (2018). Reframing transitions to school as continuity practices: The role of practice architectures. *Australian Education Researcher, 45*, 419–434. https://doi.org/10.1007/s13384-018-0272-0

Bronfenbrenner, U. (1979). *The ecology of human development: Experiments in nature and design.* Cambridge, MA: Harvard University Press.

Bronfenbrenner, U., & Morris, P. A. (2006). The bioecological model of human development. In W. Damon & R. M. Lerner (Eds.), *Handbook of child psychology, Vol. 1: Theoretical models of human development* (6th ed., pp. 793–828). New York: Wiley. https://doi.org/10.1002/9780470147658.chpsy0114

Broström, S. (2013). Play as the main road in children's transition to school. In O. Lillemyr, S. Dockett, & B. Perry (Eds.), *Varied perspectives on play and learning: Theory and research in early childhood education* (pp. 37–53). Charlotte, NC: Information Age.

Büker, P., & Höke, J. (2019). Children's voices as a bridge between education in kindergarten and teachers in primary school: Potential of children's perspectives to support professional development. In S. Dockett, J. Einarsdóttir, & B. Perry (Eds.), *Listening to children's advice about starting school and school age care* (pp. 116–132). London: Routledge.

Cook, K. D., & Coley, R. L. (2017). School transition practices and children's social and academic adjustment in kindergarten. *Journal of Educational Psychology, 109*, 166–177. https://doi.org/10.1037/edu0000139

Corsaro, W. (2011). *The sociology of childhood* (3rd ed.). Thousand Oaks, CA: Pine Forge Press.

References – Chapters 2 and 2A

Cowan, P. (1991). Individual and family life transitions: A proposal or a new definition. In P. Cowan & M. Hetherington, (Eds.), *Family transitions* (pp. 3–30). Hillsdale, NJ: Erlbaum.

Dockett, S. (2014). Transition to school: Normative or relative? In B. Perry, S. Dockett, & A. Petriwskyj (Eds.), *Transitions to school – International research, policy and practice* (pp. 187–200). Dordrecht: Springer. https://doi.org/10.1007/978-94-007-7350-9_14

Dockett, S., & Einarsdóttir, J. (2017). Continuity and change as children start school. In N. Ballam, B. Perry, & A. Garpelin (Eds.), *Pedagogies of educational transitions. European and Antipodean research* (pp. 133–150). Dordrecht: Springer. https://doi.org/10.1007/978-3-319-43118-5_9

Dockett, S., Einarsdóttir, J., & Perry, B. (Eds.). (2019). *Listening to children's advice about starting school and school age care*. London: Routledge. https://doi.org/10.4324/9781351139403

Dockett, S., Griebel, W., & Perry, B. (2017). Transition to school: A family affair. In S. Dockett, W. Griebel, & B. Perry (Eds.), *Families and the transition to school* (pp. 1–18). Cham, Switzerland: Springer. https://doi.org/10.1007/978-3-319-58329-7_1

Dockett, S., & Perry, B. (2001). Starting school: Effective transitions. *Early Childhood Research and Practice*, 3(2). http://ecrp.uiuc.edu/v3n2/dockett.html

Dockett, S., & Perry, B. (2006). *Starting school: A handbook for early childhood educators*. Sydney: Pademelon Press.

Dockett, S., & Perry, B. (2009). Readiness for school: A relational construct. *Australasian Journal of Early Childhood*, 34(1), 20–26. https://doi.org/10.1177/183693910903400104

Dockett, S., & Perry, B. (2013). Trends and tensions: Australian and international research about starting school. *International Journal of Early Years Education*, 21(2–3), 163–177. https://doi.org/10.1080/09669760.2013.832943

Dockett, S., & Perry, B. (2014a). *Continuity of learning: A resource to support effective transition to school and school age care*. Canberra, ACT: Australian Government Department of Education. https://docs.education.gov.au/system/files/doc/other/pdf_with_bookmarking_-_continuity_of_learning-_30_october_2014_1_0.pdf

Dockett, S., & Perry, B. (2014b). Universal access to preschool education – Approaches to integrating preschool with school in rural and remote communities. *Early Years*, 34(4), 420–435. https://doi.org/10.1080/09575146.2014.968100

Dunlop, A.-W. (2014). Thinking about transitions – One framework or many? Populating the theoretical model over time. In B. Perry, S. Dockett, & A. Petriwskyj (Eds.), *Transitions to school: International research policy and practice* (pp. 31–46). Dordrecht: Springer. https://doi.org/10.1007/978-94-007-7350-9_3

Dunlop, A.-W. (2015). The developing child in society: Making transitions. In M. Reed & R. Walker (Eds.), *A critical companion to early childhood* (pp. 142–153). London: SAGE. https://doi.org/10.4135/9781473910188.n13

Educational Transitions and Change (ETC) Research Group. (2011). *Transition to school: Position statement*. https://arts-ed.csu.edu.au/education/transitions/publications/Position-Statement.pdf

Edwards, A. (2011). Building common knowledge at the boundaries between professional practices: Relational agency and relational expertise in system of distributed expertise. *International Journal of Educational Research*, 50(1), 33–39. https://doi.org/10.1016/j.ijer.2011.04.007

Einarsdóttir, J., Perry, B., & Dockett, S. (2008). Transition to school practices: Comparisons from Iceland and Australia. *Early Years*, *28*(1), 47–60. https://doi.org/10.1080/09575140801924689

Government proposition 1990/91:115. *Om vissa skollagsfrågor m.m.* [Some school law issues].

Government proposition 2017/18:9. *Skolstart vid sex års ålder* [Starting school at six years old].

Graue, M. E. (2006). The answer is readiness – Now what is the question? *Early Education and Development*, *17*(1), 43–56. https://doi.org/10.1207/s15566935eed1701_3

Graue, M. E., & Reineke, J. (2014). The relation of research on readiness to research/practice of transitions. In B. Perry, S. Dockett, & A. Petriwskyj (Eds.), *Transitions to school: International research, policy and practice* (pp. 159–173). Dordrecht: Springer. https://doi.org/10.1007/978-94-007-7350-9_12

Griebel, W., & Niesel, R. (2009). A developmental psychology perspective in Germany: Co-construction of transitions between family and education system by the child, parents and pedagogues. *Early Years*, *29*(1), 59–68. https://doi.org/10.1080/09575140802652230

Griebel, W., Wildgruber, A., Schuster, A., & Radan, J. (2017). Transition to being parents of a school-child: Parental perspective on coping of parents and child nine months after school start. In S. Dockett, W. Griebel, & B. Perry (Eds.), *Families and transition to school* (pp. 21–36). Cham, Switzerland: Springer. https://doi.org/10.1007/978-3-319-58329-7_2

Hammarström-Lewenhagen, B. (2016). *Förskolans århundrade: pedagogiska nyckeltexter om förskolans framväxt och idéarv* [The preschool century: Key pedagogical texts on the growth and heritage of preschool]. Malmö: Gleerups Utbildning.

Hopps, K. (2014). Preschool + school + communication = What for educator relationships? *Early Years*, *34*(4), 405–419. https://doi.org/10.1080/09575146.2014.963032

Hopps-Wallis, K., Fenton, A., & Dockett, S. (2016). Focusing on strengths as children start school: What does it mean in practice? *Australasian Journal of Early Childhood*, *41*(2), 103–111. https://doi.org/10.1177/183693911604100214

Huf, C. (2013). Children's agency during transition to formal schooling. *Ethnography and Education*, *8*(1), 61–76. https://doi.org/10.1080/17457823.2013.766434

Jadue-Roa, D. (2019). Children's agency in transition experiences: Understanding possibilities and challenges. In S. Dockett, J. Einarsdóttir, & B. Perry (Eds.), *Listening to children's advice about starting school and school age care* (pp. 26–41). London: Routledge.

James, A., Jenks, C., & Prout, A. (1998). *Theorizing childhood*. New York: Teachers College Press.

Karila, K., & Rantavuori, L. (2014). Discourses at the boundary spaces: Developing a fluent transition from preschool to school. *Early Years*, *34*(4), 377–391. https://doi.org/10.1080/09575146.2014.967663

Lago, L. (2017). Different transitions: Timetable failures in the transition to school. *Children & Society*, *31*, 243–252. https://doi.org/10.1111/chso.12176

Lauter, L., Woo, M., Grodsky, E., & Graue, M. E. (2020). *Improving the transition to kindergarten through information sharing: Project report*. Madison Education Partnership. http://mep.wceruw.org/documents/MEP-improving-transition-research-brief.pdf

References – Chapters 2 and 2A

Lee, N. (2001). *Childhood and society. Growing up in an age of uncertainty.* Buckingham: Open University Press.

Lehrer, J., Bigras, N., & Laurin, I. (2017). Preparing to start school: Parent and early childhood educator narratives. In S. Dockett, W. Griebel, & B. Perry (Eds.), *Families and transition to school* (pp. 195–210). Cham, Switzerland: Springer. https://doi.org/10.1007/978-3-319-58329-7_13

Lillejord, S., Børte, K., Halvorsrud, K., Ruud, E., & Freyr, T. (2017). *Transition from kindergarten to school: A systematic review.* Oslo: Knowledge Centre for Education. www.kunnskapssenter.no

Little, M. (2017). School-based kindergarten transition practices and child outcomes: Revisiting the issue. *The Elementary School Journal, 118*(2), 335–356. https://doi.org/10.1086/694221

LoCasale-Crouch, J., Mashburn, A. J., Downer, J. T., & Pianta, R. C. (2008). Pre-kindergarten teachers' use of transition practices and children's adjustment to kindergarten. *Early Childhood Research Quarterly, 23*, 124–139. https://doi.org/10.1016/j.ecresq.2007.06.001

LoCasale-Crouch, J., Moritz-Rudasill, K., Sweeney, B., Chattrabhuti, C., Patton, C., & Pianta, R. (2012). The transition to kindergarten: Fostering connections for early school success. In S. Karabenick & T. Urdan (Eds.), *Transitions across cultures* (pp. 1–26). Bingley: Emerald Group.

Margetts, K. (2003). Children bring more to school than their backpacks: Starting school down under. *Journal of European Early Childhood Education Research Monograph, 1*, 5–14. https://doi.org/10.1080/1350293X.2003.12016701

Mason-White, H. (2014). *The journey to big school. Supporting Aboriginal and Torres Strait Islander children's transition to primary school.* Melbourne: SNAICC. www.snaicc.org.au/wp-content/uploads/2016/01/03316.pdf

Meisels, S. J. (1999). Assessing readiness. In R. Pianta & M. Cox (Eds.), *The transition to kindergarten* (pp. 39–66). Baltimore: Paul Brookes.

Miller, K. (2015). The transition to kindergarten: How families from lower-income backgrounds experienced the first year. *Early Childhood Education Journal, 43*(3), 213–221. https://doi.org/10.1007/s10643-014-0650-9

Moss, P. (Ed.). (2013). *Early childhood and compulsory education: Reconceptualising the relationship.* London: Routledge.

O'Kane, M., & Murphy, R. (2016). *Transition from preschool to primary school: Audit of policy in 14 jurisdictions.* Dublin: National Council for Curriculum and Assessment. www.ncca.ie/media/2468/transition-from-preschool-to-primary-school-audit-of-policy-in-14-jurisdictions.pdf

Organisation for Economic Cooperation and Development (OECD). (2017). *Starting strong V. Transitions from early childhood education and care to primary education.* Paris: OECD Publishing. https://doi.org/10.1787/9789264276253-en

Pálsdóttir, K. (2019). Connecting school and leisure-time centre: Children as brokers. In S. Dockett, J. Einarsdóttir, & B. Perry (Eds.), *Listening to children's advice about starting school and school age care* (pp. 99–115). London: Routledge.

Perry, B. (2014). Social justice dimensions of starting school. In B. Perry, S. Dockett, & A. Petriwskyj (Eds.), *Transitions to school: International research, policy and practice* (pp. 175–186). Dordrecht: Springer. https://doi.org/10.1007/978-94-007-7350-9_13

Perry, B., & Dockett, S. (2011). 'How 'bout we have a celebration?' Advice from children on starting school. *European Early Childhood Education Research Journal, 19*(3), 375–388. https://doi.org/10.1080/1350293X.2011.597969

Peters, S. (2010). *Literature review: Transition from early childhood education to school.* Waikato: New Zealand Ministry of Education. http://ece.manukau.ac.nz/__data/assets/pdf_file/0008/85841/956_ECELitReview.pdf

Peters, S. (2014). Chasms, bridges and borderlands: A transitions research "across the border" from early childhood to school in New Zealand. In B. Perry, S. Dockett, & A. Petriwskyj (Eds.), *Transitions to school – International research, policy and practice* (pp. 105–116). Dordrecht: Springer. https://doi.org/10.1007/978-94-007-7350-9_8

Petriwskyj, A. (2014). Critical theory and inclusive transitions to school. In B. Perry, S. Dockett, & A. Petriwskyj (Eds.), *Transitions to school – International research, policy and practice* (pp. 201–215). Dordrecht: Springer. https://doi.org/10.1007/978-94-007-7350-9_15

Pianta, R., & Kraft-Sayre, M. (2003). *Successful kindergarten transition: Your guide to connecting children, families, & schools.* Baltimore, MD: Paul H Brookes.

Pianta, R., Rimm-Kaufman, S., & Cox, M. (1999). An ecological approach to kindergarten transition. In R. Pianta & M. Cox (Eds.), *The transition to kindergarten* (pp. 3–12). Baltimore, MD: Paul H Brookes.

Rimm-Kaufman, S. E., & Pianta, R. C. (2000). An ecological perspective on the transition to kindergarten: A theoretical framework to guide empirical research. *Journal of Applied Developmental Psychology, 21*(5), 491–511. https://doi.org/10.1016/S0193-3973(00)00051-4

Rogoff, B. (2003). *The cultural nature of human development.* Oxford: Oxford University Press.

School Law *[Skollagen]* 1962:319. https://www.lagboken.se/Lagboken/start/skoljuridik/skollag-2010800/d_2682774-sfs-1962_319

Schulting, A., Malone, P., & Dodge, K. (2005). The effect of school-based kindergarten transition policies and practices on child academic outcomes. *Developmental Psychology, 41*, 860. https://doi.org/10.1037/0012-1649.41.6. 860

SOU (1948:27). *1946 års skolkommissions betänkande med förslag till riktlinjer för det svenska skolväsendets utveckling* [1946 School Commission Report with proposed guidelines for development of the Swedish school system]. Stockholm: Ecklesiastikdepartementet.

SOU (1951:15). *Daghem och förskolor. Betänkande om barnstugor och barntillsyn angivet av 1946 års kommitté för den halvöppna barnavården* [Home nurseries and preschools. Report on child nurseries and child supervision provided by the 1946 committee for semi-open childcare]. Stockholm: Socialdepartementet.

SOU (1972:26). *Förskolan del 1: Betänkande angivet av 1968 års barnstugeutredning* [Preschool part I: 1968 Children's Preschool Report]. Stockholm: Socialdepartementet.

SOU (1972:27). *Förskolan del 2: Betänkande angivet av 1968 års barnstugeutredning* [Preschool part II: 1968 Children's Preschool Report]. Stockholm: Socialdepartementet.

SOU (1974:53). *Utredningen om Skolans inre arbete, SIA-utredningen* [Report on the internal work of schools, SIA Report]. Stockholm: Utbildningsdepartementet.

SOU (1985:22). *Förskola – skola: betänkande* [Preschool-School Report]. Stockholm: Utbildningsdepartementet.

SOU (1997:21). *Växa i lärande – Förslag till läroplan för barn och unga 6–16 år* [Grow in learning – Proposals to curricula for children and youths 6 to 16 years]. Stockholm: Utbildningsdepartementet.

SOU (2010:67). *Utredningen om flexibel skolstart i grundskolan. I rättan tid?: Om ålder och skolstart* [Report on flexible school start in compulsory school. In the nick of time? Ages and school start]. Stockholm: Utbildningsdepartementet.

References – Chapters 2 and 2A

SOU (2015:91). *Mer tid för kunskap – förskoleklass, förlängd skolplikt och lovskola* [More time for knowledge – preschool class, lengthened obligatory school attendance and school during holidays]. Stockholm: Utbildningsdepartementet.

SOU (2016:59). *På goda grunder – en åtgärdsgaranti för läsning, skrivning och matematik* [On firm ground – an intervention guarantee for reading, writing and mathematics]. Stockholm: Utbildningsdepartementet

Turunen, T. (2012). Individual plans for children in transition to pre-school: A case study in one Finnish day-care centre. *Early Child Development and Care, 182*(3–4), 315–328. https://doi.org/10.1080/03004430.2011.646728

United Nations. (1989). *The United Nations convention on the rights of the child.* New York, United Nations. www.ohchr.org/EN/ProfessionalInterest/Pages/CRC.aspx.

van Gennep, A. (1960). *The rites of passage* (B. V. Minika & G. L. Caffee, Trans.). London: Routledge and Kegan Paul.

Victorian Department of Education and Training. (2020). *Transition: A positive start to school resource kit.* www.education.vic.gov.au/childhood/professionals/learning/Pages/transkit.aspx#link77

Wenger, E. (1998). *Communities of practice.* Cambridge: Cambridge University Press.

Wilder, J., & Lillvist, A. (2017). Hope, despair and everything in between – Parental expectations of educational transitions for young children with intellectual disability. In S. Dockett, W. Griebel, & B. Perry (Eds.), *Families and transition to school* (pp. 51–66). Cham: Springer. https://doi.org/10.1007/978-3-319-58329-7_4

Woo, M., Lauter, L., Jeppson, A., Graue, E., Grodsky, E., & Vaade, E. (2019). *Combined project briefs: Improving the transition for students, families, and teachers.* Madison, WI: Madison Education Partnership. http://mep.wceruw.org/documents/MEP-transition-combined-brief.pdf

Zittoun, T. (2016). A sociocultural psychology of the life course. *Social Psychology Review, 18*(1), 6–17.

3 What is meant by a successful or effective transition to school program?

Sue Dockett and Bob Perry

Introduction

In Chapter 2, we set the scene for the book by sharing our definition of transition to school. We introduced notions of continuity and change and emphasised the wide variety and diversity of people, institutions, and systems that are impacted when a child begins their first year of school. Most children begin school through what Lago (2019, p. 56) has called the normal "pace, rate and order" of the transition to school. In Australia and many other countries, this *normal* pattern of transition to school usually involves the child's participation in an ECEC setting in the year before commencing school, along with a transition to school program linking this setting to the destination school. There are other routes to school possible (Dockett & Perry, 2021), but most will involve some type of transition to school program or activities.

The aim of this book is to assist educators, families, children, institutions, systems, and communities in the evaluation of these transition to school programs. Often, what we want to evaluate is whether the programs are *working* or to what extent they are *working* and for whom. (There is extensive discussion about the purposes of evaluation in Chapter 4.) To achieve this aim, all involved in the evaluation need to have at least similar views of what it means for the program to be working. In this chapter, we investigate what it means not only for the transition program to be working but also what it means for it to be considered *successful* or *effective*. We know, given that transition to school programs are so firmly based in the context of the transition, that success or effectiveness will also be based in context – what appears to work very well in one context may not work nearly as well in others. This contextual nature of transition programs has been established for many years (Rimm-Kaufman & Pianta, 2000) and remains one of the key indicators of an effective program which we identified 20 years ago (Dockett & Perry, 2001a).

There are many participants in a transition to school program. Evaluating the program needs to consider whether definitions of success rely on it being considered successful or effective for all of them or whether it is sufficient for it to be successful or effective for only one or some groups of participants or for

DOI: 10.4324/9781003055112-4

only one or some individuals. More than two decades ago, Lloyd, Steinberg, and Wilhelm-Chapin (1999, p. 313) identified the complexity of this task:

> in identifying what constitutes successful transition to kindergarten, not only must many factors be considered, but they also must be considered in relation to each other . . . transition occurs on many interwoven levels (i.e., child, family, school, community) . . . transition outcomes must be conceptualised in terms of context.

This reminds us that the transition to school is both an individual and a social experience; individual experiences of changed roles, identity, and status occur within social contexts, be they the family, ECEC setting, school, or community. Determining the effectiveness of transition to school programs will involve both these individual and social dimensions.

Before determining the success or effectiveness of any program, process, or even single practice, it is necessary to be clear about the intended outcomes and how the program is to be used to achieve these. Sometimes, logic models set out this path, indicating what practices will be employed and how these link to the proposed mechanism for change and generate the anticipated outcomes (Savaya & Waysman, 2005; see also Chapter 4). Once the intended outcomes and the pathway to achieving these are determined, the level of success or effectiveness will be informed by ascertaining to what extent these were achieved and for whom (Organisation for Economic Co-operation and Development (OECD), 2017). For example, a transition to school program might have as its primary aim that all the children starting school have settled into the school and classroom routines by Week 4 of Term 1. If this is the aim, then it needs to be decided how *settling in* will be judged and whether *all* refers to all the children starting school at the beginning of the year or all at school in Week 4 or some other calculation. This will probably not be done meaningfully if only the children's skills in counting or recognising letters are measured, even though these may also be important understandings for the children to develop.

So what does it mean to meet the aims of a transition to school program, and even before answering this question, what are these aims?

What are the aims of the transition to school program?

As we noted in Chapter 2, transitions are times when "individuals change their role in their community's structure" (Rogoff, 2003, p. 150). With transition to school, these individuals may be children – both those children starting school for the first time and other children who may already be at school or part of families; adult family members – parents, carers, grandparents, aunties, uncles; educators – school and early childhood (ECEC) educators; and many other community members. To varying levels, all participants in a transition to school program will experience change. As noted in Chapter 2, *without change, there is no need for transition*. Given that we know change will occur during transition to school, is the overriding purpose of any transition to school program to assist all participants to cope with the changes that will occur, or can we expect more than this?

The purpose or aim of a transition to school program is related to its *program theory* – the rationale or ideas underpinning the program – the answer to the questions such as *Why does this program exist?* and *Why does it look the way it does?* The notion of *program theory* is considered in more detail in Chapter 4 but is introduced here to indicate its importance in determining whether or to what degree a transition to school program is successful or effective.

One of the common aims of transition programs is to promote continuity – particularly in children's learning, although other forms of continuity are also identified as important (Boyle, Petriwskyj, & Grieshaber, 2018; Dockett & Einarsdóttir, 2017; Dockett & Perry, 2014). Sometimes continuity is framed in terms of curriculum alignment (Vitiello et al., 2020), although what this looks like in practice is often hard to describe. One consequence has been that interpretations of ECEC curricula around the world have tended to become more school oriented, a process described as *schoolification* (Moss, 2013) and *schoolarisation* (Ackesjö & Persson, 2019, Chapter 2A). While transition programs to support continuity have many potential positive outcomes, they can also drift towards readiness programs (see Chapter 2).

Several descriptors of transition to school programs have been used in research and practice. These give us an idea about what the aims of these programs might be. Many researchers have reported descriptions of transition to school programs as *smooth* or *seamless* (Boyle et al., 2018; Hirst et al., 2011; Mirkhil, 2010; Packer et al., 2020; Purtell et al., 2020; Urbina-Garcia, 2019; Yeboah, 2010), with at least one of the aims being to reduce, as much as possible, the uncomfortable or stressful aspects of the transition, particularly for the children involved. Programs try to achieve such smoothness through communication and physical experiences designed to help people to get to know other people undertaking the transition and to become familiar with the new setting and what happens in that setting. Activities such as visits to the school and classrooms; conversations among children starting school, first-year-of-school teachers, and family members; conversations and other communication among preschool and schoolchildren; parent information sessions; and, once children have started school, play experiences with classmates might all be utilised to achieve the desired smoothness in the transition experience.

Positive and *optimal* are other descriptors of successful or effective transition to school that are used in both research and practice (Centre for Equity and Innovation in Early Childhood (CEIEC), 2008; Tatalović Vorkapić, 2019). The term *positive* indicates the importance of making children's first experiences with school ones that build positive self-identity, agency, and respect. While some components of a positive transition to school will involve aspects of smoothness or seamlessness, others may emphasise the changes experienced in moving from one context to another and the provision of opportunities to build transitions capital (Dunlop, 2014) as children and families meet the challenges associated with these changes.

When the label *optimal* is used for the success or effectiveness of transition to school, there is recognition that all transitions to school are based in the contexts in which they occur – contexts for children, families, early childhood settings, schools, and communities – and that the success of any transition to school is impacted by those contexts. Different contexts provide different opportunities, and different individuals will have different levels of success. There is no *one-size-fits-all* approach or absolute *best practice*: the search for such an approach will be fruitless and potentially frustrating. Nevertheless, there are likely to be some general practices or activities that can be promoted in different ways in different contexts.

Despite the increasing focus on the importance of transition to school, there is no consensus about what constitutes effective experiences or outcomes. There are indications that what is considered successful differs by group, with educators and parents expressing both similarities and differences in their preferred outcomes of an effective transition to school (Correia & Marques-Pinto, 2016; Dockett & Perry, 2004; Einarsdóttir, 2006) and children also reflecting different perspectives (Dockett, Einarsdóttir, & Perry, 2019). Sometimes judgements about the effectiveness of transition programs have been made not by considering positive outcomes but rather the absence of negative outcomes, with successful transitions "defined as the absence of any major problems" (Griebel & Niesel, 2003, p. 28).

Throughout this book, we argue that the basis for the evaluation of transition to school programs will be whatever are established as markers of the effectiveness of a transition to school program and the strategies or practices used to achieve these. These will vary according to context, the stakeholders involved, and the purpose of the evaluation (see Chapter 4). Recognising that this is a very broad approach, we outline some frameworks to guide the evaluation and describe a focus on *belonging*, which, for us, is a key factor in determining the effectiveness of a program.

Frameworks for evaluating effective transitions

In 2001, we published a set of ten guidelines for effective transition to school programs which have stood the test of time. They are reproduced here to establish a baseline for further discussion. We noted (Dockett & Perry, 2001b, pp. v–vii) that effective transition to school programs:

1 establish positive relationships between children, parents, and educators.
2 facilitate each child's development as a capable learner.
3 differentiate between "orientation to school" and "transition to school" programs.
4 draw upon dedicated funding and resources.
5 involve a range of stakeholders.

6 are well planned and evaluated.
7 are flexible and responsive.
8 are based on mutual trust and respect.
9 rely on reciprocal communication among participants.
10 take into account contextual aspects of community and of individual families and children within that community.

Guideline 6 has this book as a direct consequence, and each of the other guidelines can be seen throughout different aspects of this work. The importance of relationships (Guidelines 1, 5, 8, and 9), context (Guidelines 4, 5, 7, and 10), and the belief that children are capable and agentic (Guideline 2), which provided foundations for our ongoing work in transition to school, are clear.

Similar elements are reflected in a list of five key features of successful transition to school outlined by Ramey, Ramey, and Lanzi (2006). These are reported in Ramey and Ramey (2010, p. 23) as:

1 Children have positive attitudes towards school and learning and are motivated to do well in school.
2 Children maintain and enhance their academic and social skills via their school experiences.
3 Parents and other key adults show positive attitudes toward the school and learning in general and act as partners in their children's learning.
4 Teachers and other school personnel recognise and value children's individual and cultural differences and provide developmentally appropriate school experiences.
5 Schools, families, and communities are linked together in positive and mutually supportive relationships to enhance young children's well-being and education.

In 2011, the Educational Transitions and Change (ETC) Research Group published its *Transition to School: Position Statement* which reconceptualised "transition to school in the context of social justice, human rights (including children's rights), educational reform and ethical agendas" and established the importance of:

- understandings of all children as competent, capable, and creative, who have already learned a great deal before they enter school, regardless of their context or backgrounds;
- acknowledging and supporting children as active participants in their own transition and learning;
- recognising and valuing the strengths of all involved in transitions to school;
- genuine partnerships involving reciprocal, responsive, respectful relationships;
- critically reflecting on established policies and practices and their underlying assumptions; and
- curriculum and pedagogy relevant to children's characteristics, interests, and circumstances (p. 2).

There are clear echoes of the 2001 guidelines in this list of important considerations as well as enhancements in terms of children's capabilities and rights and more precision around evaluation of transition to school policies and practices through critical reflection. Utilising these underlying principles, The *Transition to School: Position Statement* characterises transition to school in terms of four constructs pertinent to all participants: opportunities, aspirations, expectations, and entitlements which can form a framework for the evaluation of transition to school programs. Chapter 8 provides an example of this framework and how it might be applied.

As outlined in Chapter 2, the process of a child's and family's transition to school can be said to begin when the child first takes some interest in it, often at the urging of a sibling or adult in the family. It can be said to be complete when all involved feel a sense of belonging within the new school context (Dockett & Perry, 2014). If we accept this definition for the duration of transition to school processes, then it would seem reasonable to claim that at least one of the aims of all such programs is that all participants achieve such a sense of belonging. This broad aim for transition to school will encompass many sub-aims and, perhaps, can be considered as the omnibus aim for all transition to school programs. Hence, in our quest for a description of what is meant by a successful or effective transition to school program, *belonging* would seem to be central.

Belonging as a marker of effective transition

Belonging is one of the key concepts framing *Belonging, Being and Becoming: The Early Years Learning Framework for Australia* (EYLF) (Department of Education, Skills and Employment (DESE), 2019) and is a familiar term for many educators. But what does it mean in relation to transition to school? While the focus of the EYLF is on young children, our claim that transition to school programs might aim for the achievement of a sense of belonging among all participants broadens the scope of what it means to belong.

Much has been written about the importance of a personal sense of belonging, reflected in feelings of emotional attachment as individuals are "seen, accepted and recognised" (Nergaard, 2020, p. 228). Educators note this when they observe children playing, interacting, and seeking to be physically close to others (Juutinen, Puroila, & Johansson, 2018). In early childhood contexts, belonging is connected with children's sense of well-being and regarded as a key factor underpinning the development of social interactions and interpersonal relationships, particularly friendship (Papadopoulou, 2016).

A substantial body of scholarship has explored the notion of school belonging as feeling "accepted, respected, included and supported by others in the school environment" (Goodenow & Grady, 1993, p. 61). A positive attachment to the school is aligned with well-being and academic outcomes (Arslan, Allen, & Ryan, 2020). The finding that school belonging tends to be stronger in younger children than those in later years links to the focus of this research on adolescents, particularly those making the transition to secondary school (Waters, 2016). However, we suggest that the transition to school is a significant point for building a sense of belonging and that it is a key element in considering the effectiveness of transition programs.

As well as focusing on personal feelings of belonging, attention has been paid to the social sense of belonging, such as belonging to a group or community. As an example, Joerdens (2014) describes children's membership in a classroom community of practice as they start school. Taken together, belonging can be regarded as both personal and relational (Johansson, 2017), where an individual's sense of belonging interacts with belonging to a community.

While belonging to a community has potential to promote inclusion, it also opens up possibilities for exclusion. Social rejection and exclusion are associated with negative social experiences (Sandseter & Seland, 2018) impacting on well-being and engagement (Nergaard, 2020). How belonging and exclusion are constructed and enacted is explored by Yuval-Davis (2006) as she describes the *politics of belonging*. Central to this concept are collective decisions about insiders and outsiders – who belongs and who does not – and where each community draws its boundary. There may be clear boundaries – such as for preschool or classroom groups – or boundaries that are not clear at all and where it is not clear what is required for acceptance within the group. These groupings can apply to children as well as the adults in ECEC and school contexts.

To unpack what we mean by belonging in relation to transition to school, we utilise the cartography of belonging developed by Sumsion and Wong (2011). Drawing on a range of theoretical perspectives, these authors outline ten dimensions that reflect ways of experiencing belonging: emotional, social; cultural; spatial; temporal; physical; spiritual, moral/ethical; political; and legal. While described as separate entities, these dimensions often converge, illustrating the multi-faceted and multi-layered nature of belonging.

In addition to these ten dimensions, Sumsion and Wong (2011) identify three axes of belonging that consider how belonging is enacted, by whom and for what purpose. The first of these axes – *categorisation* – explores who decides who belongs and who is excluded. The second axis – *resistance and desire* – relates to how the boundaries are drawn, maintained, challenged, or changed and includes the negotiations that are involved as individuals seek to choose where they belong. The third axis is labelled *performativity* and refers to how individuals make and remake themselves in relation to others. The stories people tell about themselves as well as the stories others tell about them contribute to this latter axis.

Awareness of this conceptual background acknowledges some of the complexity associated with belonging. It also helps to explore the everyday actions and interactions that contribute to belonging and exclusion and alerts us to look for narratives of belonging and how these are performed or enacted and what strategies are used to frame the borders of communities or groups and to keep these borders in place.

Belonging and the transition to school

As we explore belonging as a marker of an effective transition to school, it is important to note that belonging is not necessarily stable or fixed. Neither is it created passively. Rather, belonging can be fluid, changing as the context and those within it change. For example, a child might feel very comfortable and at ease in an ECEC context but feel uncomfortable in a school environment, just as a child who feels strong connections with one educator might not feel the same when interacting with a new or different educator. The same applies to adults: parents may have developed a trusting relationship with one but not another teacher; educators across ECEC and school contexts may feel part of a connected transition network but not feel like they belong to the broader ECEC or school communities.

The axes and dimensions of belonging (Stratigos, 2015; Stratigos, Bradley, & Sumsion, 2014; Sumsion & Wong, 2011) provide a frame for exploring how belonging is enacted, by whom, and for what purpose. As stakeholders experience the transition to school, close observation and reflection will identify some of the many ways children, families, educators, and other stakeholders enact belonging as well as some of the negotiations that occur as people try to work out where they belong, with whom, and how they might achieve that.

When we propose that transition to school is said to be complete when *all involved feel a sense of belonging within the new school context*, we draw on both the personal sense of belonging and the social element of belonging that links to connection with a community or group. In Table 3.1, we have tried to illustrate some of the different ways in which belonging might be noted during the transition to school. The aim here is to reflect on the question "How will we know if children/educators/families feel like they belong at school?" The examples provided are not exhaustive or necessarily the most relevant in all settings. We encourage readers to consider what might be appropriate examples in their own contexts.

In one recent project, we asked children and educators what they thought it meant to belong at school. Their responses reflected several of these dimensions. Some children in preschool and the first year of school indicated that they did not feel like they belonged at school. Their responses indicated that instead, they belonged at home with their families and that "Mum and Dad will be sad" if they were to belong anywhere else. Some older, Year 5 children interpreted belonging at school as "when you feel like you can trust the school" and "it means you are actually part of the school". Educators reflected that belonging at school was evident when children have "confidence about where they are . . . feel that the school is their school" and when "they have relationships, they want to come, and they are willing to learn . . . being respectful to the school . . . wearing the school uniform . . . picking up a lunch box . . . [making sure] the school is neat and tidy . . . being respectful".

While detailed consideration of what it means for transition to school participants to feel that they belong in a school is important and could assist in

Table 3.1 Belonging during the transition to school.

Dimension of Belonging	Definition (derived from Sumsion & Wong, 2011)	What might it look like for		
		Children	Educators	Parents
Emotional	Feeling comfortable and at ease; accepted; liked; recognised; respected	Children enter the classroom confidently. They are confident that their teacher "likes" them. Children feel comfortable seeking help as needed. Children see their efforts respected and displayed with care.	Educators are recognised by children and families. Their colleagues respect and value their role. ECEC and school educators feel welcome in each other's contexts.	Parents and family members are recognised and greeted by name when they visit the school. Educators are interested in and responsive to family experiences of the transition.
Social	Feeling part of a community; accepted by the group; participating in the activities and practices of the group	Children have friends and/or know how to make friends in the new context. Children identify as a member of the group – "I'm in class xx". Children use the language of school – assembly, recess, homework, etc.	ECEC and school educators identify as part of a transition community. They work together to support transitions and are supported by their network colleagues.	Family members are welcomed into the school and classroom and are invited to share in meaningful activities. Family members contribute to transition programs and/or activities. Parents interact as they gather at the school gate.
Cultural	Connections with a group based on some shared factor, such as ethnicity, language, interests, or professional identity. Belonging to the group helps people understand and interpret events and expectations	Children talk about the school values and what they mean for them. Current schoolchildren share their knowledge and experiences with those about to start school. Children see evidence around the school that people "like them" are successful and respected.	First-year-of-school teachers meet regularly to discuss transition. First-year-of-school teachers and ECEC educators are members of a collaborative network.	Parents take on the role of school ambassadors, sharing their knowledge of the school and its operation with new families. Families see evidence around the school that people "like them" succeed and are respected.

(*Continued*)

Table 3.1 (Continued)

Dimension of Belonging	Definition (derived from Sumsion & Wong, 2011)	What might it look like for		
		Children	Educators	Parents
Spatial	Feeling connected to a place, knowing how it operates	Children know the places around the school and feel comfortable accessing these. They know school routines.	Educators have a sense of ownership for their classroom. They personalise their spaces.	Families know the routines and rituals of school, such as drop-off and pick-up times, what happens at assembly, sport, etc.
Temporal	Connections over time	Children are afforded some time to feel settled and at ease in school. Transition programs/activities over time help children feel connected. Children can see evidence of change over time – such as how they have changed over the year or since preschool.	Educators promote continuity by building on children's prior experience and recognising what has gone on before. Educators have time to connect their colleagues as well as children and families to get to know what has happened before starting school.	Families build up connections over time as various children have progressed through the school. Family members are welcomed to spend time at the school.
Physical	Connecting with the physical context	Children feel comfortable in the different physical elements of the school. They know and are able to engage with the physical environment. Resources support children in this connection.	Educators have appropriate physical resources to engage with young children.	Families have a place in the school where they can go, for example to wait for children or talk with educators.

What is meant by a successful or effective transition to school program? 47

Dimension of Belonging	Definition (derived from Sumsion & Wong, 2011)	What might it look like for		
		Children	Educators	Parents
Spiritual	Connections based on spiritual rituals and traditions	Children's spiritual connections are respected through curriculum inclusions, appropriate resources and activities.	Educators' spiritual connections are respected.	Family spiritual connections are respected through recognition of special days and celebrations.
Moral/ethical	Belonging based on obligations and responsibilities	Children talk about how they are expected to behave when at school or wearing the school uniform. They talk about school rules.	Educators understand how their own actions can influence the ways others experience belonging.	Families feel responsible for getting children to school on time and with the necessary resources.
Political	Belonging based on citizenship and rights	Children are eager to participate in school councils or leadership groups. They are aware of how their class group functions and how their actions impact on others.	Educators participate in leadership or governance roles. Educators develop a communication strategy that is available for all parents.	Family members engage with parent organisations. Family members contribute to the newsletter.
Legal	Based on the right to belong	Children feel they have the right to be at school. Putting on their school uniform is evidence of their right to belong.	Educators have appropriate qualifications. They have a sense of ownership of their space and of what occurs within that.	Family members are respected as contributors to their children's learning and education. Family decisions about education are listened to and respected.

establishing transition activities and processes, such belonging is the end result to which transition to school programs aspire. Broström (2013, p. 40) has characterised belonging in terms of participants, particularly children, feeling "*suitable* in school. This is to feel secure, relaxed, and comfortable in the new environment; to have a feeling of wellbeing and belonging" (italics in original). It is unlikely that all participants will achieve this feeling of belonging at the same time, in the same way, and through the same experiences. So it is probably unreasonable to think that any transition to school program can meet all the needs of all the participants all of the time. In other words, efforts to promote belonging should continue throughout the years of school.

Effectiveness for whom?

For a transition to school to be effective, it is important for many groups of people to feel that they belong, especially children, families, and early childhood and school educators. Table 3.1 provides details of what this might mean for each of these groups, but there are others for whom it is important for transition to school programs to be effective, perhaps not at the personal and individual levels illustrated in Table 3.1 but at more institutional or systemic levels. For example, a school principal might deem a transition to school program at her/his school to be effective if there are no complaints from families and communities or no behavioural issues to be addressed. Some principals have indicated that they believe a successful start to the school year is one no one hears about – smooth and not noticed. While expectations such as these might be relevant to some aspects of the transition program, defining an effective transition as an absence of negatives reflects a passive approach and does not augur well for the building of positive and respectful relationships among those involved.

While individual ECEC educators are concerned that the children in their care make an effective transition to school, one complaint we often hear is that these educators seldom hear whether this happens. There may be some incidental reporting, particularly if there are younger siblings of a child starting school who are attending the setting. In this situation, ECEC educators may see parents and first-year-of-school children when they drop off or pick up the other children. However, it seems to be relatively rare for ECEC educators to be told whether their efforts in facilitating transition to school have been effective.

Example: Back to Preschool

When they did not hear anything from schools about how children from their early childhood centre were settling into their new schools, the educators took matters into their own hands. About a month after school had started, they contacted each of the children who attended the centre in the previous year and had just started school. Letters were written and sent to the children, inviting them and their families to a *Back to Preschool* evening from 5 to 7 p.m. In particular, the children were requested to wear their

What is meant by a successful or effective transition to school program? 49

school uniform. The returning children were able to play in the familiar preschool spaces, show off their uniforms, and interact with preschool staff. Educators were able to see for themselves that the children were settling into their new contexts and to be assured by children and families that all was well and they felt like they belonged at school. The evening finished with a barbecue.

In contrast, when feedback is provided to ECEC educators about how children from their setting and those around them managed the transition, the ground is laid for ECEC and school educators to feel that they both belong in the transition space.

Chapter 3A provides an example of a successful approach to evaluating the quality of cooperation among early childhood and school educators during the transition to school. Such cooperation is critical to these participants feeling that they belong in the transition to school space and that they have a great deal to offer to each other and to children and families involved. While much of the detail in Chapter 3A will become more meaningful as readers delve deeper into the book, the example of cooperation and reflection is timely as we try to establish what it is that transition to school programs should do. While reading Chapter 3A, reflect on relationships you have – or would like to have – with other educators who work in schools and in early childhood settings.

Educational systems – both school and early childhood – want to ensure that transition to school is effective, because they know that such success can have a major impact on all participants' well-being and on children's future learning (Entwisle & Alexander, 1989; Mashburn, LoCasale-Crouch, & Pears, 2018; Schulting, Malone, & Dodge, 2005). In Australia, all the state and territory education departments, as well as independent education systems, have invested a great deal of time and resources into state- or territory-wide transition to school approaches, processes, and materials. Evaluations of local transition to school programs can be part of the overall evaluations of these jurisdiction-wide programs.

Communities want the transition to school in their local areas to be effective because they benefit when their children and families feel that school is for them. Communities want to be part of such an important milestone in their children's lives because it makes their communities stronger. Many communities have long-standing commitments to transition to school through particular activities which have become part of the annual program of events.

Example: Starting school picnic

The local council in one NSW community has been running a Starting School Picnic for more than 15 years in which families are invited to share a Sunday morning in a local park in order to celebrate that young children will soon be starting school. There are activity and information stalls, the mayor performs a shared big book reading, there is a gift bag, and children who are starting school and their families are celebrated. Many people were disappointed when, in 2020, the picnic had to be cancelled because of COVID-19 restrictions.

> *Example: Community celebrations of starting school*
>
> In a small rural town in Queensland, merchants displayed their starting school photographs and their favourite children's books in their shop windows. They also invited any child starting school to come into the shop for a treat – usually a sweet. In this way, children saw that adults they knew also experienced the transition to school and seem to have survived it.

What makes an effective transition to school program?

This question cannot be answered if what is expected is a list of best practices or essential activities. As far back as 2001, and probably long before this, it was established that transition to school programs are, by their very nature, based in context (Dockett & Perry, 2001a; Rimm-Kaufman & Pianta, 2000). However, at the more general level of overall guidance, much can be said.

One thing that has been well established is that effective transition to school programs are predominantly about the building of positive, respectful, and trusting relationships among people. These are essential elements of building a sense of belonging. Hence, we can say that if a transition to school program is *not* aiming to build these relationships among all participants, then it will *not* be effective for at least some participants.

> *Example: Listening to it twice*
>
> We recall speaking through an interpreter with a group of Vietnamese-speaking parents at a Parent Information Evening held in a highly multicultural school where Arabic was the most common non-English language spoken by families. The school had thought about the backgrounds of their families and had ensured that there was an Arabic-speaking interpreter at the meeting. Everything that was said in English by staff was interpreted into Arabic. The common comment from the Vietnamese-speaking parents was that they had to sit through the presentations twice – once in English and once in Arabic – and did not understand either. The effort to build relationships with this group of parents had failed and, in fact, hardened their belief that the school disregarded them as an important part of the school community.

Transition to school is a time for both continuity and change. Children starting school have consistently told us over many years that they want school to be different from what has gone before, because that's what happens as you grow up – you meet change. At the same time, they don't want there to be so much change that they do not feel that school is for them; that they don't belong or feel suitable in school. Families have similar feelings about their children starting school. Educators often talk about continuity of curriculum, pedagogy, and/or learning. If we define curriculum as everything that happens in the school or ECEC setting (DESE, 2019, p. 9) then clearly, curricula are not continuous across the transition to school. Throughout Australia and in many other countries, there are different curricula documents mandated for ECEC settings and schools, with different outcomes and approaches. Despite this, there can be continuity of children's learning, and a mark of an effective transition to school program is that the children build on what has gone before and continue to learn in ways that suit them and in which they can be successful.

Much of this chapter has canvassed the importance of all participants in transitions to school feeling that they belong in the new contexts. The building and enacting of powerful positive relationships will go a long way towards belonging, but different people – children, family members, and educators – will require particular, personal actions in this space. Knowing each other will be critical in an effective transition.

Success breeds success, and as people effectively experience the transition to school, they will build a *school identity* – an indication of how they and others feel that they belong in the school. If a child's first and ongoing experiences of school are that it is a place where people care about them, where they can do things, where people will help them if they need it, and where they know what to do and to whom to go if something goes wrong, then it is likely that they will build a positive school identity. If the experiences are not as positive as these, it is likely that the school identity will not be as positive, and learning as well as social challenges could follow. While school identities can change, negative images of a child who feels like they do not belong in school often last, to the detriment of both the child's well-being and learning outcomes (Besi & Sakellariou, 2019). Similarly, the transition to school is a great time at which schools can help build positive identities in parents as parents of a school child, and these can last in the form of the parents' enhanced engagement with both the school and their child's future education.

Conclusion

Overall, the success or effectiveness of a transition to school program can be measured by the sense of belonging in the new context which is felt by all participants. The ways in which this might be judged will vary from context to context, and the details of what is judged will also differ. The guidelines and approaches discussed in this chapter provide a basis in establishing what current research and practice in transition to school suggest. The remainder of this book is devoted to the evaluation of transition to school programs to help ensure that those programs are as successful and effective for all involved as they possibly can be. Once we know what it is we are trying to evaluate, there are many opportunities to explore how this might be done.

3A Paderborner Qualitätsstern (PQ³)
Self-evaluation of transition to school programs for educators and teachers

Petra Büker, Julia Höke, and Jana Ogrodowski

Introduction

> We are very pleased that we have been given such a quality development tool we can use to work together with our cooperation partners. This enables us to reflect and document our work, to achieve and maintain a professional standard permanently. (Kindergarten educator)

Voices from evaluation, such as this from a pedagogical practitioner, clearly show what the instrument presented in this article is about: the aim of the self-evaluation instrument is to induce systematic reflection on the design of transition to school programs in kindergartens and primary schools and, from this, to plan jointly and implement cooperation on the basis of a criterion-based analysis of the current situation. The item-based self-evaluation instrument thus serves the purpose of quality assurance and quality development of cooperation in the transition from kindergarten to primary school.

The instrument is based on the idea of lifelong learning of the professionals and recognition of kindergartens and schools as learning organisations (Holly & Southworth, 2005). Thus, the evaluation of transition is not carried out by an external authority. Rather, it is a matter of looking at the cooperation process in dialogue. Using the tool, educators regularly refer to a set of established quality criteria to analyse whether their joint activities still correspond to the goals of strengthening children for transition and of professionalising pedagogical staff through cooperation.

Development context of the self-evaluation instrument

In Germany, kindergarten and primary school belong to different systems, and they each follow their own traditional logic within these systems (Büker & Höke, 2019). Kindergartens educate children aged between a few months and six years. Most children in Germany attend a kindergarten, but it is not obligatory. Aged six, children enter primary school, which is compulsory for everyone. Up to now, every institution has its own mandate and its own organisational structures. Kindergarten and primary school own different pedagogical traditions; historically

DOI: 10.4324/9781003055112-5

they reflect different views on children learning and playing, what constitutes quality practice, and working with parents. Due to this, children experience the change from *kindergartener* to *student* as one of the major changes in their lives. Professionals in kindergarten are called *Erzieher* (educators), and those in primary school are called *Lehrer* (teachers). Up to now both professional groups differ in their salaries and social prestige.

Only recently has a legally binding mandate been introduced across Germany, requiring cooperation between kindergartens and primary schools around the transition to school. Currently, children's preparation for school, perceptions of school readiness, and support for children's transition are positioned as issues best addressed across the institutions of both kindergarten and primary school (Höke et al., 2017).

In reaction to the disastrous PISA results in Germany in 2001, countless scientifically supervised pilot projects were created to optimise children's chances of a well-supported start in their early years. Results of these studies highlighted the importance of successful cooperation between educators in kindergarten and teachers in primary schools in multi-professional teams (Wildgruber & Griebel, 2016). Currently, only a few networks of kindergartens and primary schools have reached the highest level of cooperation, which is described as a collaboration of professionals who aim to co-construct new knowledge through the development of joint comprehension and intensive reflection processes (for standards or stages of cooperation, see Gräsel, Fußangel, & Pröbstel, 2006).

Often, networks are fragile. Cooperation can collapse if promoters leave the team, if principals do not consider the topic important, or if some of the favourable conditions are lost. However, national (Faust, Wehner, & Kratzmann, 2011) and international studies (Ahtola et al., 2011; Huser, Dockett, & Perry, 2016) show that professional collaboration must reach a high level to obtain a positive impact for transition and to enhance children's educational opportunities. This is particularly the case in contexts where the integration of children with diverse backgrounds – such as recently arrived immigrant children or those with special education needs – takes place (Arndt & Kipp, 2016).

The sustainability of cooperation structures among adults is related to the well-being of children. The self-evaluation instrument *Paderborner Qualitätsstern (PQ³)* addresses this meaningful relation. In its first edition, the instrument was developed by a team of authors from the University of Paderborn in cooperation with staff from the regional youth welfare office in Paderborn. This is why the instrument bears its name. It is particularly based on the results of the accompanying research from three pilot projects on transition in which the authors were involved (Höke et al., 2020). From the findings obtained there, it was possible to develop quality criteria identifying elements of effective cooperation during the transition to school.

In terms of research methodology, the instrument can be characterised as process-oriented or formative self-evaluation (Bortz & Döring, 2015). The practitioners involved in the cooperation measures are also evaluators, and they are the main users of the evaluation results. In addition to the cognitive function ("How have we proceeded?"; "Where do we stand in the process of cooperation?") and the legitimation function ("Are we still on the way to our self-defined goal?"), self-evaluation has an optimisation function ("What do we want to improve in the future?"), a decision-making function ("What do we need to change?"; "What next steps will we take?"), and a learning and dialogue function. The latter is the most characteristic feature of the PQ³, as the kindergarten and school professionals' work with the items and scales of the instrument allows the taking of a distanced metaperspective on the process. On this basis, reflection and communication as well as the development of new common knowledge should be promoted.

What does it mean for a transition to school program to be successful or effective? To address this question, clear evaluation criteria were defined as items, and evaluation standards were established. This process drew on co-constructivist (Gräsel et al., 2006) and process theoretical approaches (Vogt, Heim, & Zumwald, 2016) as well as bioecological perspectives (Griebel & Niesel, 2011; Perry & Dockett, 2018). While the development of a measure in this way carries the risk of setting normative values, the PQ³ tries to counteract this by encouraging evaluators to define their own goals for cooperation within their network and include those within the evaluation as well. Participants are also asked to provide feedback via an evaluation questionnaire and an online blog about the validity of the evaluation criteria and future changes that may be required. As a result, the PQ³ is now available in a third, revised edition (which explains the superscript 3). The instrument itself is therefore to be understood as a *work in progress*.

The Paderborner Qualitätsstern (PQ³)

The PQ³ identifies three levels across three areas of cooperation:

A: pedagogical activities with the children;
B: structures within the individual institutions; and
C: working in cooperation networks.

Each area of cooperation contains scales in which, in a discussion process between educators and teachers from all participating institutions, it is decided jointly to what extent they apply to the current form of cooperation. On a scale from 1 to 5, the current state of development is assessed.

The quality levels build on one another in terms of content. Level 1 is always the starting point, and together, it is discussed whether this level applies to the participant's own cooperation network. If the description of Level 1 holds, the description of Level 2 is read, and again, it is clarified whether Level 2 fits beyond Level 1. This procedure is repeated until the quality level at which all descriptive elements are considered as given is reached. A value is assigned to each level and is included into the evaluation

A: Pedagogical activities with the children

Intensive cooperation is characterised by transition between the kindergarten and primary school being regarded as a non-linear process. Instead, a common field of action is created, which is pedagogically and didactically designed by both institutions and involves children of different ages (Höke et al., 2017). This area of cooperation consists of six characteristics in total, which cover the time spent with the children, the aims, and the reflection of the implementation. Our example (Table 3A.1) focuses on the pedagogical-didactic aims.

Table 3A.1 Pedagogical and didactical aims.

The implemented cooperation activities with the children focus on ...				
familiarising kindergartners with school.	the development of positive relationships and shared experiences.	the development of positive attitudes towards school as well as developing pleasure in learning.	common topics, contents, and competency goals regarding the education plans.	the children's opportunities for participation.

The first stages in this area reflect basic cooperation goals such as familiarising the kindergarten children with the premises and getting to know future classmates and teachers as well as other school staff. From Level 3 onwards, the focus increasingly is on educational goals and joint learning. The highest quality level, 5, then aims at involving children in decisions relevant to them.

B: Structures within the individual institutions

Intensive cooperation is characterised by having an appropriate number of professionals and teachers implement and further develop the transition to school program in a structured, professional manner. The question arises as to how and in what logic of action tasks are distributed between the participating professionals, which resources are available in the individual participating institutions for shaping the transition, and what significance is attributed to cooperation in comparison to other tasks. The actions of leaders have a special influence on the attribution of relevance concerning the cooperation. This will be discussed in the following example.

The scale in Table 3A.2 focuses on two levels: the behaviour of the heads of educational institutions, from appreciative recognition of the cooperation activities

Table 3A.2 Role of the heads of educational institutions within the cooperation.

The collaboration within the cooperation ...				
is favourably considered by at least one administrator.	is accompanied appreciatively by at least one administrator. (For example, thematisation in team meetings/ conferences; creating transparency within the institutional team/the whole teaching staff)	is actively shaped by at least one administrator. (For example, participation in planning discussions; designing reliable communication structures; transparent information for parents)	is actively shaped by all administrators within the cooperation networks. (For example, conferences on a regular basis; joint participation at cooperation conferences)	is designed in an appreciative manner by a cross-institutional management team with shared responsibility. (For example, joint decision-making processes at management level)

towards active participation, and the involvement of the leaders of participating educational institutions. At the highest quality level, 5, all leaders together form a management team to promote the cooperation in the network.

C: Working in cooperation networks

Intensive cooperation is characterised by an appreciative collaboration between the different professions (for example, educators and teachers, school social workers). The different professional knowledge is integrated into the joint pedagogical work. It is also important to have a common vision, shared by all those involved, from which concrete goals and activities can be derived (a *common denominator*) and to reflect continuously and systematically on the joint work. Professional cooperation has to be embodied into the concepts of the institutions in order to promote long-term sustainability of the established cooperation. For this reason, the form of cooperation should not only depend on mutual sympathy but should (especially) be based on mutual professional appreciation. Our example focuses on the basis of the design of collaboration.

Level 1 (Table 3A.3) initially focuses the appreciation on a personal level. Personal sympathy is an influencing factor for professional contentment concerning the design of cooperation, but cooperation based solely on positive collegial relationships is likely to collapse in the event of personnel changes. Successive levels in this area focus on the fertilisation of multi-professional perspectives among the professionals, asking, for example, "Is there an exchange about the professional perspectives and particularities of childhood and primary school pedagogy?" (Level 2) and "Does a mutual professional appreciation develop from this?" (Level 3)? By Levels 4 and 5, the extent to which these different perspectives lead to something new – a new vision or a new professional perspective – is reflected upon.

Paderborner Qualitätsstern (PQ³) 57

Table 3A.3 Roles of collaboration.

The multi-professional collaboration serves to . . .				
work collaboratively with regard to the cooperation activities.	work together in cooperation activities to ensure professional exchange.	develop cooperation activities together and to promote the transitional organisation.	also learn from each other as well as expanding their own professional competencies.	also reflect on the quality of the joint cooperation activities, to evaluate and to develop them further conceptually.

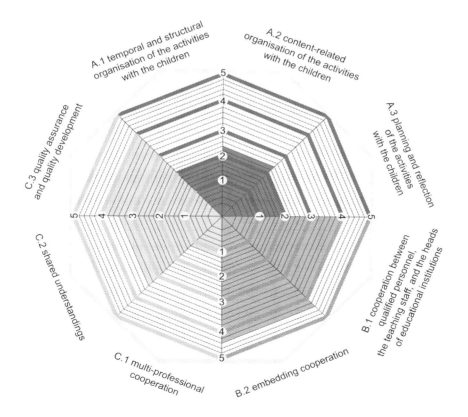

Figure 3A.1 A duly completed Paderborner Qualitätsstern.

Evaluation

After working on the individual scales from the three areas of cooperation, average values are calculated and entered into a star-shaped form (which is the reason for the label *Qualitätsstern*). By hatching the resulting areas (Figure 3A.1), it becomes clear where network-related developments have already taken place and where there may still be a need for development.

Conclusion

> The reflection questions have fully triggered discussion processes in the cooperation network and the planning of next steps has become very concrete for us through the work with the Paderborner Qualitätsstern. (Primary school teacher)

Voices from those who have used the evaluation, such as that of a primary school teacher, show that the self-evaluation instrument can achieve the desired goal in practice. The advantage of self-evaluation is that it is organised by the practitioners themselves and therefore has strong practical relevance, generating usable results. At the same time, the form of self-evaluation has the disadvantage that it is sometimes perceived as less strict than external evaluation. It is rather suspected of causing intentionally or unintentionally distorted or embellished results. In order to avoid this, we have had good experience in using an external moderator to take over the meta-evaluation and, as an evaluation expert, assess the self-evaluation activities and reflect them to the participants.

Nevertheless, each network has to find its own goal-oriented way of cooperating, adapted to the constantly changing practical conditions. In the future, the instrument is to be developed further in the direction of strengthening the participative evaluation approach. In this way, children shall be involved in the work with the PQ^3. Further development is also needed to consider some ethical challenges in the evaluation of transition to school programs. The instrument itself is and remains to be understood as *work in progress*.

We believe that the PQ^3 could be used as the basis for the development of other instruments in other contexts. It can be downloaded from the website (https://blogs.uni-paderborn.de/paderborner-qualitaetsstern) or can be requested free of charge via email by contacting the authors. Internationally, it needs to be adapted to country-specific conditions in order to use it for the planning and implementation of successful and effective transition to school programs.

References

Ackesjö, H., & Persson, S. (2019). The schoolarization of the preschool class – Policy discourses and educational restructuring in Sweden. *Nordic Journal of Studies in Educational Policy*, 5(2), 127–136. https://doi.org/10.1080/20020317.2019.1642082

References – Chapters 3 and 3A

Ahtola, A., Silinskas, G., Poikonen, P.-L., Kontoniemi, M., Niemi, P., & Nurmi, J.-E. (2011). Transition to formal schooling: Do transition practices matter for academic performance? *Early Childhood Research Quarterly*, 26(3), 295–302. https://doi.org/10.1016/j.ecresq.2010.12.002

Arndt, P., & Kipp, K. (2016). *Bildungshaus 3–10: Intensivkooperation und ihre Wirkung* [Bildungshaus 3–10: Intensive cooperation and its effects]. Leverkusen: Barbara Budrich. https://doi.org/10.1026/2191-9186/a000187

Arslan, G., Allen, K., & Ryan, T. (2020). Exploring the impacts of school belonging on youth wellbeing and mental health: A longitudinal study. *Child Indicators Research*, 13, 1619–1635. https://doi.org/10.1007/s12187-020-09721-z

Besi, M., & Sakellariou, M. (2019). Transition to primary school: The importance of social skills. *International Journal of Humanities and Social Science*, 6(1), 33–36. https://doi.org/10.14445/23942703/IJHSS-V6I1P107

Bortz, J., & Döring, N. (2015). *Forschungsmethoden und Evaluation in den Sozial- und Humanwissenschaften* [Research methods and evaluation in the social and human sciences], 5. erweit. Aufl. Berlin, Heidelberg: Springer. https://doi.org/10.1007/978-3-642-41089-5

Boyle, T., Petriwskyj, A., & Grieshaber, S. (2018). Reframing transition to school as continuity practices: The role of practice architectures. *Australian Educational Researcher*, 45, 419–434. https://doi.org/10.1007/s13384-018-0272-0

Broström, S. (2013). Play as the main road in children's transition to school. In O. Lillemyr, S. Dockett, & B. Perry (Eds.), *Varied perspectives on play and learning: Theory and research in early childhood education* (pp. 37–53). Charlotte, NC: Information Age.

Büker, P., & Höke, J. (2019). Children's voices as a bridge between education in kindergarten and teachers in primary school: Potential of children's perspectives to support professional development. In S. Dockett, J. Einarsdóttir, & B. Perry (Eds.), *Listening to children's advice about starting school and school age care* (pp. 116–132). London: Routledge.

Centre for Equity and Innovation in Early Childhood (CEIEC). (2008). *Literature review – Transition: A positive start to school*. www.education.vic.gov.au/Documents/about/research/transitionliteraturereview.pdf

Correia, K., & Marques-Pinto, A. (2016). Adaptation in the transition to school: Perspectives of parents, preschool and primary school teachers. *Educational Research*, 58(3), 247–264. https://doi.org/10.1080/00131881.2016.1200255

Department of Education, Skills and Employment (DESE). (2019). *Belonging, being & becoming: The early years learning framework for Australia*. www.dese.gov.au/national-quality-framework-early-childhood-education-and-care/resources/belonging-being-becoming-early-years-learning-framework-australia

Dockett, S., & Einarsdóttir, J. (2017). Continuity and change as children start school. In N. Ballam, B. Perry, & A. Garpelin (Eds.), *Pedagogies of educational research: European and antipodean research* (pp. 133–150). Dordrecht: Springer. https://doi.org/10.1007/978-3-319-43118-5_9

Dockett, S., Einarsdóttir, J., & Perry, B. (Eds.). (2019). *Listening to children's advice about starting school and school age care*. London: Routledge. https://doi.org/10.4324/9781351139403

Dockett, S., & Perry, B. (Eds.). (2001a). *Beginning school together: Sharing strengths*. Canberra: Australian Early Childhood Association.

Dockett, S., & Perry, B. (2001b). Introduction. In S. Dockett & B. Perry (Eds.), *Beginning school together: Sharing strengths* (pp. iii–x). Watson, ACT: Australian Early Childhood Association.

Dockett, S., & Perry, B. (2004). What makes a successful transition to school? Views of Australian parents and teachers. *International Journal of Early Years Education*, *12*, 217–230. https://doi.org/10.1080/0966 976042000268690

Dockett, S., & Perry, B. (2014). *Continuity of learning: A resource to support effective transition to school and school age care*. Canberra, ACT: Australian Government Department of Education. https://docs.education.gov.au/system/files/doc/other/pdf_with_bookmarking_-_continuity_of_learning-_30_october_2014_1_0.pdf

Dockett, S., & Perry, B. (2021). Invisible transitions: Transitions to school following different paths. *Australasian Journal of Early Childhood*. https://doi.org/10.1177/18369391211009698

Dunlop, A.-W. (2014). Thinking about transitions – One framework or many? Populating the theoretical model over time. In B. Perry, S. Dockett, & A. Petriwskyj (Eds.), *Transitions to school: International research policy and practice* (pp. 31–46). Dordrecht: Springer. https://doi.org/10.1007/978-94-007-7350-9_3

Educational Transitions and Change (ETC) Research Group. (2011). *Transition to school: Position statement*. https://arts-ed.csu.edu.au/education/transitions/publications/Position-Statement.pdf

Einarsdóttir, J. (2006). From the pre-school to primary school: When different contexts meet. *Scandinavian Journal of Educational Research*, *50*(2), 165–184. https://doi.org/10.1080/00313830600575965

Entwisle, D. R., & Alexander, K. L. (1989). Early schooling as a "critical period" phenomenon. *Sociology of Education and Socialization*, *8*, 27–55.

Faust, G., Wehner, F., & Kratzmann, J. (2011). Zum Stand der Kooperation von Kindergarten und Grundschule. Maßnahmen und Einstellungen der Beteiligten [On the status of the cooperation between kindergarten and primary school. Measures and attitudes of those involved]. *Journal for Educational Research Online*, *3*(2), 38–61.

Goodenow, C., & Grady, K. (1993). The relationship of school belonging and friends' values to academic motivation among urban adolescent students. *The Journal of Experimental Education*, *62*(1), 60–71. https://doi.org/10.1080/00220973.1993.9943831

Gräsel, C., Fußangel, K., & Pröbstel, C. (2006). Lehrkräfte zur Kooperation anregen – eine Aufgabe für Sisyphos? [Encouraging teachers to cooperate – A task for Sisyphus?]. *Zeitschrift für Pädagogik*, *52*(2), 205–219. www.pedocs.de/volltexte/2011/4453/pdf/ZfPaed_2006_2_Graesel_Fussangel_Proebstel_Lehrkraefte_Kooperation_anregen_D_a.pdf

Griebel, W., & Niesel, R. (2003). Successful transitions: Social competencies help pave the way into kindergarten and school. In A.-W. Dunlop & H. Fabian (Eds.), *Transitions, European Early Childhood Education Research Journal Monograph Series*, *1*, 25–34. https://doi.org/10.1080/1350293X.2003.12016703

Griebel, W., & Niesel, R. (2011). *Übergänge verstehen und begleiten* [Understand and accompany transitions]. Berlin: Cornelsen Scriptor.

Hirst, M., Jervis, N., Visagie, K., Sojo, V., & Cavanagh, S. (2011). *Transition to primary school: A review of the literature*. https://minerva-access.unimelb.edu.au/bitstream/handle/11343/123771/Transition-to-Primary-School-A-literature-review.pdf?sequence=1

Höke, J., Bührmann, T., Büker, P., Hummel, R., Meser, K., Miller, S., & Stölner, R. (2017). Bildungshäuser als 'Dritter Raum' im Übergang zwischen Kita und Grundschule – Kritische

Blicke auf ein Jahrzehnt Intensivkooperation [Bildungshäuser as a third room in transition between day care and elementary school – Critical views of a decade of intensive cooperation]. *Zeitschrift für Grundschulforschung, 10*(1), 91–106.

Höke, J., Büker, P., Ogrodowski, J., & Vollmann, B. (2020). *Paderborner Qualitätsstern zur Einschätzung der Kooperation im Übergang Kita – Grundschule. Paderborn.* PQ³. [Padeborn quality star for assessing the cooperation in the transition from day care centre to elementary school] Universität Paderborn. 3., stark überarb. Auflage. Unter Mitarbeit von Alina Bruyn und Theresa Driller. https://blogs.uni-paderborn.de/paderborner-qualitaetsstern/

Holly, P., & Southworth, G. (2005). *The developing school.* London: Falmer Press.

Huser, C., Dockett, S., & Perry, B. (2016). Transition to school: Revisiting the bridge metaphor. *European Early Childhood Education Research Journal, 24*(3), 439–449. https://doi.org/10.1080/1350293X.2015.1102414

Joerdens, S. (2014). "Belonging means you can go in": Children's perspectives and experiences of membership of kindergarten. *Australasian Journal of Early Childhood, 39*(1), 12–21. https://doi.org/10.1177/183693911403900103

Johansson, E. (2017). Toddler's relationships – A matter of sharing worlds. In L. Li, G. Quinones, & A. Ridgway (Eds.), *Studying babies and toddlers: Cultural worlds and transitory relationships* (pp. 13–27). Singapore: Springer. https://doi.org/10.1007/978-981-10-3197-7_2

Juutinen, J., Puroila, A.-M., & Johansson, E. (2018). "There is no room for you!" The politics of belonging in children's play situations. In E. Johansson, E. Emilson, & A.-M. Puroila (Eds.), *Values education in early childhood settings* (pp. 249–264). Cham, Switzerland: Springer. https://doi.org/10.1007/978-3-319-75559-5_15

Lago, L. (2019). Different transitions: Children's different experiences of the transition to school. In S. Dockett, J. Einarsdóttir, & B. Perry (Eds.), *Listening to children's advice about starting school and school age care* (pp. 55–68). London: Routledge.

Lloyd, J. W., Steinberg, D., & Wilhelm-Chapin, M. K. (1999). Research on transition to kindergarten. In R. C. Pianta & M. Cox (Eds.), *The transition to kindergarten* (pp. 305–316). Baltimore, MD: Paul H Brookes.

Mashburn, A. J., LoCasale-Crouch, J., & Pears, K. (Eds.). (2018). *Kindergarten transition and readiness.* Cham, Switzerland: Springer.

Mirkhil, M. (2010). Important ingredients for a successful transition to school. *International Research in Early Childhood Education, 1,* 60–70. https://files.eric.ed.gov/fulltext/EJ1151145.pdf

Moss, P. (Ed.). (2013). *Early childhood and compulsory education: Reconceptualising the relationship.* London: Routledge.

Nergaard, K. (2020). The heartbreak of social rejection: Young children's expressions about how they experience rejection from peers in ECEC. *Child Care in Practice, 26*(3), 226–242. https://doi.org/10.1080/13575279.2018.1543650

Organisation for Economic Cooperation and Development (OECD). (2017). *Starting strong V. Transitions from early childhood education and care to primary education.* Paris: OECD Publishing. https://doi.org/10.1787/9789264276253-en

Packer, R., Thomas, A., Jones, C., & Watkins, P. (2020). Voices of transition: Sharing experiences from the primary school. *Education,* 3–13. https://doi.org/10.1080/03004279.2020.1805487

Papadopoulou, M. (2016). The "space" of friendship: Young children's understandings and expressions of friendship in a Reception class. *Early Child Development and Care, 186*(10), 1544–1558. https://doi.org/10.1080/03004430.2015.1111879

References – Chapters 3 and 3A

Perry, B., & Dockett, S. (2018). Using a bioecological framework to investigate an early childhood mathematics education intervention. *European Early Childhood Education Research Journal, 26*(4), 604–617. https://doi.org/10.1080/1350293X.2018.1487161

Purtell, K., Valauri, A., Rhoad-Drogalis, A., Jiang, H., Justice, L., Lin, T.-J., & Logan, J. (2020). Understanding policies and practices that support successful transitions to kindergarten. *Early Childhood Research Quarterly, 52*, 5–14. https://doi.org/10.1016/j.ecresq.2019.09.003

Ramey, C., & Ramey, S. (2010). The transition to school. Concepts, practices, and needed research. In S. L. Kagan & K. Tarrant (Eds.), *Transitions for young children* (pp. 19–32). Baltimore, MD: Paul H Brookes.

Ramey, C., Ramey, S., & Lanzi, R. (2006). Children's health and education. In I. Sigel & A. Renninger (Eds.), *The handbook of child psychology* (Vol. 4, pp. 864–892). Hoboken, NJ: Wiley.

Rimm-Kaufman, S. E., & Pianta, R. C. (2000). An ecological perspective on the transition to kindergarten: A theoretical framework to guide empirical research. *Journal of Applied Developmental Psychology, 21*(5), 491–511. https://doi.org/10.1016/S0193-3973(00)00051-4

Rogoff, B. (2003). *The cultural nature of human development*. Oxford: Oxford University Press.

Sandseter, E. B. H., & Seland, M. (2018). 4–6 year-old children's experience of subjective well-being and social relations in ECEC institutions. *Child Indicators Research*, 11, 1585–1601. https://doi.org/10.1007/s12187-017-9504-5

Savaya, R., & Waysman, M. (2005). The logic model. *Administration in Social Work, 29*(2), 85–103. https://doi.org/10.1300/J147v29n02_06

Schulting, A., Malone, P., & Dodge, K. (2005). The effect of school-based kindergarten transition policies and practices on child academic outcomes. *Developmental Psychology, 41*, 860. https://doi.org/10.1037/0012-1649.41.6.860

Stratigos, T. (2015). Assemblages of desire: Infants, bear caves and belonging in early childhood education and care. *Contemporary Issues in Early Childhood, 16*(1), 42–54. https://doi.org/10.1177/1463949114566757

Stratigos, T., Bradley, B., & Sumsion, J. (2014). Infants, family day care and the politics of belonging. *International Journal of Early Childhood, 46*(2), 171–186. https://doi.org/10.1007/s13158-014-0110-0

Sumsion, J., & Wong, S. (2011). Interrogating "belonging" in belonging, being and becoming: The early years learning framework for Australia. *Contemporary Issues in Early Childhood, 12*(1), 28–45. https://doi.org/10.2304/ciec.2011.12.1.28

Tatalović Vorkapić, S. (2019). Children's well-being during transition periods in Croatia: The proposal of empirical validation of Ecological-dynamic model. In L. Gómez Chova, A. López Martínez, & I. Candel Torres (Eds.), *INTED2019 proceedings, 13th international technology, education and development conference* (pp. 265–276). Valencia, Spain: INTED. https://doi.org/10.21125/inted.2019.0130

Urbina-Garcia, A. (2019). Preschool transition in Mexico: Exploring teachers' perceptions and practices. *Teaching and Teacher Education*, 85, 226–234. https://doi.org/10.1016/j.tate.2019.06.012

Vitiello, V., Pianta, R., Whittaker, J., & Ruzek, E. (2020). Alignment and misalignment of classroom experiences from pre-K to kindergarten. *Early Childhood Research Quarterly*, 52, 44–56. https://doi.org/10.1016/j.ecresq.2019.06.014

Vogt, F., Heim, D., & Zumwald, B. (2016). Kooperationsqualität: Strukturqualität, Prozessqualität, Wirkungen und Forschungsdesiderate [Cooperation quality: Structural quality, process quality, effects and research desiderata]. In A. Kreis, J. Wick, & C. Krosorok Labhart (Hrsg.), *Kooperation im Kontext schulischer Heterogenität* [Cooperation in the context of school heterogeneity] (pp. 15–31). Münster: Waxman.

Waters, L. (2016). Fostering school belonging in secondary schools using a socio-ecological framework. *The Educational and Developmental Psychologist*, *33*(1), 97–121. https://doi.org/10.1017/edp.2016.5

Wildgruber, A., & Griebel, W. (2016). *Erfolgreicher Übergang vom Elementar- in den Primarbereich. Empirische und curriculare Analysen* [Successful transition from elementary to primary school. Empirical and curricular analyses]. München: DJI.

Yeboah, D. (2010). Enhancing transition from early childhood phase to primary education: Evidence from the research literature. *Early Years*, *22*(1), 51–68. https://doi.org/10.1080/09575140120111517

Yuval-Davis, N. (2006). Belonging and the politics of belonging. *Patterns of Prejudice*, *40*(3), 197–214. https://doi.org/10.1080/00313220600769331

4 Evaluation of transition to school programs – an introduction

Sue Dockett and Bob Perry

Introduction

Internationally as well as nationally, we have witnessed increasing interest in children's transition to school. In many contexts, this has been accompanied by increased funding and support for programs. At the same time, there has been an increase in efforts to monitor, review, appraise, and/or evaluate programs and an increased use of terms such as *accountability*, *surveillance*, and *compliance* (Organisation for Economic Co-operation and Development (OECD), 2017; Pianta, Cox, & Snow, 2007). The chapter begins with consideration of evaluation as a measure of both worth and merit before exploring the purposes and types of evaluations relevant to transition to school programs. This links with Chapter 4A, which provides a detailed example of a needs analysis. We then outline frameworks for evaluation and introduce the concepts of participatory evaluation, participatory action research, and the project approach, considering their application for the evaluation of transition to school programs.

What is meant by evaluation?

Dictionary definitions of evaluation refer to the process of judging the worth or value of something. A more detailed definition is provided by Fournier (2011, p. 140), who refers to:

> an applied inquiry process for collecting and synthesizing evidence that culminates in conclusions about the state of affairs, value, merit, worth, significance, or quality of a program, product, person, policy, proposal, or plan. Conclusions made in evaluations encompass both an empirical aspect (that something is the case) and a normative aspect (judgment about the value of something).

This definition emphasises the purposeful nature of evaluation as well as the focus on both merit – the relative quality of something measured against specific criteria – and worth – the value of something in a particular context (Mertens,

2015). Both elements are important as we consider the evaluation of transition to school programs. For example, a program that meets a goal of providing extensive information for children and families before they start school may have considerable merit, but if many children and families cannot access the information, it may have limited worth in that context.

Evaluating transition to school programs

Transition programs consist of a plan or schedule of activities and practices that aim to promote positive transition to school experiences for all involved. There are many different forms of transition programs and many possible approaches to evaluation. For example, some programs are large scale and funded, while others are much more locally developed programs with limited resources; some will be the subject of external evaluation, while others will be evaluated internally. While the evaluation of all programs is important, it is likely to look different for different programs and different contexts. In this chapter, we provide an overview of evaluation possibilities particularly focused around the small-scale evaluations that are likely to be undertaken within educational communities. While we focus on evaluating programs, specific practices within programs may also be the subject of evaluation.

All evaluation involves processes of inquiry. High-quality evaluation utilises processes similar to those of applied research around project design, data generation, analysis, interpretation, and reporting. Just as in research, these processes are important in introducing rigour and establishing the trustworthiness of the evaluation. Before we explore these processes, we consider some of the purposes of evaluation.

Purposes of evaluation

While there are many purposes of evaluation, underpinning each is the notion of informing decision-making, whether it be about the need for a program, the nature and content of the program, its implementation, or outcomes. Some of the purposes and related questions for transition programs to be addressed by evaluation could include:

Is the transition program needed?

- Why is it needed?
- How do we know?
- What programs already exist?
- How effective are existing programs and for whom?

Does the program meet the needs of stakeholders?

- Is the program reaching stakeholders?
- Is the program relevant and appropriate for stakeholders?

Can the program be improved?

- What are the challenges, constraints, or unintended consequences of the program?

How does the program operate?

- What happens during the program?
- What is involved for stakeholders?
- Is the program delivered as planned?
- Does the program meet any required standards?

How effective is the program?

- Does it meet the program goals?
- What are the outcomes for stakeholders?
- Should the program be continued?

How efficient is the program?

- What are the program costs and benefits?
- How are resources allocated and used?

Why does the program work (or not work?)

- Does it work for all stakeholders?
- Does it work in all contexts?
- How does it work?
- What elements do not work?

It is unlikely that locally based transition programs involving a small number of early childhood (ECEC) and school settings as well as some community participants will have the time, resources, or personnel to ask all of these questions. Rather, some priorities will need to be established to act as foci for the evaluation. Whatever these foci, it will be important to involve relevant stakeholders in appropriate ways. This is particularly important when the outcome of the evaluation provokes change, as there is much more likely to be *buy-in* to those changes if people feel that they have been involved meaningfully in the evaluation process.

Types of evaluation

Typically, three types of evaluation are used to answer the sorts of questions listed above: needs analysis, process evaluation, and outcome or impact evaluation (Morrison & Harms, 2018).

Needs analysis

Needs analysis is undertaken to find out what is needed within a particular context. It requires a systematic approach to seeking information to inform decisions about programs in answer to questions such as "Is the transition program needed?"

Example: Finding out what is already available

A school in one inner-city community was looking to expand its program from a focus on orientation to transition. The existing orientation program featured two visits to the school, for two hours each, over two consecutive Tuesdays in Term 4. As part of their planning, the school team contacted local ECEC settings, arranged visits, and sought information about existing transition practices. They surveyed existing and prospective families about their preferences. Realising that much was already happening in their community around transition, they concluded that there was no need for them to embark on constructing a totally new, school-based program. Rather, they embarked on building collaborations with ECEC educators to generate a community transition program that incorporated a wide range of activities offered by families, ECEC settings, and the school.

The practice review reported in Chapter 4A is an example of a needs analysis, as it identified and mapped existing supports and effective practices relevant for children experiencing vulnerability in the state of Victoria. From this extensive review, the authors identified recommendations that offered directions and priorities for the future development of the statewide policy and practice framework. The needs analysis described in the earlier example involved seeking information from families and ECEC settings about existing as well as desired transition practices and, from this, deciding how to structure a community transition to school program.

Process evaluation

Process evaluation focuses on what occurs as a program is implemented. It analyses what happens during the program – from the initial planning through to implementation, considering factors such as who participates and how participants are accessed; how, when, and where the program operates; who delivers the program; decisions made as the program is implemented; and intended as well as unintended occurrences. In addition, perceptions of those involved, as well as those who observe the program, can contribute to process evaluations. Process evaluations are often described as formative evaluations – conducted during the development or delivery of a program with the intent of providing feedback to improve that program.

The focus on the development and implementation of the program seeks to identify reasons for its success (or otherwise) as well as providing information about how the program could be improved or implemented in different contexts (Mathison, 2011). Process evaluations can address questions such as: "Does the program meet the needs of stakeholders?"; "Can the program be improved?"; and "How does the program operate?" Process evaluations may also focus more specifically on what practices are considered effective and how these are implemented. Some examples of process evaluations are noted in what follows.

Example: Evaluating a transition practice

Parent information evenings were a standard activity in the transition program at Bluetooth School. Across several years, attendance had been dwindling, and despite extensive advertising, not one parent attended the most recent session. Responses to a follow-up survey conducted through ECEC settings and community organisations indicated that parents felt that they had already accessed much of the information they needed, using both social media and word of mouth. Other responses indicated that being unable to take younger children to the meeting prevented attendance; the timing of the session was problematic; and parents preferred opportunities to meet individually with educators to talk about their child rather than presentations of generic information. These data, along with indications of what information parents did want, were used to change the program by developing a communication plan that co-ordinated web-based and written information with small-group sessions in which a few parents and teacher could meet to share and seek information at a more personal level.

Example: Evaluating a transition program

Educators from Muskheart Preschool and Baloghia School developed a transition program for their local community that involved a series of child and educator visits to the different settings and coordinated information for parents and activities at the local library. The program ran over a 10-week period on set days each week. During the program, it became evident that some groups of preschool children had greater access to the program than others because of their scheduled days of preschool attendance. To address this, the remaining five weeks of the program were spread across different days of the week to promote access for preschool children with varying attendance patterns.

Example: Evaluating a statewide initiative

The *Transition: A Positive Start to School* initiative was launched in Victoria in 2009. Semann and Slattery (2015a) were commissioned to review the use of transition practices, including transition statements and the strategies used to evaluate transition programs. Using mixed methods, the consultation sought the views of stakeholders (ECEC, school, and outside-school-hours care educators, family members, and Prep children) through focus groups, teleconferences, surveys, and informal consultations. Analysis of data from the consultation generated principles to guide the future development and implementation of the statewide program.

Process evaluations can employ many strategies to inform decisions, including surveys of participants, observations of practice, reflections, journals, or self-reports (see Chapter 7). These strategies can provide opportunities for participants to share their perspectives. However, some quantitative data – such as the number of people participating in specific transition practices, the amount and type of follow-up interactions with ECEC settings or schools, analysis of documents, or the number of transition to school statements shared – can also be used to describe the operation and possible outcomes of the program.

Process evaluations pay attention to specific contexts and the interaction between these and the program. Involving children, families, and educators in reflection on their participation and engagement can start the process of documenting what seems to work, as well as what does not, for whom, and in what contexts. Process evaluations are often considered formative evaluations, as they examine the program as it unfolds and help to modify it in ways that help achieve the program goals. For example, if the transition program aims to involve families, yet few families have engaged with it, formative evaluations can identify practices that are not working and recommend changes to make them more appropriate.

The involvement of a mentor, critical friend, transition network, or community of practice can support process evaluations. For example, prompts or provocations from a mentor who is not involved in the day-to-day delivery of the program can facilitate reflections that may not be generated by self-reports. As well, the sense of being engaged in a social and collaborative process of evaluation can help remove the focus from any one individual and can help build ownership of any changes that follow.

The involvement of someone external to the program can also encourage participation in the process evaluation. Sometimes, potential participants may be wary of identifying challenges or concerns for fear it will be regarded negatively and impact them later. Examples might include educators who fear damaging their relationships with ECEC settings or schools if they appear to be critical of people or processes and parents who may be uncomfortable criticising a transition program or the way in which it is implemented in the belief that they or their child may be regarded negatively. Engaging with an external mentor or evaluator can address some of the ethical challenges associated with the generation and sharing of data as well as help to maintain confidentiality.

Outcome evaluation

Outcome evaluations investigate the impact of the program on those taking part, addressing questions such as "How effective is the program?"; "How efficient is the program?" and "Why does the program work (or not work)?" Outcomes can include those intended and unintended, as well as short- and longer-term outcomes. *Impact assessment* is another term for examining the outcomes of a program. Summative evaluation is also associated with reporting program outcomes.

Outcome evaluations assume that something will change as a result of the program and that change can be measured in some way. This usually means utilising quantitative measures, often comparing data before and after the program. To ensure that any change is due to the program itself, outcome evaluations seek to establish causal relationships, such as demonstrating that a specific transition program led to specific outcomes, through the use of experimental designs. There are many forms of experimental designs, including the *gold standard* random control trial, such as in the following example.

Example: Evaluating a parent program

Giallo et al. (2010) reported a randomised control study designed to assess the effectiveness of a parent program which aimed to "enhance parents' knowledge and confidence in their ability to help their child make a smooth transition and manage any difficulties that might arise at this time" (p. 3). Twenty-one schools participated in the evaluation, with 10 allocated to the intervention and 11 to the control group. Parents in the intervention schools were offered the parenting program, while parents in the control schools accessed the standard transition activities offered by the schools. Participating parents completed pre-intervention surveys which established baseline characteristics for each group. Both groups of parents also completed a number of self-report measures seeking information about parental self-efficacy, sense of competence, parental involvement, and any concerns about their child's health or development. Follow-up surveys were completed by parents in the term children started school and at the end of the following term. Statistical analyses of these data resulted in the conclusion that "participation in the transition to school parent program had a positive effect on parental self-efficacy to help their children make the transition to school, and was associated with greater parent involvement at school during the children's first term at school" (p. 12).

While randomised control studies do seek to establish causal relationships, the time, resources, and expertise required to implement these means that they are probably unrealistic options for most locally based transition programs. In many settings, it would be difficult to establish distinct and separate intervention and control groups with sufficient participants to employ the statistical analysis required to establish causality. Further, the notion of excluding some people from something like a transition program sits uneasily with educators promoting social justice and ethical engagement. Nevertheless, using such studies to review large-scale programs that involve substantial funding and have the potential to make significant differences across populations or systems is an important exercise.

Apart from randomised control trials, there are other strategies for evaluating the outcomes of a program. These include designs that survey participants before and after the program but have no control group. Some outcome measures might interview participants after a program and seek information about how they believe they have changed. Others might rely on the number of participants who maintained participation in the program or reflect on the proportion of participants involved in different activities or across the program. For example, a program might be considered effective if it reached 90% of potential participants. While these measures can be important, they do not necessarily establish a causal link or do not attest to the quality of the program. In these instances, some data gathered through process evaluation could provide additional information about outcomes and effectiveness.

The generation of before and after data (pre- and post-transition program) can provide some evidence of the perceptions, experiences, and expectations of stakeholders. Strategies for generating this information can include questionnaires and conversations (see also Chapter 7).

Example: Surveying families

As the end of the preschool year approached, several families were seeking information from educators about their children's transition to school, what would happen at school, how they could prepare for it, and how they might manage the change. As children from the preschool group were to attend many different schools, the ECEC educators felt unsure about providing specific advice that was relevant for all schools. A group of educators and parents created an initial questionnaire identifying what information was sought by families and a follow-up questionnaire seeking details of whether this information had been provided and, if so, when and how. They shared their results with schools in the local area. These results served as a basis for reviewing information exchange about transition among ECEC settings, families, and schools.

Example: Children's expectations and experiences

In preparation for a visit to the local school as part of their transition program, ECEC educators held conversations with children to identify what they wanted to know about school. The educators transcribed the children's questions onto a large piece of butcher's paper and put these on display in the classroom, where both parents and children could refer to them. Children's questions included:

- Are there swings at school?
- Who will help me if I fall over in the playground?
- Can we play at school?
- Where is my brother?

After the transition visit, the ECEC educators added another piece of paper on which the information children had gleaned was recorded. Conversations generated further questions from the children about school to add to the questions that had not yet been answered. Another piece of paper was used to record these in preparation for the next visit.

Example: Impact of a professional learning program for educators

In one regional area, a professional learning program included focus on the role of school principals in creating *ready schools* and supporting positive transition programs and experiences. Participants completed questionnaires, detailed their expectations of the program and the outcomes they anticipated for themselves and their school approach to transition, and engaged in conversations with the external evaluator prior to commencing the professional learning program, which consisted of several input sessions, site visits, and mentoring exchanges. Similar strategies were used to generate data once the program had been completed. Analysis indicated changes in principals' views of what constituted optimal transitions, interactions with ECEC educators, and community networks, as well as enhanced leadership practice around transition to school.

Process, outcome, or both?

In the light of limited resources, it is likely that some priorities need to be established to provide foci for the evaluation of transition programs. While we have described needs assessment, process evaluation, and outcome evaluation as distinct, the reality is that many evaluations seek information about the program, how it operates, and how it can be improved, as well as its effectiveness. There is no one *right* focus for the evaluation of transition programs. Rather, the nature of the evaluation needs to be relevant to the evaluation questions asked as well as the context and resources available. In many instances, it may be appropriate to start with a small-scale evaluation, focusing on some transition practices and their perceived effectiveness. This will be particularly important where such evaluation is undertaken internally – where it is on top of the regular roles and responsibilities of educators and other stakeholders. Starting small can also assist in building expertise or in developing strategies to access external expertise to support the evaluation process.

The evaluation of transition to school programs often seeks both process and outcome information, aiming to evaluate what happens in the program and how to improve this, as well as considering the effects of the transition program. This was the case in the evaluation of the *Linking Schools and Early Years* project described in what follows.

Example: Process and outcome evaluation

The *Linking Schools and Early Years* project aimed to "ensure that all children enter the formal education system ready to engage with the many opportunities offered by their new learning environment" and "to ensure that schools are prepared for children of all abilities and backgrounds when they first attend, and that families, services and communities are ready to support the development of children" (valentine & Katz, 2010, p. 1). The evaluation plan identified three aims which incorporated both process and outcome elements (Valentine & Katz, 2010, p. 6):

1   To determine the overall impact of the project towards achieving the project goals (outcome)
2   To identify the effectiveness of strategies and activities implemented towards achieving the project goals across and within project sites (outcome and process)
3   To identify barriers and enablers to achieving the project goals (process).

Each of these aims was broken down into a series of questions, which were addressed through a combination of questionnaires and interviews. Other data sources included demographic data and relevant documents.

Evaluation frameworks

If the aim of an evaluation is to improve the program, it is important to explore how a program works and how this contributes to outcomes. One way to focus an evaluation is to consider the *program theory*. Program theory simply refers to the theory underpinning the evaluation. It does not necessarily refer to grand theories but to the rationale or ideas underpinning the program. These ideas might be clear in answers to the question "Why it is important to have this transition to school program?" For example, if the answers relate to building relationships and a sense of belonging, the strategies adopted within the evaluation would probably focus on observations and conversations with participants about what it means to belong and the relationships that support this. If the answers relate to preparing children for school, the evaluation measures will probably focus on assessing children's school-related behaviours. In identifying the theory behind the program, the aim is to ask not only if the program works but also how and why it works (Chen, 2012).

Sometimes we design transition programs based on experience, what we think is possible, or what we have seen elsewhere, as well as what we believe to be important. Spending some time articulating the theory behind the program can create spaces for reflection, unpacking what we take for granted, and sharing perspectives with others. For example, in a network of ECEC and school educators, clarifying why each thinks transition is important and what they see as the goals of transition is an important step in promoting collaboration (see also Chapter 7A). While it is likely to highlight a range of differences, it is also possible to identify some commonalities that will be necessary for the program to operate. In their toolkit supporting evaluation within Aboriginal and Torres Strait Islander child and family services, SNAICC (n.d, p. 5) describes the theory of change as the description of how a program intends

> to achieve meaningful change ... it is not just a description of what the intended changes are. Rather, it is a depiction of how your program is

supposed to work and what it is intended to achieve . . . it outlines the cause-and-effect relationship between the program's activities and the long-term outcomes it creates for its targeted stakeholders . . . A theory of change . . . provides a basis to both design and evaluate programs . . . [it enables the telling] of the unique change you create as a result of your activities.

Planning an evaluation often starts with a model of what a project looks like and how it is expected to work. These plans are often visual and can be referred to as *logic models*, *road maps*, *blueprints for change*, or *frameworks for action*. Regardless of the term used, the aim of the models is to outline the logic of the program – that is, how change is expected to occur. Sometimes logic maps are presented as linear. However, relationships between the elements of programs can also be displayed in web diagrams or concept maps. Logic models guide evaluation by framing the story of the project and linking outcomes to elements through the program theory (Savaya & Waysman, 2005). Typically, logic models set out the relationships between the following elements: aim of the program, the context/s in which the program operates, the inputs into the program, activities of the program, program outputs, and program outcomes. An example of an evaluation of a transition to school program framed by a logic model is provided by Newell and Graham (2008).

Realist evaluation, outlined by Pawson and Tilley (1997), is one example of using theory to consider why a program might work, for whom it works, and in what circumstances: "realist approaches assume that nothing works everywhere or for everyone, and that context really does make a difference to programme outcomes" (Westhorp, 2014, p. 4). The essence of realist evaluation is the identification of mechanisms that promote change. Mechanisms are defined as responses to activities that influence decision-making: "the interaction between what the programme provides and the reasoning of its intended target population" (Westhorp, 2014, p. 5). For example, a transition program might incorporate a series of visits to the school by children and families using the logic that this will build familiarity with the people and places at school, leading to a sense of belonging and the building of relationships which, in turn, result in an effective transition to school. What happens on the school visits could include information sessions for families and children, spending time in the classroom, school tours, meeting teachers, and many other transition practices. In this example, the transition program promotes the activity of the visit, but the mechanism it aims to engage is the reasoning by children and families that school is a familiar place in which they belong. It is the reasoning rather than the visits themselves that promotes change. Similar logic underpins activities for educators, where reciprocal visits to ECEC and school settings and participation in a transition network are possible activities to build a sense of familiarity and belonging (the mechanism for change) and generate the outcome of an effective transition to school for all involved. Table 4.1 provides an example of the relationships between activities, mechanisms, and outcomes.

Table 4.1 Mechanism for change.

Focus participants	Activity	Mechanism for change	Outcome
Children starting school	School visits	Sense of belonging characterised by familiarity with the school setting and based on trusting and respectful relationships.	Effective transition to school
Parents/family members	School visits		
Educators	Reciprocal visits Transition network		

Identifying the possible mechanisms involved in an effective transition to school can aid in both designing the transition program and focusing the evaluation. Attention to mechanisms can lead to the identification of multiple possible activities and practices that support the mechanism for change. In the earlier example, it could generate a list of transition practices that support the building of relationships and promote familiarity with the school context.

Example: Realist evaluation

Astbury (2009) conducted a realist evaluation of pilot transition to school programs in Victoria. Investigation of the perceptions and experiences of those educators implementing the pilots resulted in findings across four key areas: the importance of school transition, factors affecting the implementation of transition, emerging evidence of promising practices, and implications for statewide implementation of promising transition practices.

An evaluation model

The *Evidence of Impact Model* (Harper, Maden, & Dickson, 2020) provides one framework to guide the evaluation of the short- and longer-term impact of programs. While it was developed in relation to large-scale health evaluations in the UK, the model considers impact at the micro, meso, and macro levels in a framework that will be familiar to many educators utilising bioecological theory (Bronfenbrenner & Morris, 2006) to plan transition programs. The other attractions of the model are the emphasis on qualitative data to support decisions made in specific contexts and the possibilities of evaluating programs as they develop over time and involve a range of participants.

The model evaluates change at five levels: the first two reflecting the micro level of individuals (the self and personal practice), the third and fourth levels incorporating the meso level of teams and organisations, and the macro level of professional or societal change. Paraphrasing this model and considering its application for transition programs, the following levels of impact and evaluation possibilities are noted:

Table 4.2 Evidence of impact model applied to transition programs.

Level of impact	Examples
1	*Level 1* considers the self and the personal impact of the program for individual children, parents, families, and/or educators. Evaluation could focus on children's reported changes in attitudes or emotions, families' feelings of being partners in their child's education, or the relationships between educators in different sectors.
2	*Level 2* focuses on personal practice, asking how what was learned in the transition program is applied in practice. Attention might be paid to changes in actions by the participants, such as children knowing where to go for specialist lessons, families communicating with the school, or educators participating in transition network meetings. The focus at this level is how participants put into practice the things they have gained from the transition program.
3	*Level 3* explores changes in the actions, expectations, and practices of the transition team as a result of the transition program. For example, "Have the priorities of the transition team changed?"; "What effects are noted from working in a team across sectors?"; and "What collaboration has been promoted or challenged?"
4	*Level 4* indicates whether the transition program has had effects at the organisational or local community level. For example, "Have schools or ECEC settings changed their practice as a result of participating in the transition program?"; "Has the program generated interest in the local community?"; and "If there is a transition network, has the work of that network changed?"
5	*Level 5* focuses on the professional sector or wider society, asking questions such as "Have approaches been shared with other transition teams?" and "Has the program generated broader interest?"

Considering the micro, meso, and macro levels of change reminds us of the importance of reflecting on individual as well as social change. In the transition to school space, it recognises that we need to consider what happens for individual children and adults, as well as what happens for the starting-school cohort, families, and educators. Attending to the application of knowledge or information also provides further avenues for examining program impact. The emphasis on macro-level changes also situates transition programs as important within each community.

Evaluating promising practices

One of the guidelines established early in our research reiterated the importance of contextual aspects of community and individual families and children within that community (Dockett & Perry, 2001). Recognising the importance of responsiveness and arguing that there is no *one-size-fits-all* transition to school program can prompt focus on practices that *fit* within a context and that, while effective in one context, may not be generalisable. These are considered promising practices.

Sometimes, the term *promising practices* is used to avoid using more definite terms such as *best practice* (Bohan-Baker, & Little, 2002; Watson, 2008). In the health and welfare fields, promising practice can sit between emerging and proven or *best* practices (Canadian Homelessness Research Network, 2013). In general, promising practices are those that appear to be effective in a specific context and where there is some evidence to support their effectiveness, but the evidence is not sufficient to make generalisable conclusions.

Example: A framework for promising practices

In building a repository of promising practices across community development and early childhood services supported by the Australian federal government, Soriano, Clark, and Wise (2008) outlined six criteria for program inclusion – that the practice be effective, be evidence based, contribute to the existing evidence base, be replicable, be innovative, and be sustainable. While not all criteria needed to be demonstrated for a practice to be considered promising, those nominating the project for inclusion in the repository were required to provide details of:

- What works?
- Why does it work?
- Under what circumstances does it work?
- For whom does it work?
- Outcomes.

As practices were verified, they were added to the *Child Family Community Australia Promising Practice Profiles* (Australian Institute of Family Studies, 2014).

Reporting the evaluation of pilot transition programs in Victoria, Astbury (2009, p. 5) noted that "while it is too early to evaluate the outcomes and impact of pilots, a number of pilots were able to identify emerging benefits". These were labelled promising practices and included the practices of reciprocal visits, transfer of information, joint professional development, local transition networks, and buddy programs. These practices have been the focus of several further evaluations (Scull & Garvis, 2015; Semann & Slattery, 2015b, 2016; Smith et al., 2011).

To be described as promising, there needs to be some evidence of effectiveness that is relevant to the aim of the program – the program theory. To evaluate promising practices, it is necessary to describe the practice/s, identify the proposed mechanism for change and how this connects to the practice/s, consider what is involved in the effective implementation of the practice/s in context, and generate evidence to document its effectiveness. This could involve asking some of the following questions:

- What is the practice?
- What is the connection between the practice/s and the program theory?

- What is the community context in which it operates?
- Why was it expected to work?
- What evidence was generated to show the effectiveness of the practice?
- Who contributed to the evidence and how?
- How was the evidence analysed?
- What were the results?
- How will the results influence future implementation of the practice?
- How will the results be shared?

Participatory evaluation

Participatory evaluation refers to any evaluation that actively involves participants or stakeholders in decision-making throughout the project (Coghlan, 2011). It is about more than consulting stakeholders in some way – such as interviewing them or asking them to complete a questionnaire. Participatory evaluation is a collaborative process. It may be undertaken solely by stakeholders or may involve an external person in the role of evaluation partner, facilitator, and/or technical adviser, working with participants as they plan and implement the evaluation. Participatory evaluation often has multiple goals directed towards not only understanding the program being evaluated but also fostering participant ownership of processes and outcomes and effecting change at the individual and community/organisational level. Involving stakeholders in evaluation has the advantage of incorporating different perspectives and ways of viewing the situation. A further advantage is that those involved in the evaluation are likely to adopt the findings and use these to change their own practice.

In participatory evaluations, stakeholders may be involved in all aspects of the evaluation: identifying the focus of the evaluation, developing the program theory or logic model, identifying questions to be asked about the program and the strategies to seek answers, data generation, data analysis and interpretation, reporting, and planning for change based on the evaluation outcomes (Zukoski & Luluquisen, 2002). It may be unrealistic to expect all stakeholders to have the technical skills required to participate in all these elements. Rather than excluding participants, participatory evaluations often include a training element to help stakeholders build up their repertoire of skills. A further advantage of participatory evaluation is the involvement of people who know the program well – from the inside. They bring tacit as well as explicit knowledge and experience that can add depth to the evaluation. Their insider involvement can also help drive continued commitment to the evaluation within the setting or organisation.

Potential disadvantages of participatory evaluation include perceptions of the evaluation as subjective and therefore not as rigorous or objective as an evaluation carried out solely by external evaluators; possible challenges in accessing technical skills; the commitment of time and resources among stakeholders; and the potential for some stakeholders to control the agenda and exclude others (Coghlan, 2011; Guijt, 2014).

When considering whether evaluations are genuinely participatory, Weaver and Cousins (2007) direct attention to five elements: control of technical decision-making, diversity of stakeholders involved in the evaluation, power relationships among participating stakeholders, manageability of the implementation of the evaluation, and the depth of participation. These elements provide a framework for promoting participatory evaluation, as well as analysing those studies utilising participatory processes.

Practitioner inquiry

Baumfield, Hall, and Wall (2013) position practitioner inquiry as a step between reflection and action research, such that it can be "a step in a process that begins with reflection and leads to sustained action research or . . . as the trigger to further development through reflection or action research. In either case, a crucial stage is the forming of questions arising directly from practice" (pp. 4–5). The focus of practitioner inquiry for transition to school is educators reflecting on their own educational practice, identifying an issue or area for the inquiry, establishing processes for the inquiry, and determining the audience with whom to share the results of the inquiry.

Chapter 7 provides an example of a statewide approach to practitioner inquiry, built on the notion that "educators need to be *inquirers into professional practice* who question their routine practices and assumptions and who are capable of investigating the effects" [italics in the original] of their actions (Reid, 2004, p. 3). Further, Reid (2004, p. 4) suggests that reflective questions, such as those that follow related to transition, form the basis of practitioner inquiry.

- What practices do we use to support transition to school?
- Why are we doing this?
- What are the effects of these practices?
- What alternatives are possible? Are these likely to result in more just outcomes?

Participatory action research

Sometimes parallels are drawn between participatory evaluation and participatory action research (PAR). Both can be described as based on a "democratic and participative orientation to knowledge creation" (Bradbury, 2015, p. 1) that focuses on the critical involvement of stakeholders in decision making about a project, seek to influence the practice of those involved, and consider the interplay of theory, practice, and reflection. One difference between participatory evaluation and participatory action research can be timing: participatory evaluation generally focuses on a project that is already in place (Cousins & Whitmore, 1998), while participatory action research generally focuses on emerging programs or processes "conducted by and for those taking the action" (Sagor, 2000, p. 1).

Participatory action research (PAR) usually involves those within a particular community or context working through a local issue with a view to improving practice. PAR is typically led by practitioners but may also involve collaboration with external mentors or facilitators.

Like action research, PAR involves a systematic approach to exploring and making positive changes to everyday practices (Reason & Bradbury, 2006). It is important to note that neither action research nor PAR is a single method. Rather, they are collaborative processes of inquiry focused on developing practical knowledge (Reason & Bradbury, 2006). Cyclical processes of planning, acting, observing, and reflecting form the basis of collective, reflective inquiry (Rosier et al., 2015). Action research becomes PAR when those who are impacted by the policy or practice have input into the research (or evaluation) process, not as subjects but as active participants. The principle of working with rather than on participants is an essential element of PAR.

PAR approaches reflect understandings that practices – such as the transition to school – are shaped by and inextricably linked to the sites in which they unfold. The approach captures lived experiences of practices in real time, at real sites, by real people (Kemmis, McTaggart, & Nixon, 2014). Considering its application to the evaluation of transition programs and practices and adapting the potentials noted by Kemmis et al. (2014, pp. 5–6), PAR sets the context for educators to:

- understand and develop the ways transition practices occur *from within* the practice traditions informing them;
- create and use shared language to engage in conversations and critical discussions with those participating in transitions practice;
- participate in and develop transitions actions and interactions;
- develop and participate in communities of practice focused on transition;
- both individually and as a group, transform transitions practice by "confronting and overcoming . . . untoward consequences of their practice" (p. 6) – when practices are irrational, unsustainable, or unjust.

PAR can create contexts in which stakeholders are supported to examine, reflect on, and seek to improve their own practice. By promoting systematic links between the processes of planning, acting, observing and reflecting, and sharing understandings, stakeholders are encouraged to take responsibility for examining and reflecting critically on their own practice, testing out ideas, and asking difficult or complex questions (Crane & O'Regan, 2010).

Example: Participatory action research to inform transition to school

McLeod and Anderson (2020) utilised participatory action research to explore perceptions of school readiness and its role in transition to school. Working collaboratively, the project supported educators in ECEC settings and schools to examine their own practice both individually and collectively.

The authors highlighted the importance of trusting relationships among participants which enabled reflexivity and supported participants as they reflected on and critically examined their practice.

The essence of participatory approaches to evaluation is that they intentionally include those people who are most impacted by the evaluation in their design and implementation. The inclusion of a range of stakeholders and perspectives contributes to the democratisation of knowledge (Wood, McAteer, & Whitehead, 2019), recognising that many people bring valuable insights to the project and that stakeholders are well positioned to construct their own narratives and generate new knowledge as they make sense of their own experiences. However, the genuine participation of a range of stakeholders requires a climate of mutual trust and respect as well as strong ethical commitment to valuing diverse experiences and knowledge. As well, facilitation skills, appropriate time, and resources will be required to reap the potential benefits of participatory evaluation.

The project approach

While discussions of participatory evaluation often focus on adult stakeholders, there is also potential for children to participate in meaningful and relevant ways. One focus has been the project approach (Katz, Chard, & Kogen, 2014; Mitchell et al., 2009), which begins with children and educators discussing issues and developing questions which then form the focus of in-depth investigations. In its initial phase, the project approach draws on participants' prior knowledge and experiences to identify issues and specific questions to be investigated. Brainstorming sessions are a common strategy during this phase of selecting a topic. The second phase involves data collection and analysis. The final phase of the project can be marked by an event or culminating activity that shares the outcomes of the project.

Example: Children's advice about transition

Children in an Icelandic preschool were participants in a project focused on their forthcoming transition to school. At the start of the project, the children brainstormed what they knew about school and identified areas they wanted to know more about. The preschool teacher accompanied the children as they made visits to the local school and sought to find answers to their questions. She communicated with the first-year-of-school teacher to plan the visits around the children's questions. She also documented the visits through notes and photographs and, on returning to the preschool, engaged with the children in the analysis of these, asking "questions about transitioning to school, challeng[ing] them to think critically about the process and invit[ing] them to use different methods of communicate their ideas" (Ólafsdóttir & Einarsdóttir, 2019, p. 81). This analysis was shared with the first-year-of-school teacher and used to plan later visits. At the end of the project, the children presented their findings to their parents.

Reflecting on the project, the preschool teacher noted the importance of ongoing support for the preschool children – from their peers, older children and adults – as they made the transition to school. While the school visits provided the context for relevant activities, it was noted that "transition to school is . . . not about how many times the children visit the primary school; it is about listening to them and supporting them in different ways so that they can feel secure and a sense of belonging in the new school environment" (Ólafsdóttir & Einarsdóttir, 2019, p. 82).

Conclusion

While much attention has been directed towards theorising transition, developing, and implementing transition to school programs, less attention has been paid to evaluating programs. This chapter provides a base to support focus on evaluation by considering what is meant by evaluation and how this might apply to transition to school programs. Purposes and types of evaluation are explored, and the relevance of evaluation frameworks and models is outlined. This discussion is complemented by Chapter 4A, which details a large-scale needs analysis. Throughout this chapter, we have highlighted the importance of participatory processes and the involvement of stakeholders in evaluations. In Chapter 5, we link these elements to planning evaluation of transition to school programs.

4A Support for children and families at risk of experiencing vulnerability in early years transitions

Andrea Nolan and Anna Kilderry

Introduction

This chapter links with Chapter 4 by reporting on a statewide Department of Education and Training (DET) evaluation, called a *Practice Review*, conducted in Victoria, Australia. The Practice Review evaluated the types of support and resources available for children and families at risk of experiencing vulnerability in early years transitions, collecting perspectives of early years professionals, teachers, and families. Key findings from the study point to:

- the importance of collaborative professional networks;
- the identification of effective and promising practices and resources;
- the significance of respectful, responsive, and supportive relationships with families; and
- the need to build professional knowledge, skills, and attitudes around transition and children and families who experience vulnerability.

Aims of the practice review

In 2015 the Victorian Auditor General released the *Report on Education Transitions*, highlighting that while most Victorian children were being effectively supported in their transition to primary school, children experiencing developmental vulnerability were particularly at risk of falling further behind during the transition process. It was noted that 1 in 5 Victorian children started their first year of school with a developmental vulnerability. Recommendations contained in the Auditor General's Report led to a stronger emphasis by governments on the support provided to children and families experiencing vulnerability during transition to school to enhance their life opportunities. Importance was placed on providing these children and their families with a coordinated approach in which services work together collaboratively, enabling a more targeted approach. This context led to the Victorian Government commissioning the *Support for children and families at risk of experiencing vulnerability: Practice Review* (Nolan et al., 2017).

This statewide Practice Review identified and mapped some of the existing supports and effective practices in relation to early years transitions for children

DOI: 10.4324/9781003055112-7

at risk of experiencing vulnerable circumstances. Outcomes of the Practice Review included recommendations for policy and practice relating to how best to support ECEC professionals to work in transdisciplinary teams for improving transitions for families and children at risk of experiencing vulnerability. Children experiencing vulnerability were defined in the review as those vulnerable to child abuse, neglect, and exclusion or where "the capacity of parents and family to effectively care, protect and provide for their long term development and well-being is limited" (Victorian Government, 2013, p. 1). The Practice Review focused on children and families affected by trauma, especially children known to Child Protection and Family Services, at risk of intergenerational poverty, who were refugees, and in "out of home" care. Some of the children and families experiencing vulnerability, who took part in the Practice Review, came from culturally or linguistically diverse or Indigenous and Koorie backgrounds or had a disability or developmental delay. However, they were not the focus of this particular review.

Designing the evaluation: respectful, ethical, and fit-for-purpose

When designing the Practice Review, we were cognisant of the importance of hearing about the experiences from a range of early years professionals, teachers, and families about transition to school practices within ECEC services. In particular, we were interested in the ways in which transitions were supported (or not) for children and families at risk of experiencing vulnerable and disadvantaged circumstances. Therefore, the methodology took into consideration diverse families' cultural sensitivities, power imbalances such as those between families and professionals and researchers, and how it can take time for participants to build trusting relationships with researchers. An ethic of care was embedded into all research activities, and we took note of the preferred forms of communication of various participants and participant groups, along with people's limited time to take part in the project.

We also ensured the project design was flexible enough to address issues of data collection across different situations, locations, and personnel and with more marginalised stakeholders. For example, we were careful to consider parents/carers and families experiencing vulnerability and disadvantage and what that might mean for engaging and retaining participants. We found that our fit-for-purpose multi-faceted approach to data collection was responsive to and respectful of participants, supported recruitment, and minimised attrition.

We instigated a statewide survey and conducted small to medium-sized focus groups as well as conducting some individual interviews, especially with families who did not want to share their personal insights with others. The way we referred to children and families as *experiencing vulnerability* rather than the term *vulnerable children and families* was carefully considered in discussion with Department of Education and Training (DET) (Victoria) colleagues. The two terms illustrate how a small change in discourse can position children and families differently. The term families *experiencing vulnerability* refers to a situation, one that is not necessarily fixed, whereas referring to a *vulnerable family* casts a judgement and can be seen as a negative label.

The survey was designed with two purposes:

1 as a mapping exercise to assist with identifying and collecting information relating to existing supports, effective practices, resources, and transition to school programs and
2 identifying effective transition to school networks and professionals who could be potential interview and focus group participants.

A specially designed communication protocol was developed to guide the focus groups and interviews, allowing for both in-person meetings and telephone and video interviews. The reason for these alternative methods of communication was based on our previous research experience of conducting focus groups with diverse families, many of whom were experiencing hardship and who – for a wide range of reasons – were unwilling or unable to attend in-person meetings. Provision was made for interpreters of local community languages if required by parents, carers, or families.

From our previous research, we were aware of some of the sensitivities when working with vulnerable communities and Indigenous Peoples in respectful, caring, and responsive ways. As a first step, we consulted community Indigenous Elders, enquiring about respectful and culturally sensitive ways to engage Aboriginal and Torres Strait Islander families in the Practice Review. These valuable insights, along with our previous knowledge and experience, provided us with some initial ways to approach and engage respectfully with Indigenous families. Building respectful and trusting relationships with local community Elders before any family engagement could take place was paramount. Another important aspect was the views of community Elders on the project aims and outcomes and how these aligned with their views. Most importantly, the project aims and outcomes had to benefit children, families, and local communities. Once positive relationships with local community Elders were formed and trust was established and the aims of the project agreed upon, we were then able to engage with Indigenous families as part of the project.

Implementing an inclusive methodology was one of our main objectives, one in which family members would be comfortable with the information gathered about themselves and their children, and with their experience of the research overall. The methodology was tailored to suit the preferred ways of communication, ensuring it was flexible, respectful, and responsive for all participants.

Practice review outcomes

As research in the area has reported, building strong partnerships between all key transition to school stakeholders is important. Acknowledging the complexity of diverse children and families' life circumstances, such as families experiencing vulnerability and disadvantage, it is vital that all stakeholders work together to provide a strong support network during times of transition. However, at times, partnerships are not well formed, are not reciprocal, and can lack the understanding across stakeholder groups that is required for practice change. It is important to build awareness and understanding across the ECEC and primary sectors so that knowledge and skills are valued and shared by all parties, with the aim of enhancing transition to school programs and providing all children with the support they require when transitioning to school. A coordinated service system within a transitions network, for example, provides an opportunity for a tailored approach to transition, ensuring children experiencing vulnerability or disadvantage can receive the support that is needed. The main Practice Review recommendations are summarised in what follows.

Collaboration

Formal transition to school networks have the capacity to work with families in holistic ways, such as streamlining referral processes, reducing duplication, supporting families in differentiated ways, and sharing information across services. It is important that schools are key players in these networks and that the networks are sustainable and built into existing work practices and policies.

Evaluation

Having a systematic process to document and assess transition to school programs and initiatives enables promising practices to be identified and replicated across local communities and sectors. The assessment of the impact of many programs, strategies, and actions supporting families and children experiencing vulnerability is often informal, ad-hoc, or non-existent.

Staff capacity building

Professional skills and knowledge benefit from enhancement with regard to working respectfully and inclusively with children and families experiencing vulnerability and disadvantage during early years transitions. Professional learning delivered cross-sector supports, transdisciplinarity, and consistency of practice. Initial teacher education has a role to play in adequately equipping educators and teachers to work in respectful and knowledgeable ways with children and families experiencing vulnerabilities.

Designated leader

Programs reported the benefits of having a designated leader to support the group to keep transition to school on the agenda of networks, raising awareness of the complexity of transitioning children and families within the locality.

Communication and confidentiality protocols

Programs that shared information have a better-informed services system and promote the building of trust between services and personnel more effectively.

A nominated "key" transition person in primary schools

Programs that had a dedicated key transition person enabled trusting relationships to develop with children and families and other transition stakeholders. This person could be a primary school teacher or support worker. Having a dedicated person in this role enhanced understandings, supported the tailoring of transition processes, and facilitated the sharing of information between the school and family.

Resource funding

Time management was considered a major barrier for all services to be able to support children and families experiencing vulnerability adequately in transitioning to school. Through having designated time and resources, professionals can be more supportive of diverse children and families and their needs during transition.

Conclusion

In conclusion, we have learned that evaluations of transition to school programs need to be conceptualised within particular parameters, taking into consideration the localised context and the time that is required to form respectful relationships with participants. This transition to school evaluation highlighted some *success* stories, along with some not-so-positive experiences, from a range of transition to school stakeholders, highlighting the varied quality of transition to school initiatives. The Practice Review has begun the much-needed work in the state of Victoria to evaluate the type and range of support children and families experiencing vulnerability making early years transitions require and should have access to. We maintain that more formal, rigorous evaluations, such as the Practice Review, need to be developed and implemented before large-scale systemic change can occur.

References

Astbury, B. (2009). *Evaluation of transition: A positive start to school pilots*. Melbourne: Centre for Program Evaluation, University of Melbourne. www.education.vic.gov.au/Documents/about/research/transitionpilotevaluation.pdf

Australian Institute of Family Studies. (2014). *Promising practices profiles*. http://www3.aifs.gov.au/institute/cafcappp/ppp/index.html

Baumfield, V., Hall, E., & Wall, K. (2013). *Action research in education: Learning through practitioner enquiry* (2nd ed.). London: SAGE. https://doi.org/10.4135/9781526402240

References – Chapters 4 and 4A

Bohan-Baker, M., & Little, P. (2002). *The transition to kindergarten: A review of current research and promising practices to involve families.* Cambridge, MA: Harvard Family Research Project. https://eric.ed.gov/?id=ED473924

Bradbury, H. (2015). Introduction: How to situate and define action research. In H. Bradbury (Ed.), *The SAGE handbook of action research* (3rd ed., pp. 1–9). Los Angeles, CA: SAGE. https://doi.org/10.4135/9781473921290

Bronfenbrenner, U., & Morris, P. A. (2006). The bioecological model of human development. In W. Damon & R. M. Lerner (Eds.), *Handbook of child psychology, Vol. 1: Theoretical models of human development* (6th ed., pp. 793–828). New York: Wiley. https://doi.org/10.1002/9780470147658.chpsy0114

Canadian Homelessness Research Network. (2013). *What works and for whom? A hierarchy of evidence for promising practices research.* Toronto: Canadian Homelessness Research Network Press. www.homelesshub.ca/sites/default/files/attachments/PPFramework_Part1.pdf

Chen, H. (2012). Theory-driven evaluation: Conceptual framework, application and advancement. In R. Strobl, R. O. Lobermeier, & W. Heitmeyer (Eds.), *Evaluation von Programmen und Projekten für eine demokratische Kultur* [Evaluation of programs and projects for a democratic culture] (pp. 17–40). Wiesbaden: Springer, VS. https://doi.org/10.1007/978-3-531-19009-9_2

Coghlan, A. (2011). Participatory evaluation. In S. Mathison (Ed.), *Encyclopedia of evaluation* (pp. 292–296). Thousand Oaks, CA: Sage. https://doi.org/10.4135/9781412950558

Cousins, B. J., & Whitmore, E. (1998). Framing participatory evaluation. *New Directions for Evaluation, 80*, 5–23. https://doi.org/10.1002/ev.1114

Crane, P., & O'Regan, M. (2010). *On PAR. Using participatory action research to improve early intervention.* Canberra: Australian Government Department of Families, Housing, Community Services and Indigenous Affairs. www.dss.gov.au/sites/default/files/documents/05_2012/reconnect_0.pdf

Dockett, S., & Perry, B. (Eds.). (2001). *Beginning school together: Sharing strengths.* Watson, ACT: Australian Early Childhood Association.

Fournier, D. (2011). Evaluation. In S. Mathison (Ed.), *Encyclopedia of evaluation* (p. 140). Thousand Oaks, CA: Sage. https://doi.org/10.4135/9781412950558

Giallo, R., Treyvaid, K., Matthews, J., & Kienhuis, M. (2010). Making the transition to primary school: An evaluation of a transition program for parents. *Australian Journal of Educational & Developmental Psychology, 10*, 1–17.

Guijt, I. (2014). Participatory approaches. *Methodological Briefs: Impact Evaluation 5.* Florence: UNICEF Office of Research. www.unicef-irc.org/publications/pdf/brief_5_participatoryapproaches_eng.pdf

Harper, L., Maden, M., & Dickson, R. (2020). Across five levels: The evidence of impact model. *Evaluation, 26*(3), 350–366. https://doi.org/10.1177/1356389019850844

Katz, L., Chard, S., & Kogen, Y. (2014). *Engaging children's minds: The Project Approach* (3rd ed.). Santa Barbara, CA: Praeger.

Kemmis, S., McTaggart, R., & Nixon, R. (2014). *The action research planner: Doing critical participatory action research.* Singapore: Springer. https://doi.org/10.1007/978-981-4560-67-2

Mathison, S. (Ed.). (2011). *SAGE research methods.* Thousand Oaks, CA: SAGE. https://doi.org/10.4135/9781412950558

McLeod, N., & Anderson, B. (2020). Towards an understanding of "school" readiness: Collective interpretations and priorities. *Educational Action Research, 28*(5), 723–741. https://doi.org/10.1080/09650792.2019.1654902

Mertens, D. (2015). *Research and evaluation in education and psychology* (4th ed.). Thousand Oaks, CA: SAGE.

Mitchell, S., Foulger, T., Wetzel, K., & Rathkey, C. (2009). The negotiated project approach: Project-based learning without leaving the standards behind. *Early Childhood Education Journal*, 36(4), 339–346. https://doi.org/10.1007/s10643-008-0295-7

Morrison, J., & Harms, A. (2018). *Advancing evidence-based practice through program evaluation: A practical guide for school-based professionals.* London: Oxford University Press. https://doi.org/10.1093/med-psych/9780190609108.001.0001

Newell, S., & Graham, A. (2008). *Goonellabah transition program – "Walking together, learning together": Final evaluation report.* Canberra: Australian Government, Department of Families, Housing, Community Services & Indigenous Affairs.

Nolan, A., Kilderry, A., Beahan, J., Lanting, C., & Speldewinde, C. (2017). *Early years transitions. Support for children and families at risk of experiencing vulnerability: Practice review report.* Melbourne: Department of Education and Training, Victoria. www.education.vic.gov.au/Documents/childhood/professionals/learning/Transition%20to%20School%20Vulnerability%20Project%20Practice%20Review.pdf

Ólafsdóttir, S., & Einarsdóttir, J. (2019). Following children's advice in transition from preschool to primary school. In S. Dockett, J. Einarsdóttir, & B. Perry (Eds.), *Listening to children's advice about staring school and school age care* (pp. 69–83). London: Routledge.

Organisation for Economic Cooperation and Development (OECD). (2017). *Starting strong V. Transitions from early childhood education and care to primary education.* Paris: OECD Publishing. https://doi.org/10.1787/9789264276253-en

Pawson, R., & Tilley, N. (1997). *Realistic evaluation.* London: SAGE.

Pianta, R., Cox, M., & Snow, K. (Eds.). (2007). *School readiness and the transition to kindergarten in the era of accountability.* Baltimore, MD: Paul H Brookes.

Reason, P., & Bradbury, H. (2006). Introduction: Inquiry and participation in search of a world worthy of human aspiration. In P. Reason & H. Bradbury (Eds.), *Handbook of action research* (pp. 1–10). London: SAGE.

Reid, A. (2004). *Towards a culture of inquiry in DECS.* Occasional Paper Series, No 1. Adelaide: Department of Education and Children's Services.

Rosier, K., Lohoar, S., Moore, S., & Robinson, E. (2015). *Participatory action research.* Canberra: Australian Institute of Family Studies. https://aifs.gov.au/cfca/publications/participatory-action-research

Sagor, R. (2000). *Guiding school improvement with action research.* Alexandria, VA: Association for Supervision and Curriculum Development.

Savaya, R., & Waysman, M. (2005). The logic model. *Administration in Social Work*, 29(2), 85–103. https://doi.org/10.1300/J147v29n02_06

Scull, J., & Garvis, S. (2015). *Transition: A positive start to school.* Melbourne: Department of Education and Training, Victoria. https://research.monash.edu/en/publications/transition-a-positive-start-to-school

Semann & Slattery. (2015a). *Transition: A positive start to school initiative.* Melbourne: Department of Education and Training, Victoria. www.education.vic.gov.au/Documents/about/research/finalsconstransition.pdf

Semann & Slattery. (2015b). *Transition: A positive start to school. Supporting reciprocal visits.* Melbourne: Department of Education, Victoria. www.education.vic.gov.au/Documents/about/research/transpositivestarttoschool.PDF

Semann & Slattery. (2016). *Transition to school. Supporting reciprocal visits (Koorie focus).* Melbourne: Department of Education and Training, Victoria. www.

education.vic.gov.au/Documents/childhood/professionals/learning/Transition%20 to%20School%20%20Supporting%20Reciprocal%20Visits%20Koorie%20focus.pdf

Smith, K., Kotsanas, C., Farrelly, A., & Alexander, K. (2011). *Research into practices to support a positive start to school.* www.education.vic.gov.au/Documents/about/research/pospracmelbuni.pdf

SNAICC. (n.d.). *Aboriginal and Torres Strait Islander child and family services evaluation readiness toolkit.* www.snaicc.org.au/sector-development/monitoring-and-evaluation/

Soriano, G., Clark, H., & Wise, S. (2008). *Promising practices final report.* http://www3.aifs.gov.au/institute/cafcappp/evaluation/pubs/pppfinalreport.pdf

valentine, K., & Katz, I. (2010). *Linking schools and early years project evaluation. Evaluation framework (2010–2013).* Social Policy Research Centre. www.rch.org.au/uploadedFiles/Main/Content/lsey/LSEY_Evaluation_Plan_FINAL.pdf

Victorian Auditor-General. (2015). *Education transitions.* www.audit.vic.gov.au/sites/default/files/20150318-Education-transitions.pdf

Victorian Government. (2013). *Vulnerable children action plan: An overview of the Department's response to Victoria's vulnerable children: Our shared responsibility strategy 2013–2022.* Melbourne: State of Victoria. http://youthlaw.asn.au/wp-content/uploads/2016/07/Victorias-vulnerable-children-Our-Shared-Responsibility.pdf

Watson, J. (2008). *Blended learning: The convergence of online and face-to-face education.* Vienna, VA: North American Council for Online Learning. https://files.eric.ed.gov/fulltext/ED509636.pdf

Weaver, L., & Cousins, J. (2007). Unpacking the participatory process, *Journal of Multidisciplinary Evaluation, 1*(1), 19–40. https://journals.sfu.ca/jmde/index.php/jmde_1/article/view/144/159

Westhorp, G. (2014). *Realist impact evaluation.* London: Overseas Development Institute. www.odi.org/sites/odi.org.uk/files/odi-assets/publications-opinion-files/9138.pdf

Wood, L., McAteer, M., & Whitehead, J. (2019). How are action researchers contributing to knowledge democracy? A global perspective. *Educational Action Research, 27*(1), 7–21. https://doi.org/10.1080/09650792.2018.1531044

Zukoski, A., & Luluquisen, M. (2002). Participatory evaluation: What is it? Why do it? What are the challenges? *Policy & Practice, 5.* http://depts.washington.edu/ccph/pdf_files/Evaluation.pdf

5 Planning an evaluation of transition to school programs

Sue Dockett and Bob Perry

Introduction

In this chapter, we explore the practical aspects of planning to evaluate transition to school programs. We start by outlining some broad parameters for evaluation then consider identifying the evaluation focus, potential participants in the evaluation, and approaches to data generation and analysis, as well as the ways in which findings may be communicated and used. Some of the ethical challenges involved in the evaluation of transition to school programs are explored. Chapter 5A elaborates these elements by describing the planning and implementation of an evaluation of the transition program in one school.

Planning the evaluation

Planning the evaluation should be part of the overall planning of the transition program rather than something that is considered as the program nears its end. Planning the evaluation as an integral part of the program provides clarity and direction and helps to identify the data that can be generated as the program is delivered. However, aspects of the evaluation plan may change as the program is implemented or as other issues arise. For example, many evaluation plans will have changed for the 2020–2021 cohort of children and their families in response to the changed circumstances related to COVID-19. While the aims of the evaluation may remain the same, the methods to gather data are likely to have changed, as may some of the data that are considered relevant.

Included among the ten *Guidelines for Effective Transition to School Programs* (Dockett & Perry, 2001), developed early in our research agenda, was the statement that *Effective transition programs are well planned and evaluated*. Unpacking this, the following elements were identified:

- stakeholders are involved in the planning and evaluation of programs;
- transition programs are reviewed systematically;
- effective local data collection and analysis informs the planning and evaluation of programs;
- a range of appropriate evaluation strategies is employed.

DOI: 10.4324/9781003055112-8

This guideline and the elements inform the following description of planning an evaluation.

Purpose of the evaluation

Before developing an evaluation plan, it is important to have a clear idea of the program to be evaluated and its aims and purposes, as well as the intended audience for the evaluation. It is likely that different audiences will have different views about what they expect the program evaluation to deliver, as well as the nature of the evaluation and the types of data to be used in the evaluation. For example, a statewide or systemwide evaluation may seek information about how the program is delivered across different contexts, as well as information about efficiency and sustainability, with the purpose of up-scaling both program and outcomes. A more locally based evaluation may seek information about how the program works in this community, with the purpose of making improvements for this group of stakeholders.

Spending some time developing some form of logic model or identifying the program theory will help unpack the intended purpose of the evaluation. This is a particularly important step when bringing together people with different views, experiences, and expectations (see also Chapters 3A, 7A).

The purpose of the evaluation will vary according to the program and the context, as well as the people involved. The purpose will also be tied to the nature of the evaluation. For example, several evaluations have been initiated in Victoria to review the *Transition: A Positive Start to School* initiative. Depending on the stage of the roll-out of this initiative, the evaluations have had different purposes. An early evaluation (Astbury, 2009, p. 9) explored transition practices and programs that were being piloted in 30 sites across the state, with the purpose of recommending "what is needed for successful, state-wide implementation of transition statements and processes". Included in this brief was the aim of identifying promising practices from these sites that might be relevant in a statewide implementation of the initiative.

As the initiative was rolled-out, a statewide evaluation was conducted (SuccessWorks, 2010, p. 3), with the purpose of evaluating "the Transition Initiative in its first full year of implementation to ensure that what has been designed is both effective and sustainable. The evaluation will inform the refinement, improvement and further development of the Transition Initiative for subsequent years".

Further evaluations included some with a specific focus, such as exploring the efficacy of specific promising practices (Smith et al., 2011) and the use of transition statements (Department of Education and Early Childhood Development, 2011), as well as others with a broader focus. An example of the latter was a statewide consultation undertaken by Semann and Slattery (2015, p. 8) with the purpose of obtaining "qualitative feedback from key stakeholders to strengthen the Department's understanding of current transition approaches, including the use of Transition Statements and supporting resources, to consider what is working well and where improvements can be made".

Several possible questions relating to the purpose of the evaluation were listed in the previous chapter. At this point, it is also useful to determine what resources are available for the evaluation. Questions to be asked could include:

- What is the context for the program?
- What is the purpose of the program?
- Why is the program being evaluated? For example, is it to improve the program, check that it is being delivered appropriately, or demonstrate outcomes of the program?
- What is the outcome of the evaluation expected to be? For example, a report, a revised program, set of recommendations, or another outcome?
- What resources are available for the evaluation?
- Will the evaluation draw on external expertise or be conducted solely by stakeholders?
- How will the evaluation be used? Who will use the evaluation?

Focus of the evaluation

In most education contexts, resources are limited. Some priorities will need to be set to decide what will be included in the evaluation and make it manageable. Decisions will need to be made about the design of the evaluation, the questions to be addressed, who will lead the evaluation, and which stakeholders will be involved. These decisions direct attention to specific aspects of the program. Some evaluations will be guided by an advisory committee; some will be led by an external researcher/s; and some will be conducted by stakeholders. Combinations of these options are also likely.

Some of the questions to be asked include:

- What is to be evaluated? Is it the entire transition program or some specific transition practices?
- What are the boundaries of the evaluation – what is to be excluded?
- Who are the stakeholders to be involved in the evaluation?
- What constraints are there – for example, timing, budget, resources?
- What are the evaluation questions to be asked?
- What model of evaluation will be used? Is it a needs analysis, process evaluation, outcome evaluation, realist evaluation, participatory evaluation, participatory action research, the project approach, some other form of evaluation, or some combination of these models?
- What are the criteria for the program or practice to be described as successful or effective?
- How are stakeholders involved in developing or affirming these criteria?

Some evaluations aim to consider all aspects of a program, its delivery, and its outcomes. The evaluation of the Goonellabah Transition Program (Newell & Graham, 2008) is one such example, where a comprehensive evaluation plan was developed to monitor the program "implementation, acceptability and impact" (p. 3) for children, families, and staff involved with the program.

Many other evaluations will focus on a particular aspect of the transition program. The specific focus needs to be decided in collaboration with stakeholders and will depend on the resources available. It will be influenced by the type of evaluation to be undertaken – needs analysis, process evaluation, outcome evaluation, or some combination of these. It could, for example, include exploring the intent and impact of some practices – such as reciprocal visits, parent information sessions, communication between stakeholders, or the effectiveness and sustainability of a transition network. Another possible focus could be the participation of stakeholders across specific practices. In some recent evaluations, strategies to include and respond to the perspectives of children have provided the focus (Dockett, Einarsdóttir, & Perry, 2019). The focus of the evaluation is reflected in the questions that frame the evaluation and the stakeholders invited to participate.

Planning evaluation activities

This step involves planning the activities that make up the evaluation. A key part of this process is matching data-generation methods and participants with the evaluation questions. For example, an evaluation of the transition expectations and experiences of families from culturally and linguistically diverse communities required consideration of culturally appropriate methods and involved interpreters (Dockett & Perry, 2005). In a similar vein, an evaluation focused on children's perspectives of their transition required interactions with children using methods appropriate to both the children and the context (Perry & Dockett, 2011).

Many methods are available for use in generating data (see Chapters 6 and 7). For example, data can be generated through methods such as observation, interviews, questionnaires, diaries, photo-voice, drawing, brainstorming, concept mapping, or conversations. Other data can be derived from attendance patterns, specific tasks and assessments, or already-existing data sets. Many other methods also are possible. It is important to match the methods with the evaluation questions, the contexts in which the evaluation takes place, and those involved in the evaluation. It may be that some stakeholders prefer to participate in specific ways or with specific members of the evaluation team. For example, in some of our studies, participants have indicated a strong preference for engaging in conversational interviews rather than filling out written or online questionnaires. In other instances, some children and adults have preferred to engage in group conversations, while others have preferred one-on-one interactions. In some contexts, it has been appropriate for female members of the evaluation team to interview other women; in other situations, while gender has not been raised, perceptions of power and influence remained issues to consider. Whatever the method/s used, ethical issues need to be addressed.

Questions to be considered when planning the evaluation activities include:

- What are the ethical issues invoked by the evaluation?
- How are these ethical issues to be addressed?
- What data generation strategies will be used?
- Why are these the most appropriate?
- Who contributes data?
- Who records the data?
- When and where are data to be generated?
- What is the time frame for the evaluation?
- What is the best timing for data generation?
- How will data be stored?
- Is there a diversity of stakeholders involved?
- How will data be analysed?
- What resources and/or expertise are available?
- Is some additional training needed for members of the evaluation team?
- Who is responsible for managing the evaluation?
- What plans are there to monitor/evaluate the evaluation?

Evaluation implementation

Developing a work plan for the evaluation is an integral part of this step. While such a plan provides details of what is to happen and when and who is to be involved, it is also important that the plan is both flexible and responsive. When evaluating transition programs, it is always possible that some potential participants will be unavailable or planned activities will not be possible. Where involvement in the evaluation occurs on top of other responsibilities, time and resource demands can influence implementation. Effective communication among members of the evaluation team is critical.

Questions to be asked as the evaluation is implemented include:

- Who is responsible for making the evaluation happen?
- What resources are available to support the evaluation?
- Who has responsibility for different aspects of the evaluation?
- What reporting and communication processes are in place to ensure the evaluation proceeds as planned?
- What back-up plans are in place for implementation?
- What is the timing of the evaluation? How does this fit with other expectations for those involved?
- What opportunities are there to modify evaluation plans as circumstances change and data are generated?

Data analysis and synthesis

There is the potential for any evaluation to generate a great deal of data. Appropriate analysis of these data will play a major role in the success (or otherwise) of the evaluation. Depending on the nature of the data, qualitative and/or quantitative analyses or a combination of both will be appropriate. Visualising data, such as in charts, graphs, word clouds, or social mapping, can help identify relationships within the data. The steps of analysis and synthesis also involve combining the range of data and analyses to address the evaluation questions.

Data analysis is about making sense of the data and relating this back to the evaluation questions. Some questions may be quite simple to answer. For example, if one of the questions considered the reach of the transition program, calculation of the numbers of participating family members, children, and educators can provide at least part of the answer. Analysis of demographic information about who participated, when they participated, and in what activities may also be useful. Analysis of the perceived usefulness of activities might be calculated from a rating scale (see Chapter 7).

However, personal reflections on the program and stories about participation will draw on qualitative approaches such as thematic or content analysis, which identify patterns across narrative data that can be used to answer the evaluation questions (Patton, 2015). It may be possible to code data into different categories and count responses for each of those categories or to review the data to identify any main themes and then revisit the data to investigate what different people have said in relation to these themes. The development of codes and themes involves a rigorous and transparent process and takes time. It can often be a fluid process, informed by ongoing data generation, reflection, and revision as the evaluation progresses. An example of analysing children's responses is provided in Chapter 6, and a further example identifying codes and categories from data generated by adults is provided in Chapter 7.

In qualitative evaluations, it is appropriate for data analyses to begin once data have been generated rather than at the end of a project. For example, initial coding of data can highlight areas where misunderstandings have occurred or identify additional areas for investigation. As one example, in early studies, when we asked young children what it meant to be *ready for school*, we were often told about children's routines – getting out of bed, having breakfast, getting dressed and so on (Perry, Dockett, & Tracey, 1998). Rephrasing questions to ask if there was "Anything you needed to know or be able to do before you went to school?" changed the focus of responses.

Possible questions related to data analyses include:

- What data have been generated?
- What are appropriate strategies for analysis?
- Who has the skills/expertise to analyse the data?
- How are stakeholders involved in data analyses and synthesis?
- What mechanisms are in place to check that interpretations of data match the meanings of participants?
- How do the data address the evaluation questions?
- How do ongoing data analyses contribute to modification of the evaluation?

Planning an evaluation of programs 97

Reporting the results of the evaluation

The evaluation report provides a clear overview of the processes involved and utilises data (evidence) to answer the evaluation questions. From this, the evaluation report may also make recommendations about aspects of the program, the program delivery, or the impact and outcomes of the program. The report also details any limitations of the evaluation and may point to future projects. It may be that different forms of the report need to be developed for different audiences. These could include versions in different languages, an accessible format, a summary of the report, and versions that report back to child as well as adult participants (see also Chapter 9). In all instances, ethical approaches must be adopted.

As an example, the brochures illustrated in Figure 5.1 were developed to report the transition to school expectations and experiences of families and

Figure 5.1 Reporting to different audiences.

children from diverse linguistic backgrounds. Many of the families that had contributed to the evaluation did so with the aid of interpreters. After a series of translations into English and then back into the original language, along with further interactions to check meanings and interpretations, a series of brochures reported the project and provided a resource for families from the different language groups involved (Dockett & Perry, 2005).

Possible questions related to reporting include:

- How are results communicated to different audiences?
- What procedures are in place to ensure ethical standards of reporting are met?
- How are stakeholders involved in the sharing of results?
- Who has ownership of the report?
- To whom are the results available?

Ethical considerations

Evaluations occur within social and political contexts (Barnett & Camfield, 2016). They are undertaken with a view of providing evidence of the worth and merit of programs or activities. Evaluations have the potential to generate results that prompt change to both policy and practice that may impact on those working in settings, as well as those accessing them. It is probably not surprising that issues of power come into play.

All evaluations need to address ethical principles. Some large-scale projects and external evaluations will need to be presented to Human Research Ethics Committees (National Health and Medical Research Council, 2018) or to system/organisation review panels. While smaller-scale evaluations may not require such approval, the need to conduct the evaluation in accordance with ethical principles remains (Scott, 2013). The same principles apply to all participants in the evaluation – be they children or adults.

Voluntary participation is a cornerstone of ethical practice. Voluntary participation requires the provision of information about the project, including what is involved for participants and any potential harm or risk, why the project is important, and how data will be used and reported. Information may need to be provided in several forms to be accessible to different audiences. Other elements of voluntary participation include the right to withdraw from the project without consequence and steps to prohibit the exploitation of participants. In many studies, formal processes of consent may be required. When children are involved, additional processes often are necessary to ensure that they are provided with relevant and meaningful information and offered appropriate opportunities to choose their levels of participation. Figure 5.2 provides an example of one page of an information booklet for children prepared for the evaluation reported in Chapter 5A. The booklet was read to children whose parents had consented to their involvement in the evaluation. The children had time to reflect on their possible participation, ask questions, and then decide whether they wished to participate. They were offered the same opportunities throughout the project.

Planning an evaluation of programs 99

Expectations and experience of starting primary school

Child assent form

We would like to ask you some questions about starting school.

You might like to have a conversation with us, take some photos, draw some pictures, or tell us in some other way about starting school.

Figure 5.2 Example of an information booklet for children.

While most were happy to participate, at least in some aspects of the evaluation, others declined.

Ethical principles are based on respect for participants. In practice, this involves protecting the privacy and confidentiality of participants and, when sharing data, ensuring that this is done in ways that do not denigrate them or present them in inappropriate ways. Cultural sensitivity is required at all times.

It is possible that the evaluation team may have access to sensitive information. For example, transition programs seeking to involve people living in any community, including those described as at risk, disadvantaged, vulnerable, or marginalised in some way, may generate information about complex social and physical issues. Sensitive approaches to evaluation in communities which have experienced trauma are critical and may require external assistance to ensure all involved have appropriate support. Supporting ethical participation will require sensitivity, empathy, flexibility, and responsiveness rather than strict adherence to a schedule or methods of generating data. Strategies must be developed to assess risk and or possible harm for those involved and for the appropriate management of such information, cognisant of moral and legal responsibilities related to disclosure.

As well as reflecting the research ethics focus on protecting individuals, it is important to consider ethics in a broad sense. This includes considering the ethical aspects of who is invited to participate in the evaluation and how – as well as who is not invited – which stakeholders are involved in the evaluation team and how, and the power relationships that might exist in each context (Barnett & Camfield, 2016). Consider, for example, how the relationships between parents and their children's first-year-of-school teacher might impact on what information is contributed about transition experiences implemented by that teacher. In a similar vein, consider some of the challenges inherent in a teacher being critical of transition approaches and contributing to a report that presents the program (and possibly some individuals or the organisation) in a poor light. Attention to ethics in evaluation requires that we all consider issues or power, values, norms, and expectations and that we do so in a fair and transparent way. It also reminds us that the evaluation of transition programs usually involves contact with a range of people in a range of circumstances.

Conclusion

This chapter provides an overview of the planning involved in evaluations, framed around a series of questions that might be asked at each stage from planning through to implementing and reporting. It also highlights the importance of ethical issues throughout the evaluation process. An example of the application of the different phases of an evaluation is provided in Chapter 5A. Elements of the evaluation, such as data-generation methods for engaging with children and adults, are explored in more detail in Chapters 6 and 7, respectively.

5A Putting it into practice
Planning and implementing an evaluation

Sue Dockett

Purpose of the evaluation

What is the context for the program?

Marathon Public School (pseudonym) is a primary school located in a major city. In 2019, it had a primary school enrolment of approximately 500. In addition, approximately 120 children attended preschools operated under the auspices of the school. One of these preschools is located on the school site, the other two in nearby suburbs. The 2019 Index of Community Socioeducational Advantage (ICSEA) (Australian Curriculum, Assessment and Reporting Authority, 2020) for the school was 1041, somewhat above the national average of 1000. There was a stable staff across the preschools and school, though some educators were relatively new to teaching in the first-year-of-school.

In 2019, there were five first-year-of-school classes, each with an enrolment of approximately 20 children. School educators responsible for these classes met regularly with a member of the school executive to plan collaboratively. Preschool educators met with the same member of the school executive but at different times from the school educators. There were limited opportunities for preschool and school educators to meet and work together.

A transition to school program had operated across the preschools and the school for some years. One teacher described this program as "more of an orientation program" than a transition program, as it consisted of two one-hour visits from the preschool children to one of the first-year-of-school classrooms. Another teacher noted

> that's the way we have done it for a long time. In my first year of working here I was told "this is what we are doing . . . this is what we have done previously, so we will do it again. It's just how it will continue to happen". It wasn't until we did it last year that we thought about how we could do it differently, because what we are doing is not enough.

Educators identified concerns around the organisation of the school visits, particularly as these were likely to be the only visits made by children from the

DOI: 10.4324/9781003055112-9

off-site preschools. More frequent ad hoc visits to the school occurred for those children and educators attending the preschool on site. Educators were also interested in exploring opportunities for preschool and school educators to plan collaboratively, in seeking the perspectives of children and families, and considering ways they could be more involved in the transition program.

The evaluation involved a team of three external evaluators working with educators from the school and preschools. It was framed around seeking people's expectations of transitions experiences (Term 4, 2019), followed by reflection on their experiences (Term 1, 2020). This time frame was impacted by COVID-19 and the associated restrictions. One consequence of the changed circumstances was that fewer people, particularly parents, were involved in the second phase of the project, and follow-up interactions from the external evaluators during the year were limited.

Purpose of the program

The aim of the existing transition program was to help children and families become familiar with the school and its environment. Being familiar with the school was linked to children experiencing a positive transition and engaging positively with school and those in the school. Familiarity with the school was also an aim for parents, with the expectation that family members who were familiar with the school were likely to become engaged with the school over time.

Why evaluate the program?

Educators identified several elements of their transition program that seemed to be effective, as well as other elements that they thought could be improved. Evaluation of the program was seen as a way to identify what worked and why, as well as what could be improved.

The different experiences of children, families, and educators from the different preschools highlighted a range of different transitions opportunities. Educators were concerned that some children were "missing out" on transition experiences and, as a result, were unfamiliar with the school, its people, and its expectations.

At the time of planning the evaluation, there had been limited consideration of child or parent perspectives in the transition planning and implementation. The potential to engage with external collaborators afforded opportunities to examine the existing transition program, as well as the expectations and experiences of those involved, and to consider some recommendations for change.

What was the outcome of the evaluation expected to be?

The evaluation was expected to result in a report including recommendations about possible changes and improvements to the program, based on greater awareness of what was important for children, families, and educators. Educators and the school executive were supportive of making changes to the transition program, guided by the recommendations. In addition, recommendations from the evaluation aimed to prompt ongoing reflection on transition, not just into school but across the school.

What resources were available for the evaluation?

The involvement of external collaborators to drive the evaluation meant that the main resource required from participants was time. Educators allocated time to meet with the evaluation team to outline their perceptions of transition and the program as well as their expectations for the evaluation. With the relevant permissions, educators shared information with children and families, inviting them to participate in the evaluation, and followed these up as appropriate.

Did the evaluation draw on external expertise?

External expertise guided the evaluation. This was partly because the expertise was available but also because of the timing of the evaluation, which commenced late in the school year, when transition practices were already in place and when other participants had limited time available.

Focus of the evaluation

What was evaluated?

The focus of the evaluation was the overall transition program. This was an open-ended focus, encouraging consideration of any practices identified by participants as contributing to transition or with the potential to do so. The evaluation was concerned with the expectations and experiences of the transition to school, so there was no pre-determined focus on children's academic outcomes.

Which stakeholders were involved in the evaluation?

The invitation to be involved was issued to all stakeholders – educators across the preschools and school, children about to start school, and family members. In addition, school children from Year 4 – potential buddies for the new school children – were invited to take part. However, with the tight timing of the evaluation, there was a limited number of participants.

What constraints were there?

The main constraint was time. As external evaluators were involved, approval for the evaluation had to be sought from the relevant Human Research Ethics Committee as well as the relevant education system. The timing of these processes meant that the evaluation could not begin until late in school Term 4.

What evaluation questions were asked?

Discussions between the educators and external colleagues contributed to the following evaluation questions:

- What do stakeholders expect will happen in their 2019–2020 transition to primary school program?
- What do stakeholders experience in their 2019–2020 transition to primary school program?

Stakeholders were identified as preschool children, current school children, adult family members, and educators in the preschool and school settings.

What model of evaluation was used?

The evaluation was framed as a process evaluation, focused on identifying what happened in practice and how this could be improved.

What were the criteria for the program to be described as successful or effective?

The aim of the transition program was to build familiarity with the school for children and families and for this, in turn, to generate an effective transition to school. Criteria to judge the effectiveness of the program related to the sense of familiarity expected and then experienced by stakeholders.

Evaluation planning

What were the ethical issues invoked by the evaluation?

Many ethical issues were relevant. As this evaluation involved external people, approval to conduct the project was sought and received from the relevant ethics committee and school system.

Issues of access were highlighted by the short time frame. While the educators were able to participate in the evaluation in their workplaces, family members had a range of time constraints and limited availability to talk with the evaluators. Hence, a small number of family members only were involved in telephone conversations. This was exacerbated during 2020, when families were experiencing challenges due to COVID-19. As a result, a non-representative group of mothers participated in the evaluation.

Informed consent was sought from all participants. Adult participants were provided with written information and invited to sign a consent form for the participation of themselves and their children. After consent had been obtained from parents, a consent booklet was read to the younger children, explaining what the evaluation was about and how they might be involved. They were asked to indicate their preference for involvement – yes, they wanted to be involved;

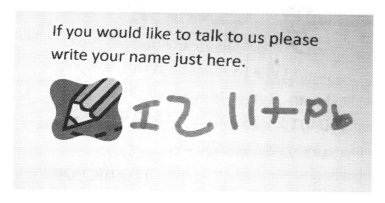

Figure 5A.1 Child permission.

no, they did not want to be involved; or they were not sure and needed to think about their decision. They were also invited to write their name, if they so wished (Figure 5A.1). The same process was applied when involving children prior to, as well as after, starting school. Older children were provided with written information and invited to indicate their consent by writing their name.

Confidentiality presented an issue, as educators knew which parents had returned signed consent forms and which children had agreed to be involved. Educators also knew that each of their colleagues was participating in the evaluation. As the external evaluators led the conversational interviews with participants, educators were aware of who was involved but not the information that was shared. Data were stored in secure, password-protected files on a secure server and de-identified for analysis. All data were anonymised in the report.

How were data generated?

Two data-generation phases were identified: towards the end of the school year when the transition program was being implemented and early in the new school year when the new children had started school. Conversational interviews were conducted with the adult stakeholders during each phase. These took place at a time and location convenient for participants. All educators were interviewed in their workplaces – preschool or school. During the second interview, educators were asked to comment on the image featured on the *Transition to School: Position Statement* (Educational Transitions and Change (ETC) Research Group, 2011) (Figure 5A.2). During the first phase, parents preferred to participate in telephone interviews. COVID restrictions impacted on the second phase of the evaluation, particularly in accessing parents. With permission, interviews were audio-recorded. At the request of one participant, written notes replaced audio-recording.

Children were also invited to participate in conversational interviews. Before they started school, these took place in the preschools. Children were not

Figure 5A.2 Transition to School: Position Statement image.
Source: Image Bernard Caleo. Copyright Sue Dockett and Bob Perry.

removed from the preschool room; rather, a small area of the room was available for use. While this sometimes meant that children were distracted, it also meant that they were easily able to indicate when they wished to conclude the activity. Preschool children were invited to draw something about starting school and to comment on it as well as responding to questions from the evaluators.

Once they had started school, the same children were invited to repeat the task of drawing something about school while talking with the evaluators. A small area off the main classroom was used, within sight of the teacher and where children could easily return to class activities when they wished. Both in the preschool and school classrooms, small groups of two or three children took part in the conversations, although some school children chose to meet individually with members of the evaluation team.

Older children – initially in Year 4 and the following year in Year 5 – also engaged in conversational interviews. They participated in small groups with the evaluators, with the interviews taking place in a corridor near their classrooms. In the first interview, they too were invited to draw about school. Some chose to do so; others preferred not to do so. During the second conversational interview, these older children were invited to comment on the image from the *Transition to School: Position Statement* (Figure 5A.2) and/or write down five words about children starting school.

Timing of the evaluation

While the time frame for the evaluation was short, it was an appropriate time to consider the transition program. As a process evaluation, it was important to consider what was happening as the transition program was enacted.

Data analysis

Narrative data were transcribed by the external evaluators. Processes of constructivist grounded theory (Charmaz, 2016) were used to code data and create a coding framework. The results were documented in a spreadsheet, which recorded the number of occurrences for each code in each conversation. Hence, total numbers of coded occurrences for each group of participants (frequency) and total numbers of conversations for each group of participants in which coded occurrences appear (source) were calculated. For each group of participants, codes were ranked according to frequency. Visual data – children's drawings – were considered illustrative of their comments and so were not analysed separately.

Stakeholders were not involved in the analysis, partly due to COVID restrictions. An interim report outlining progress with the evaluation was shared with educators and feedback sought prior to the second round of data generation.

Reporting the results of the evaluation

A written report was shared with the educators. A PowerPoint presentation provided an overview of the report, with a key focus on the recommendations. Opportunities to share the report with other participants were curtailed by COVID restrictions. The results were made available to the school and the organisations that had provided ethical approval.

What was learned from the evaluation?

The evaluation highlighted expectations that the main purposes of the transition program were to build positive relationships and help children and families feel comfortable, safe, and secure within the new school environment.

Experiences of participants also highlighted the importance of relationships and, in the main, it was felt that there were opportunities to build these in the current program but that these could be enhanced, particularly for those children and families attending the off-site preschools. Reporting their experiences of the transition, participants repeated their emphasis on feeling comfortable, safe, and secure and indicated that this seemed to have been achieved for many children and families. The new schoolchildren related this to knowing the rules and routines of school, while the older children located this within the relationships formed with other children – highlighting the importance of friends.

Educators and parents identified challenges around some of the transition activities – such as visits to the school by the off-site preschools – as well as what occurred during those visits.

Five themes were identified across the data:

- The importance of relationships
- Affective/emotional elements of the transition to primary school
- Transition activities and their effectiveness

- Place and transition
- Routines and rules at school

After addressing the evaluation questions, the report concluded with a series of recommendations aimed at maintaining effective practices and working collaboratively to improve practices that were considered ineffective, unfair, or in need of change.

What changed as a result of the evaluation?

While the evaluation reinforced that the transition to school program was meeting its overall aim of familiarity with the school for participants, a number of refinements were made both during and after the evaluation. Two aspects stand out. Firstly, preschool and school educators became known to each other and more familiar with their respective professional roles. Regular joint meetings were instituted and sharing of activities and planning increased. This was of particular benefit to the educators from the off-site preschools. Secondly, the first-year-of-school teachers changed the format by which new children started school on Day 1, allowing greater time for the teachers to spend with individual children and family members and for the children to settle into their classrooms at a more relaxed rate than was previously possible.

It is expected that other changes will be made gradually as a result of the evaluation. However, as with so many other aspects of schooling, COVID-19 has curtailed the planning and implementation of some of these changes.

References

Astbury, B. (2009). *Evaluation of transition: A positive start to school pilots*. Melbourne: Centre for Program Evaluation, University of Melbourne. www.education.vic.gov.au/Documents/about/research/transitionpilotevaluation.pdf

Australian Curriculum, Assessment and Reporting Authority (ACARA). (2020). *Guide to understanding the Index of Community Socioeducational Advantage (ICSEA)*. www.myschool.edu.au/media/1820/guide-to-understanding-icsea-values.pdf

Barnett, C., & Camfield, L. (2016). Ethics in evaluation. *Journal of Development Effectiveness*, 8(4), 528–534. https://doi.org/10.1080/19439342.2016.1244554

Charmaz, K. (2016). The power of constructivist grounded theory for critical inquiry. *Qualitative Inquiry*, 23(1), 34–45. https://doi.org/10.1177/1077800416657105

Department of Education and Early Childhood Development. (2011). *2011 Follow-up evaluation, Transition: A positive start to school*. www.education.vic.gov.au/Documents/about/research/transeval2011keyfindings.pdf

Dockett, S., Einarsdóttir, J., & Perry, B. (Eds.). (2019). *Listening to children's advice about starting school and school age care*. London: Routledge. https://doi.org/10.4324/9781351139403

Dockett, S., & Perry, B. (2001). Starting school: Effective transitions. *Early Childhood Research and Practice*, 3(2). http://ecrp.uiuc.edu/v3n2/dockett.html

Dockett, S., & Perry, B. (2005). Starting school in Australia is "a bit safer, a lot easier and more relaxing": Issues for parents from culturally and linguistically diverse backgrounds. *Early Years*, *25*(3), 271–281. https://doi.org/10.1080/09575140500251889

Educational Transitions and Change (ETC) Research Group. (2011). *Transition to school: Position statement*. https://arts-ed.csu.edu.au/education/transitions/publications/Position-Statement.pdf

National Health and Medical Research Council. (2018). *National statement on ethical conduct in human research (2007) – updated 2018*. www.nhmrc.gov.au/about-us/publications/national-statement-ethical-conduct-human-research-2007-updated-2018

Newell, S., & Graham, A. (2008). *Goonellabah transition program – "Walking together, learning together": Final evaluation report*. Canberra: Australian Government, Department of Families, Housing, Community Services & Indigenous Affairs.

Patton, M. (2015). *Qualitative research and evaluation methods* (4th ed.). Thousand Oaks, CA: SAGE.

Perry, B., & Dockett, S. (2011). "How 'bout we have a celebration?" Advice from children on starting school. *European Early Childhood Education Research Journal*, *19*(3), 375–388. https://doi.org/10.1080/1350293X.2011.597969

Perry, B., Dockett, S., & Tracey, D. (1998). At preschool they read to you, at school you learn to read. *Australian Journal of Early Childhood*, *23*(4), 6–11. https://doi.org/10.1177/183693919802300403

Scott, D. (2013). *Demystifying ethical review*. CFCA Resource Sheet. Australian Institute of Family Affairs. https://aifs.gov.au/cfca/publications/demystifying-ethical-review

Semann & Slattery. (2015). *Transition: A positive start to school initiative*. Melbourne: Department of Education and Training, Victoria. www.education.vic.gov.au/Documents/about/research/finalsconstransition.pdf

Smith, K., Kotsanas, C., Farrelly, A., & Alexander, K. (2011). *Research into practices to support a positive start to school*. www.education.vic.gov.au/Documents/about/research/pospracmelbuni.pdf

SuccessWorks. (2010). *Evaluation of transition: A positive start to school initiative*. www.education.vic.gov.au/Documents/about/research/evaluationtrans.pdf

6 Generating and analysing data for the evaluation of transition to school programs – perspectives of children

Sue Dockett and Bob Perry

Introduction

The last few decades have seen major advances in promoting children's perspectives and valuing their voices and views across a range of areas (Groundwater-Smith, Dockett, & Bottrell, 2015). The participation of children in investigations of transitions to school is no exception, as multiple studies across diverse contexts have engaged with children about their transition experiences (Corsaro & Molinari, 2005; Dockett, Einarsdóttir, & Perry, 2019; Joerdens, 2014; Peters, 2003; Sandberg, 2017; White & Sharp, 2007). Chapter 6A provides a detailed account of one such study.

This chapter focuses on how children's engagement can contribute to the evaluation of transition programs. This involves more than promoting children's participation in transitions and more than reporting their experiences. It extends to asking "How can children's perspectives inform decisions about the worth and merit of transition programs?"

Children's perspectives of their transition experiences are directly relevant when considering the purposes of evaluation:

- Is a transition program needed?
- Does the program meet the needs of stakeholders?
- Can the program be improved?
- How does the program operate?
- How effective is the program?
- Why does the program work (or not work?)

As some of those directly experiencing the transition program, children have insight into what is needed in a particular context and how that might impact on their experiences. For example, before they start school, their views on what they need or would like to know or, once they have started school, their reflections on what information was important for them and what supported – or did not support – them can all contribute to a needs analysis.

Children's insights about how the transition program operates for them, what they consider important, what they like – or don't like – about the program,

DOI: 10.4324/9781003055112-10

and why, are relevant when considering process evaluations. Their advice can inform both current and future programs.

Children's perspectives also have an important role in outcome evaluations. While there are several standardised measures to assess children's academic school readiness and/or school adjustment, these tend to privilege adult knowledge over children's experiences and perspectives. Sometimes, children's perspectives are considered but filtered by the interpretations of adults (Dockett, Einarsdóttir, & Perry, 2009). On the basis that transition programs involve multiple stakeholders, seeking input from as many of these as possible promotes the inclusion of different perspectives and contributes to the breadth of the evaluation.

Children are well positioned to share both intended and unintended consequences of transition programs or activities and to comment on the effectiveness and efficiency of these. This is particularly the case when considering social and emotional outcomes. Further, engaging with children prior to the school start, as well as after, provides opportunities to generate pre- and post-transition measures and to compare and contrast these (Wong, 2015).

Even when it is not possible to compare children's perspectives from before they started school to after, those who have directly experienced the transition program have much to offer in helping to understand the effectiveness of the program for them as individuals, as well as for their cohort. Attending to children's perspectives reminds us that it is important to provide transition programs accessible to all but also to emphasise the importance of contextual and situated transition practices (Broström, 2019) rather than a *one-size-fits-all* approach.

Often forgotten in the evaluation of transition programs are the voices of older children who themselves have experienced not only the transition to school but the regular incremental transitions across school years. In many schools, older children participate in buddy programs and have different interactions with school starters than adults. Siblings too can be important contributors to transition programs. Involving these older children can not only generate different perspectives on current programs but also offer suggestions for improving future transition programs (Dockett & Perry, 2005a, 2013; Perry & Dockett, 2011). It also provides opportunities for these older children to reflect on how they have managed and continue to manage transitions as they build up transitions capital (Dunlop, 2014).

Why involve children in evaluation of transition programs?

Responses to this question reflect changing views of children's competence (Lansdown, 2005a) and recognition of their rights to have a say on things that matter for them afforded by the UN *Convention on the Rights of the Child* (United Nations, 1989). Other important reasons to include children's perspectives are that listening is the basis for respectful relationships, which, in turn, support ongoing engagement; and, in the very practical sense, children's perspectives often offer different insights and raise different issues from those of adults. Some of our earliest transitions research indicated similarities in the issues adults (parents and educators) considered important for transition and differences between these groups and the issues mentioned by children. For example, parents and teachers highlighted the importance of children's adjustment to the school environment as an indication of an effective transition to school, while children highlighted the importance of knowing the rules and their feelings (dispositions) about school (Dockett & Perry, 1999, 2002).

Adults who recognise children's competence and promote their participation rights have used a range of methods to create supportive contexts in which children feel comfortable to share their views. Several of these are relevant for evaluating transition programs and are featured in this chapter. However, listening – even in its broadest sense (Rinaldi, 2005) – is not sufficient for children's perspectives to contribute to judgements about programs. Lundy (2007) has argued that for children's perspectives to be taken seriously, we need to advocate for *space*, where children have the opportunity to express their views; *voice*, where children are supported to share their views; *audience*, where their views are listened to; and *influence*, where their views are acted upon. Each of these elements is important in the implementation of the strategies and methods we outline in the chapter.

Participatory evaluation

Chapter 4 described participatory evaluation as that which involves participants or stakeholders in decision-making throughout the project. To be genuinely participatory, children would need to be involved in all aspects of the evaluation, from planning the focus, determining methods to be used, participating in data generation, analysis, and interpretation, to reporting the results of the evaluation and planning for change. While all of this is possible (Perry & Dockett, 2011), it is also rarely the case. It may be that time and resource constraints present challenges, that some of the participants of transition programs are not known at the time the program is planned, or that organisational and systems issues preclude children's ongoing participation in the evaluation. However, this should not mean that children's participation is sidelined.

Lansdown (2005b) distinguishes three levels of engagement: consultation, participation, and self-initiation. *Consultation* recognises the value of different perspectives and seeks information from children that can be used by adults to influence policy and/or practice that directly impacts upon those children. For example, educators might seek children's views about the buddy program, staggered starts to the first day of school, or inviting parents to stay in the classroom. While it does not have to be so, consultation tends to be driven by adults and seeks information about issues usually identified by the adults. Many of the reports of children's involvement in the evaluation of transition programs report such consultation.

Example: Consulting children

Children attending one preschool and who were soon to start school were asked:

- How do you feel about going to big school?
- How do you feel about leaving preschool?
- Is there something the teachers at preschool or big school could do to make it better?

Children's comments reflected both excitement and anxiety about starting school, tinged with some sadness at leaving friends from preschool. Discussion of how teachers could facilitate the transition included one child's suggestion that they "have a celebration". This was accepted enthusiastically by the others, who added to the idea by suggesting the timing – "on the first day I have at school", what to wear – "party clothes", and who to invite – "everyone who goes to school next year" and "our preschool teachers" as well as "our big school teachers". Their advice was followed, and a celebration of starting school was held.

(Perry & Dockett, 2011)

Participatory processes move beyond consultation by involving children in all aspects of the evaluation. This means that children, in partnership with adults, shape the evaluation by having input into decisions about what is to be evaluated, how, and by whom and engage in discussions about data analysis, results and reporting.

Example: Children and educators working together

Together with their preschool teacher, a group of Icelandic preschoolers explored their own transition processes. In initial discussions, they outlined what they already knew about school and then posed questions about what they wanted to find out in their visits to the school. During their first visit to the school, they explored the building and playground. This provided the basis for planning future visits and activities. The preschool teacher documented the children's investigations through field notes, records of discussions, and photographs. These, together with children's discussions, provided the data for future planning and the evaluation.

(Ólafsdóttir & Einarsdóttir, 2019)

The next level of *self-initiated processes* sees children themselves defining the agenda, selecting methods, implementing, and reporting the evaluation. In these processes, adult roles lean towards facilitation and technical support rather than direction.

Example: Buddies evaluating the transition program

With the planned introduction of a buddy program, current Year 5 students were invited to discuss ways the program might operate, what they thought they could contribute, and what they anticipated would be of benefit for those involved. Initial conversations focused on experiences some of the Year 5 children had had with buddies when they started school. They devised buddy application forms for their peers and established criteria for the selection of buddies. Supported by their teachers, the Year 5 buddies identified times they could support new children as well as some joint activities both before and after the new children started school. To evaluate the buddy program, the now Year 6 buddies – with input from their teachers – developed brief surveys for those involved seeking information about what they did or did not like about the program and what worked or did not work for them. Each older buddy read the questions to their younger buddy and recorded responses. Written surveys were distributed to parents and teachers. The Year 6 buddies collated survey responses in their report, which concluded with recommendations for changes to the buddy program. Specifically, they recommended more time for group games, providing coffee/tea for parents during the visits, more use of the school newsletter to introduce new children to the school, and development of a booklet about the school for the children to take home.

(Dockett & Perry, 2005a)

The process followed by these children is similar to that espoused by the Open University's Children's Research Centre (http://wels.open.ac.uk/research/childrens-research-centre/) and Southern Cross University's Centre for Children and Young People (www.scu.edu.au/centre-for-children-and-young-people/).

Involving children in evaluations

While it is possible to draw on several methods to elicit children's perspectives, it is also important to situate these within the overall interpretive framework we all bring to our interactions. This involves reflecting on our image of the child and expectations of their competence and rights. For example, if we have a strengths-based view of children, we will tend of focus on using methods that are familiar and comfortable for them rather than methods that highlight any perceived "deficits". Similarly, if our perspectives are framed by rights-based practice, it is likely we will select methods based on active engagement that offer children participation choices (Dockett, Einarsdóttir, & Perry, 2011).

Chapter 4 outlined the importance of exploring the theory underpinning transition programs and the proposed mechanisms for change. The example of including school visits (activity) with the aim of building familiarity with the school setting and helping develop a sense of belonging (mechanism for change) was linked with the anticipated outcome of an effective transition to school (Table 4.1). Identifying the mechanism helps to focus the evaluation. This example sets the scene for exploring children's expectations and experiences of the school visits, investigating their familiarity with the school environment and sense of belonging.

In the following section, we draw on several studies to provide examples of questions and methods that might be used to explore children's perspectives of school visits and their sense of familiarity and belonging. We start by sharing some children's perspectives of school visits made as part of their transition program and link these to the proposed mechanism for change – building familiarity and a sense of belonging at school. We then consider data that reflect familiarity and belonging and act as indicators of an effective transition. From this, we explore how these perspectives contribute to evaluation of the transition program. More detail about using specific methods as well as the potential advantages and disadvantages of each can be found in Dockett and Perry (2005b), Einarsdóttir (2007a), and Groundwater-Smith et al. (2015).

Children's perspectives of school visits

Children can share a great deal of information when they engage freely and actively in conversations or informal interviews (see Chapter 6A). The notion of conversation – the reciprocal exchange of information – is important, as few people respond well to interrogations. A range of prompts can be used to guide conversations – including children's books about starting school, old school photos, school uniforms or equipment, and visits to school. In some instances, children will prefer to have conversations in small groups rather than individually. Large-group conversations sometimes are effective but have the potential for some children to be more dominant than others and for the silence of others to be overlooked.

Sometimes, children will be comfortable conversing with ECEC educators, family members, school teachers, or other adults. Some studies have found it effective to engage older buddies in recording conversations with their younger counterparts (Dockett & Perry, 2005a; Yeo & Clarke, 2005), while others have reported the delight of children who have recently started school on meeting their preschool teachers and conversing with them (Einarsdóttir, 2011). Several studies make use of drawings, photos, and/or videos in conjunction with conversations (Dockett, Einarsdóttir, & Perry, 2017; Einarsdóttir, Dockett, & Perry, 2009; Jadue-Roa, 2019; Murray & Harrison, 2005; Salmi & Kumpulainen, 2019). In all instances, attention to ethical protocols (see Chapter 4) is critical.

Documenting conversations can support the revisiting of topics and the sharing of information. Records of school visits can prompt conversations about different experiences when children will attend different schools, as well as encourage children who have visited the same school to reflect on and discuss their shared experiences.

Example: About school

An ECEC educator recorded the following comments from Shayla after a transition visit to the school he would be attending the following year.

Educator: What did you find out about school?
Shayla: You have to listen to the teacher at your school . . . because if you don't listen to the teacher, they'll get upset. The people will be crying if you don't listen to the teacher . . . you have to be

116 *Sue Dockett and Bob Perry*

quiet drawing and the teacher will be happy if you be quiet . . . and at storytime when the teacher's reading, quietly laugh.

Over several days, later conversations with other children in the group also referred to crying:

Zara: It's not OK to cry at school 'cause people will think you are a baby.
Educator: Is it Ok to cry at school if you feel sad or if you miss your family?
Tristan: If you don't know where the toilets are.
Zara: If you aren't in the classroom.
Educator: Who could help you feel happy?
Tristan: Teacher . . . or a kid . . .

(An edited version of this example appears in Dockett & Perry, 2014, p. 75)

The connection between crying and babies, with the implication that babies did not belong at school, was also reflected in brainstorming sessions and children's drawings of what they did when they went to visit the school (Figures 6.1–6.2).

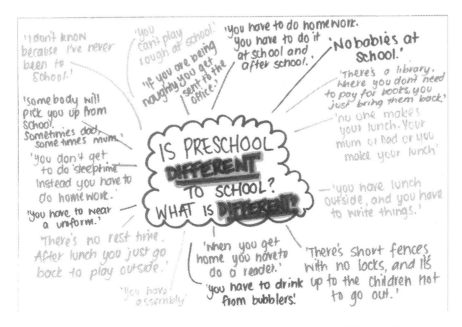

Figure 6.1 Brainstorm: Is preschool different to school? What is different? (Dockett & Perry, 2014, p. 74)

Evaluation of programs – perspectives of children 117

Figure 6.2 Jonah: We went to assembly. There's no babies at assembly.

Tristan's concern with toilets also reappeared in his conversations and drawings. While not referred to as often, the issue of toilets and toileting was raised by several other children. Ada commented that her big brother at school had told her the toilets were always dirty and smelly, and Evie's sister had told her not to go there because of the "big kids".

Building familiarity and belonging

ECEC educators raised these issues with parents and teachers at the schools children would be attending. Further conversations with the children confirmed some anxiety about the move to school; children's comments indicated that they connected starting school with *being big* but were worried that they would not know what to do. Of concern for the educators was that children were unlikely to develop a sense of familiarity and belonging at school if they – or others – felt they were behaving *like babies* or did not know where to go. Activities were added to the transition program – at the ECEC centre and school – to discuss the range of emotions children might be feeling, strategies they might use to regulate these, and where and how they might seek help.

As well, during the next school visit, the teacher and buddies led the children on a school tour, pointing out different buildings and places. On each

Figure 6.3 Tristan: ". . . have a door to the toilets and you shut the door to the toilets. No one told me where the toilets are . . . I think about the toilets. Now I know where the toilets are."

subsequent visit, they included a visit to a specific place – the toilets, canteen, hall, library, oval – and discussed what happened in that place. As in other studies (Tatlow-Golden et al., 2017), toilets were a topic of both fascination and some concern for several children. During the tours, children took turns to take some photos of things they thought were important to know about. Tristan took a photo of the school toilets (Figure 6.3).

Gillian's map of the school (Figure 6.4) also highlighted the importance of toilets.

Children's concerns about crying and toileting were identified as the transition program was implemented. They affirmed that a transition program was needed and provided evidence for the process evaluation of how the transition program operated. They also established the basis for an impact assessment, identifying areas where the transition program could make a difference for the children.

How do we know if children are familiar with the school and feel like they belong?

It is important to find out from the children themselves how they have experienced the transition. Conversations, sometimes supported by drawings or

Evaluation of programs – perspectives of children 119

Figure 6.4 Gillian: "I'm drawing my school and everything in my school. I'm drawing me . . . the toilets. This is a map so the kids know where to go. First stop, toilets."

photos, can be useful starting points. Several schools have worked with children currently in their first year of school to develop booklets for the next cohort starting school, describing these as "Things new children need to know, What we have learned since we started school?" or "What might the children at preschool ask me about big school?" (Figure 6.5). In several instances, these books refer to toilets (Figure 6.6) and to knowing what to do (Figures 6.7–6.8) and where to go (Figure 6.9) or not to go (Figure 6.10) as important things to know about.

Opportunities for those who have started school to share these books with those soon to start school can prompt wide ranging conversations, indicating what the current schoolchildren regard as important and how they have managed this, as well as highlighting what the prospective children want to know.

Children's reflections on their transition experiences also provide evidence of their perceptions of their own changing identity, role and status. Reflections might be generated by discussions of drawings (Figure 6.11) or through measures such as the *Reflection Task* (Perry & Dockett, 2005), (Figure 6.12), which encourage children to think about those changes.

120 Sue Dockett and Bob Perry

Figure 6.5 What might the children at preschool ask me about big school?

Figure 6.6 What if I need to go to the toilet in class time?

Figure 6.7 What do new children need to know? They need to know how to buy food at the canteen.

Figure 6.8 They need to know what to do in assembly. Now I know that I have to be quiet at assembly.

Figure 6.9 They need to know where to go to get a drink – at the bubblers.

Figure 6.10 They need to know they're not allowed to 'out of bounds' because you're not allowed to go there.

Evaluation of programs – perspectives of children 123

Figure 6.11 That's me not crying at school.

Figure 6.12 Reflection.

Observations of children's actions and behaviour provide evidence of their familiarity with the school environment. As discussed in Chapter 3, *belonging* is a multi-dimensional concept (Sumsion & Wong, 2011) that may be expressed in several ways. On several occasions we have asked children in their first year of school if they felt like they belonged at school. Perhaps reflecting the complexity of the concept – or the strangeness of the question – children have replied with comments such as "No, I belong at home with my Mum and Dad" and "Teachers belong at school, not kids". As an alternative strategy to ascertain children's sense of belonging at school, conversations about photos and drawings that emphasise *my* school, *my* classroom, or *my* teacher (Figures 6.13–6.15) provide some initial clues.

Figure 6.13 This is me next to my classroom.

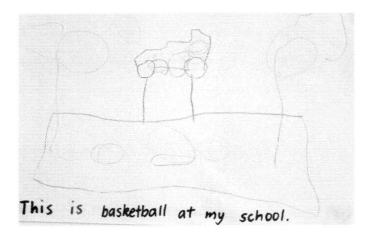

Figure 6.14 This is basketball at my school.

Evaluation of programs – perspectives of children 125

Figure 6.15 This is my teacher.

Other prompts for exploring familiarity and belonging include rating scales (Figure 6.16). Children's initial responses can be explored by additional prompts, such as those listed next.

126 Sue Dockett and Bob Perry

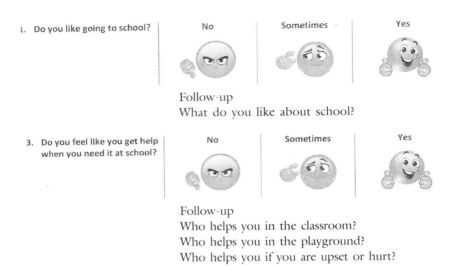

Figure 6.16 Rating scale for children (Dockett & Perry, 2019)

Data analysis

Many methods can be used to elicit children's perspectives of their transition to school. Appropriate analysis and interpretation of these data are necessary if they are to contribute to the program evaluation. Some data will be quantifiable. For example, it is possible to count how many times children mentioned specific issues as they talked about, drew, or took photos of their transition experiences. In addition to frequency, the source and strength of data can be reported. In this instance, the source refers to the number of children who referred to specific issues rather than the number of mentions, and the strength indicates how often each child mentioned the issue. For example, 20 children drew pictures and talked about what was important for children to know about school. The word *toilet* was mentioned 15 times (frequency) by five children (source). Further, one child mentioned it eight times (strength), while none of the remaining four children mentioned it more than twice. Interpretation of these data suggests that toilets were a major concern for one child, of interest to several others, but not of particular concern (at least at this time) for the remaining 15 children. This sort of information can inform both group and individual transition programs.

In our early work (Dockett & Perry, 2001, 2002), we analysed the responses of parents, teachers and children when they were asked to identify five things about starting school that were important to them. Reading and re-reading the responses, as well as discussion and debate among the research team, identified eight categories of responses:

> **Adjustment**: social adjustment to the school context, including interpersonal and organisational adjustment

Disposition: children's attitudes towards, or feelings about, school or learning

Educational Environment: concern about the nature of the school environment

Family issues: issues related to family functioning or involvement with the school

Knowledge: ideas, facts, or concepts that needed to be known in order to enter school

Physical: physical attributes, needs, or characteristics of children, including issues about safety, health, and age

Rules: fitting in with the school and school expectations

Skills: small units of action that could be observed or inferred from observable behaviour

A frequency count indicated that 32% ($n = 410$) responses from parents and 35% ($n = 445$) of teacher responses highlighted issues of adjustment, while 33% ($n = 106$) of responses from children focused on rules and 32% ($n = 103$) referred to the category of disposition. These data were reported in graphical format, rankings (Table 6.1), and in narrative forms.

While the percentages and rankings illustrated the pattern of responses, they were elaborated and explained through examples that drew on qualitative data. These indicated that parents' notions of adjustment referred primarily to social and interpersonal areas such as being accepted by the group. Teachers focused on organisational adjustment, considering how children fitted into the organisation of the class group, for example, by sharing the teacher's attention, listening, and taking turns. Children were adamant that they need to know the rules of school and talked about how their dispositions and feelings about school relied on them having friends. Just as is reported in Chapter 6A, adults and child perspectives are often different.

Table 6.1 Ranking of response categories across groups – highest to lowest (Dockett & Perry, 2001).

Children	Parents	Early Childhood Educators
Rules	Adjustment	Adjustment
Disposition	Educational environment	Disposition
Adjustment	Disposition	Skills
Knowledge	Physical	Educational environment
Physical	Family issues	Physical
Skills	Skills	Knowledge
	Rules	Family issue
	Knowledge	Rules

Data analysis is about describing patterns in the data. There will be many ways to do this and many patterns to be discerned. Some patterns will be identified clearly through quantitative analysis, while in other instances, qualitative analysis will be required. Sometimes, a combination of approaches will be the most appropriate. Data analysis takes time and requires access to appropriate resources. If we genuinely seek children's perspectives, we need to rely on their construction of meaning rather than our interpretation of data. This requires constant checking with the children involved as we analyse data.

Analysis of visual data – photos, drawings, videos – can be challenging for those who did not take the photo or make the drawing or video (Gubrium & Harper, 2013). Rather than seeking to analyse images on their own, we combine the visual with the narrative and treat them as one unit (Einarsdóttir et al., 2009).

When analysing narrative data, it is possible to apply an already-established coding frame (such as the one given earlier) to new data. It is also possible to construct a new system of coding the data from the ground up, using processes such as constructivist grounded theory (Charmaz, 2016), identify themes across the data (thematic analysis – see Chapter 6A), and identify specific content within the data (content analysis) (Denzin & Lincoln, 2017). It is important that whatever process is adopted is rigorous and yields trustworthy results.

Regardless of which of these approaches is adopted, the first step in analysing qualitative data is to become familiar with it. This might mean sharing data with other members of the transition or evaluation team. It is possible for children to be a part of this team and for them to have input into the analysis process. For example, when creating a class photo-essay about *What children need to know when they start school* (Dockett & Simpson, 2003), all photos taken by the children were available on the classroom computer. Comments contributed as the photos were taken were matched with the photos and checked by children. In group discussions, children then decided which images and which comments were to be included in the book.

Once familiar with the data, the search for patterns begins. Generally, the process starts with listing words or issues that occur across the data set. For example, initial codes could include *toilets* and *crying*, noted in examples earlier in this chapter. Mention of other feelings related to school – perhaps excitement, nervousness, feeling scared – could all be grouped together under a theme or category of emotional reactions to school. References to other physical aspects of school – maybe the classroom, playground, office – could also contribute to a category or theme of school spaces. Once initial patterns are described, these need to be reviewed continually against the data. When the patterns are affirmed, defined, and named, they and the processes used to generate them can be reported.

Trustworthiness comes from data analysis that is conducted in precise, consistent, and openly described ways (Guba & Lincoln, 1989). Trustworthy data analysis provides enough detail for readers to assess whether the results are credible and dependable and to consider whether similar results would be obtained in other circumstances (transferability). Credibility refers to the match between participants' views and how these are interpreted; dependability involves following a logical process of analysis and documenting this. When these three elements – credibility, dependability, and transferability – have been established, the analysis process attains confirmability.

Confirmability is established when it is clear that analysis is derived from data contributed by participants rather than any specific views or biases of the researcher or evaluator (Jensen, 2012). When considering data contributed by children, attention to confirmability is needed to ensure that the children's perspectives, rather than adult interpretations of these, drive the analysis. Keeping an audit trail of the steps and strategies involved in generating, analysing, and interpreting data and reflexivity are two processes often used to establish confirmability.

Reflexivity – critical reflection on what has happened, the interactions and relationships involved, the values, opinions, and experiences we all bring to situations – can add to the credibility of analysis as it involves challenging ourselves to understand things differently and confront biases we may have (Dowling, 2012). While reflection describes what has happened and why this might be the case and considers other possibilities, reflexivity asks us to examine what happens next as adults engage with children and facilitate their participation (Graham, Powell, & Truscott, 2016). Reflexivity can be both an individual and a shared process.

The impact of children's perspectives

What happens as a consequence of listening to children and taking their perspectives of transition seriously? Children's input can change programs: identifying the need for different programs or activities, contributing to changes in the operation of the program, and providing evidence of the effectiveness of transition programs. However, it is not enough for the adults to know this – it is equally important to include children in the reporting of the evaluation or, if this is not possible, to report to the children involved. Reporting with and to children demonstrates respect for their involvement and their contributions. Ongoing reporting that identifies changes made as a result of their involvement builds on this respect and can contribute to their sense of belonging. In each context, decisions will need to be made about who is responsible for keeping children informed and how this may be achieved. Far from being disinterested in changes happening in transition, older children in schools have indicated that they are indeed interested and often keen to propose ongoing improvements to programs, based on their expanding experiences of transition and growing transitions capital (Dunlop, 2014).

Involving children in reporting may involve seeking input into decisions of what to include in a written report or presentation – for example, seeking their permission to include photos or images they have contributed or comments they have made and describing the context in which these might be made

130　*Sue Dockett and Bob Perry*

accessible to others. Children (and/or their families) may be happy to share an image within the ECEC or school community; they may be less comfortable with the same image enlarged multiple times and used on posters and public presentations. Children may also be involved in presentations or reporting, such as in the following example.

> *Example: Voices of Children Expo*
>
> At the conclusion of a project involving 14 schools and ECEC settings seeking children's perspectives of transition to school, the children were invited to share their findings with other participants in the project at the Voices of Children Expo. The expo was hosted by the local council and participating children, family members, members of the transition to school network who had supported the project, and council officers were invited to listen to what the children had decided to share and to help celebrate the achievements attained throughout the project. Children from each site involved in the project led the presentations, assisted by their educators.
>
> (Perry & Dockett, 2008)

Ethical challenges and children's perspectives

It is important to report the outcomes of evaluations and to utilise these to inform current and future programs. However, the standard ethical principles of respecting privacy and confidentiality also apply. For example, names and identifying information may be removed and informed consent sought for the use of images.

Many of the efforts to seek children's perspectives of transition will occur in ECEC settings and/or schools. Many will also involve people whose roles and identities are familiar to the children. This can be an advantage, as children are often comfortable sharing information with familiar others. It can also be a disadvantage, as children may feel that they have no choice in sharing information with educators who have a habit of expecting responses.

Issues of consent for participation need to be considered. For example: Is the evaluation considered part of the education program? What information is provided to children (and families)? How is the information provided? Who needs to provide consent for children's participation? What if children choose not to participate? Can they participate in some aspects but not others? Projects involving former preschool teachers (Einarsdóttir, 2011) or buddies as interviewers (Yeo & Clarke, 2005) have attempted to address some of these power issues. However, David, Edwards, and Alldred (2001) note that the power relations within schools make it very difficult for children to exercise participation choices. The same is probably the case in ECEC settings.

Part of the rationale for seeking children's perspectives rests on perceptions of competence and children's positioning as experts on their own lives (Qvortrup, 1994). Another part recognises the diversity of children's experiences and their perspectives. The ethical challenges associated with these expectations include considering which children's perspectives are to be sought and shared, and whether these are considered representative for all children. Across many of our investigations, some children have chosen not to share their perspectives; in some school situations, children's participation has been limited by adults because of decisions about behaviour, work that needed to be completed, or adult views that they would not be able to contribute. How are the perspectives of these children to be considered? We are often reminded that children are not a homogeneous group; one child does not speak for all; and that we need to draw on methods and analysis that acknowledge the diversity of children's experiences and expectations.

The diversity of children's experiences can raise questions about whether children are responding seriously or are responding in ways that seek to please others and whether the information they share can be trusted or believed. We acknowledge that each of these situations is possible – just as it is for adults. Rather than regarding children's input as unreliable, it is important to create contexts that recognise children's capabilities and provide multiple opportunities, methods, and spaces for children to share their perspectives with people they know and trust (Dockett & Perry, 2007). Lundy's (2007) four elements, outlined at the beginning of this chapter – space, voice, influence, and audience – are relevant here.

Conclusion

There is much to be gained by including children's perspectives in the evaluation of transition programs. There are also many methods and strategies to support children to share these perspectives. Regardless of the method used, care needs to be taken to respect and value children's participation, generate and analyse data, and report these in appropriate ways to appropriate audiences. While much can be gleaned from involving children as they are about to start school, as well as once they become school children, older children who have built up transitions capital also are often eager to provide ongoing reflections to improve programs.

6A Listening to the voices of Jamaican children about their transitional experiences

Zoyah Kinkead-Clark

Introduction

In the limited research which has been done on children's transitions from pre-primary to primary school in Jamaica, the focus has predominantly been from the perspectives of adults, namely parents and educators (Harris-Mortley, 2019; Kinkead-Clark, 2015; Smith, 2010). While these studies have proved incredibly helpful in enabling key stakeholders to understand the unique issues which shape children's readiness to transition from one environment to another, they have also highlighted gaps in our knowledge. In this case, one such gap is our limited understanding of children's experiences and perceptions of their own transition from pre-school to primary school.

Hearing the voices of children relevant to their transitional experiences provides a unique opportunity to support their development and overall success not only as they progress through their early academic lives but also as they develop the requisite skills to navigate through the many demands and expectations of primary school (Dockett & Perry, 2003; Mirkhil, 2010). A number of studies (Clarke & Sharpe, 2003; Einarsdóttir, 2007b, 2013; Salmi & Kumpulainen, 2019) have documented that how children view their transitional experiences is contingent on their preschool environments and their social maturity to adapt to the new changes in primary school. Mirkhil (2010), similar to Dockett and Perry (2003), highlighted the multi-dimensionality of children's transitional experiences to primary school and cautioned against ignoring the richness and unique value children add to the discourse surrounding this period of their lives.

This chapter therefore seeks to illuminate the Jamaican story. It focuses on how Jamaican children in the early childhood years understand and perceive their transitional experiences. In this case, transitional experiences refers to the period before and after they transition from one school environment to another and the unique experiences they encounter as a part of this experience.

Overview of extant literature on Jamaican children's transitions

In comparison to other contexts, very little is known about Jamaican children's transitions or their readiness to transition to primary school. Harris-Mortley (2019)

DOI: 10.4324/9781003055112-11

and Kinkead-Clark (2015, 2018) discussed the perspective of teachers and parents as it pertained to this. Smith (2010), on the other hand, assessed early childhood programs to determine their effectiveness in facilitating children's preparedness for learning as they transitioned to primary school. Minott and Leo-Rhynie's (2015) research examined gender differences in Caribbean children's readiness to transition to primary school; and O'Sullivan (2015) examined the factors which support and impede children's successful transitions from pre-primary to primary school.

The results of these studies indicated that much of the focus for teachers rested solely with children's cognitive skills and their social preparedness for primary school (Kinkead-Clark, 2015, 2018). Harris-Mortley (2019) also noted that pre-primary teachers focused heavily on students' mastery of content knowledge because of the privileging of this by Grade 1 (first grade) teachers in primary school. Teachers indicated that the frequent dependence on high-stakes assessments in primary school and perceived measures of teacher effectiveness as being either *good* or *bad* in the eyes of school administrators, parents, and the general community at large, compelled them to focus heavily on content knowledge as the measure of children's readiness to transition from pre-primary to primary school (Kinkead-Clark, 2018).

It is also important to note that parents have also bought into the position held by teachers regarding children's preparedness to transition to primary school, according to Kinkead-Clark (2015) and O'Sullivan (2015), while many Jamaican parents focused on the provision of physical resources as an important aspect of their role in supporting children's preparedness to transition to primary school. The parents also focused on the content knowledge of their children. It is this issue among many, which O'Sullivan (2015) noted impeded children's preparedness for transitioning to primary school.

Methodology

Data for this study were gathered through interviews with six preschool children (three boys and three girls) who were in the final term of preschool. The average age of each child was 66 months. Interviews lasted approximately 20 to 30 minutes each. Each child was interviewed once. All interviews were transcribed and analysed thematically.

Due to the unique factors which come into play when young children are interviewed, the general recommendations proposed by Ponizovsky-Bergelson et al. (2019) were followed. Some of these include: the mindfulness of power relations, the use of open-ended questions, and following up each response with an affirmation/validation.

Findings

Three themes emerged from the findings;

1 *Feeding off* adult expectations
2 What about play?
3 Am I ready?

Feeding off *adult expectations*

All the children who participated in the study had some idea of what primary school would be like, based on what they were told by adults. *Feeding off* adult expectations therefore emerged as a theme because children used these responses/comments to help them get a sense of what awaited them when they moved on to primary school. All children interviewed explained that they had heard from an adult what primary school would be like. Usually, teachers were the source of this information, but in two instances, the parents had also contributed to the image children had conceptualised about primary school. Some of the comments children shared which reflect this included:

- My mother told me . . . .
- My teacher said . . . .
- My father said . . .
- When my teacher talks about it . . .
- I know because my teacher said . . .

These comments indicate that the children leaned heavily on the advice shared by adults which helped them understand what they needed to do to get ready for primary school and how they should do it. In this case, the children expressed that they had been told by adults that primary school would be very different from pre-primary school and that they needed to be prepared for it. In most cases children were aware that they were expected to be *big children*, which implied the children were expected to display more maturity, independence, and self-sufficiency. When the children were probed as to what they understood about being *big children*, varying responses were garnered, including:

- I have to finish my work in class now
- I need to be able to tie my own shoelace
- We need to know our spelling words and maths
- No more playing around at school
- I will be in the big class now
- I have to study my book

Essentially the children indicated that going to primary school would be a new experience unlike what they encountered in pre-primary school. While two of the children were prepared for this, the other four children expressed some concern about the absence of play from primary school. This provided a basis for the next theme: What about play?

What about play?

The importance of play to young children's development has been well documented in extant literature. For the children who participated in this study, this was also the case and emerged as a major concern when they considered moving on to primary school. When the children were asked what they would miss most about preschool when they moved on to primary school, all children agreed they would miss opportunities to play.

When asked to explain why they would miss play, the children expressed that they had been told that primary schools focused on *work*, and unlike pre-primary schools, there were no learning centres or toys to play with in the classroom. Messages about the absence of play from primary school were given by both parents and preschool teachers. In this regard Jerome (pseudonym), one of the participants, explained; "My mother says I romp too much and when I go to primary school I will have to settle down and study my book".

Lisa shared a similar concern "My teacher (preschool) told me when I go to primary school I need to know my spelling words and maths . . . if I don't finish my work then I can't go to play".

David, another participant in the study, expressed a similar concern about missing play. He explained, "My teacher told me there were no toys in grade one. I like to play at school so I really hope we can play with toys or bring one to school . . . I really like to play".

Am I ready?

The transitional process from one school to the next may be fraught with trepidation for some children. The findings of this study suggest that this was certainly the case with four of the participating children. Questions about their personal readiness stemmed from two areas: their ability to manage their perceptions of the academic demands of primary school and their ability to forego all they had become used to in pre-primary school.

The children made frequent reference to comments made by their pre-primary teachers and parents about the content they would need to know in preparation for primary school. This was of concern to three students who acknowledged that, based on their own assessment of their own academic capabilities, they did not have the academic skills to manage grade one. Two children acknowledged that while they believed they had the academic skills, they were concerned about their readiness to leave the comforts of their pre-primary schools.

Lisa, one of the girls interviewed, explained: "I know when I go to primary school the work will be very hard . . . my teacher told me . . . so I have to work really hard. I hope I can manage the work".

Jason, one of the boys, shared a similar concern: "Grade one is for big children you know. You have to know a lot of things like reading and writing and spelling . . . I know how to do some of that but not all . . . my mother really wants me to do my best when I go there".

Jerome expressed concern for his friends. He wanted to be reassured his friends from his preschool would still be around when he moved on. He explained, "Miss, I will really miss my friends. I hope that my friends will be in the same class like me so we can still talk and play together".

Discussion and conclusion

The findings of this study illuminate the depth of thought young children put into transitioning to primary school. It highlights that while they listen to the input of adults, children give meaning to the voice of adults to come up with their own ideas about how they will navigate the transitional process. This problematises the notion that transitions must only be interpreted and discussed through the eyes of adults.

The findings of this research support the works of Clarke and Sharpe (2003), Einarsdóttir (2007b, 2013), and Salmi and Kumpulainen (2019), who reiterate the value of gleaning children's voices in order to understand their transitional experiences. It is, however, especially important that we do this in Caribbean countries, where children's voices are frequently not listened to or, in many instances, are often ignored.

References

Broström, S. (2019). Children's views on their learning in preschool and school: Reflections and influence in practice. In S. Dockett, J. Einarsdóttir, & B. Perry (Eds.), *Listening to children's advice about staring school and school age care* (pp. 84–98). London: Routledge.

Charmaz, K. (2016). The power of constructivist grounded theory for critical inquiry. *Qualitative Inquiry*, 23(1), 34–45. https://doi.org/10.1177/1077800416657105

Clarke, C., & Sharpe, P. (2003). Transition from preschool to primary school: An overview of the personal experiences of children and their parents in Singapore. *European Early Childhood Education Research Journal*, 11(sup1), 15–23. https://doi.org/10.1080/1350293X.2003.12016702

Corsaro, W., & Molinari, L. (2005). *I Compagni: Understanding children's transition from preschool to elementary school*. New York: Teachers College Press.

David, M., Edwards, R., & Alldred, P. (2001). Children and school-based research: "Informed consent" or "educated consent". *British Educational Research Journal*, 27(3), 347–365. https://doi.org/10.1080/01411920120004834 0

Denzin, N., & Lincoln, Y. (Eds.). (2017). *The SAGE handbook of qualitative research* (5th ed.). Los Angeles: SAGE.

Dockett, S., Einarsdóttir, J., & Perry, B. (2009). Researching with children: Ethical tensions. *Journal of Early Childhood Research*, 7(3), 283–298. https://doi.org/10.1177/1476718X09336971

Dockett, S., Einarsdóttir, J., & Perry, B. (2011). Balancing methodologies and methods in researching with young children. In D. Harcourt, B. Perry, & T. Waller (Eds.), *Researching young children's perspectives: Ethics and dilemmas of educational research with children* (pp. 68–81). Milton Park, Oxon: Routledge.

Dockett, S., Einarsdóttir, J., & Perry, B. (2017). Photo elicitation: Reflecting on multiple sites of meaning. *International Journal of Early Years Education*, 25(3), 225–240. https://doi.org/10.1080/09669760.2017.1329713

Dockett, S., Einarsdóttir, J., & Perry, B. (Eds.). (2019). *Listening to children's advice about starting school and school age care*. London: Routledge. https://doi.org/10.4324/9781351139403

Dockett, S., & Perry, B. (1999). Starting school: What do the children say? *Early Child Development and Care*, *159*, 107–119. https://doi.org/10.1080/0300443991590109

Dockett, S., & Perry, B. (2001). Starting school: Effective transitions. *Early Childhood Research and Practice*, *3*(2). http://ecrp.uiuc.edu/v3n2/dockett.html

Dockett, S., & Perry, B. (2002). Who's ready for what? Young children starting school. *Contemporary Issues in Early Childhood*, *3*(1), 67–89. https://doi.org/10.2304/ciec.2002.3.1.9

Dockett, S., & Perry, B. (2003). Children's views and children's voices in starting school. *Australasian Journal of Early Childhood*, *28*(1), 12–17. https://doi.org/10.1177/183693910302800104

Dockett, S., & Perry, B. (2005a). "A buddy doesn't let kids get hurt in the playground": Starting school with buddies. *International Journal of Transitions in Childhood*, *1*, 22–35.

Dockett, S., & Perry, B. (2005b). Researching with children: Insights from the Starting School Research Project. *Early Childhood Development and Care*, *175*(6), 507–521. https://doi.org/10.1080/03004430500131312

Dockett, S., & Perry, B. (2007). Trusting children's accounts in research. *Journal of Early Childhood Research*, *5*(1), 47–63. https://doi.org/10.1177/1476718X07072152

Dockett, S., & Perry, B. (2013). Siblings and buddies: Providing expert advice about starting school. *International Journal of Early Years Education*, *21*(4), 348–361. https://doi.org/10.1080/09669760.2013.867837

Dockett, S., & Perry, B. (2014). *Continuity of learning: A resource to support effective transition to school and school age care*. Canberra, ACT: Australian Government Department of Education. https://docs.education.gov.au/system/files/doc/other/pdf_with_bookmarking_-_continuity_of_learning-_30_october_2014_1_0.pdf

Dockett, S., & Perry, B. (2019). *Revision of outcomes and indicators of a positive start to school project*. Unpublished report prepared for the Victorian Department of Education and Training.

Dockett, S., & Simpson, S. (2003). "This is school . . . where people come to learn for school": What children need to know when they start school. *Early Childhood Folio*, *7*, 14–17. https://doi.org/10.18296/set.0699

Dowling, M. (2012). Reflexivity. In L. Given (Ed.), *The SAGE encyclopedia of qualitative research methods* (p. 748). Thousand Oaks, CA: SAGE.

Dunlop, A.-W. (2014). Thinking about transitions – One framework or many? Populating the theoretical model over time. In B. Perry, S. Dockett, & A. Petriwskyj (Eds.), *Transitions to school: International research policy and practice* (pp. 31–46). Dordrecht: Springer. https://doi.org/10.1007/978-94-007-7350-9_3

Einarsdóttir, J. (2007a). Research with children: Methodological and ethical challenges. *European Early Childhood Education Research Journal*, *15*(2), 197–211. https://doi.org/10.1080/13502930701321477

Einarsdóttir, J. (2007b). Children's voices on the transition from preschool to primary school. In A.-W. Dunlop & H. Fabian (Eds.), *Informing transitions in the early years* (pp. 74–91). Maidenhead: Open University Press.

Einarsdóttir, J. (2011). Icelandic children's early education transition experiences. *Early Education and Development*, *22*(5), 737–756. https://doi.org/10.1080/10409289.2011.597027

Einarsdóttir, J. (2013). Transition from preschool to primary school in Iceland from the perspectives of children. In K. Margetts & A. Kienig (Eds.), *International perspectives on transition to school: Reconceptualising beliefs, policy and practice* (pp. 67–78). London: Routledge.

Einarsdóttir, J., Dockett, S., & Perry, B. (2009). Making meaning: Children's perspectives expressed through drawings. *Early Child Development and Care, 179*, 217–232. https://doi.org/10.1080/03004430802666999

Graham, A., Powell, M., & Truscott, J. (2016). Exploring the nexus between participatory methods and ethics in early childhood research. *Australasian Journal of Early Childhood, 41*(1), 82–89. https://doi.org/10.1177/183693911604100111

Groundwater-Smith, S., Dockett, S., & Bottrell, D. (2015). *Participatory research with children and young people.* London: SAGE.

Guba, E. G., & Lincoln, Y. (1989). *Fourth generation evaluation.* Newbury Park, CA: SAGE.

Gubrium, A., & Harper, K. (2013). *Participatory visual and digital methods.* Walnut Creek, CA: Left Coast Press.

Harris-Mortley, S. H. (2019). *Jamaican kindergarten and first grade teachers' expectations for readiness skills.* Unpublished PhD thesis, Walden University, Minneapolis. https://scholarworks.waldenu.edu/dissertations/8289

Jadue-Roa, D. (2019). Children's agency in transition experiences: Understanding possibilities and challenges. In S. Dockett, J. Einarsdóttir, & B. Perry (Eds.), *Listening to children's advice about staring school and school age care* (pp. 26–41). London: Routledge.

Jensen, D. (2012). Confirmability. In L. Given (Ed.), *The SAGE encyclopedia of qualitative research methods* (pp. 112–113). Thousand Oaks, CA: SAGE.

Joerdens, S. (2014). "Belonging means you can go in": Children's perspectives and experiences of membership of kindergarten. *Australasian Journal of Early Childhood, 39*(1), 12–21. https://doi.org/10.1177/183693911403900103

Kinkead-Clark, Z. (2015). "Ready for big school": Making the transition to primary school – A Jamaican perspective. *International Journal of Early Years Education, 23*(1), 67–82. https://doi.org/10.1080/09669760.2014.999027

Kinkead-Clark, Z. (2018). Teachers' tensions and children's readiness. Taking a discursive approach to understanding readiness for primary school. *Early Years*, 1–13. https://doi.org/10.1080/09575146.2018.1481826

Lansdown, G. (2005a). *The evolving capacities of the child.* Florence: UNICEF Innocenti Research Centre.

Lansdown, G. (2005b). *Can you hear me? The rights of young children to participate in decisions affecting them.* Working paper No. 36. The Hague: Bernard van Leer Foundation.

Lundy, L. (2007). "Voice" is not enough: Conceptualising article 12 of the United Nations Convention on the Rights of the Child. *British Educational Research Journal, 33*(6), 927–942. https://doi.org/10.1080/01411920701657033

Minott, C., & Leo-Rhynie, E. (2015). Transition from pre-school to primary school: How ready are Caribbean girls and boys? *Caribbean Journal of Education, 37*(1&2), 48–76.

Mirkhil, M. (2010). "I want to play when I go to school": Children's views on the transition to school from kindergarten. *Australasian Journal of Early Childhood, 35*(3), 134–139. https://doi.org/10.1177/183693911003500317

Murray, E., & Harrison, L. J. (2005). Children's perspectives on their first year of school: Introducing a new pictorial measure of school stress. *European Early*

Childhood Education Research Journal, 13, 111–127. https://doi.org/10.1080/13502930585209591

Ólafsdóttir, S., & Einarsdóttir, J. (2019). Following children's advice in transition from preschool to primary school. In S. Dockett, J. Einarsdóttir, & B. Perry (Eds.), *Listening to children's advice about starting school and school age care* (pp. 69–83). London: Routledge.

O'Sullivan, C. (2015). Transition from pre-primary to primary school. *Caribbean Journal of Education, 37*(1&2), 176–203.

Perry, B., & Dockett, S. (2005). *"As I got to learn it got fun": Children's reflections on their first year of school.* Proceedings of the Australian Association for Research in Education 2004 annual conference. Sydney. www.aare.edu.au/data/publications/2004/doc04324.pdf

Perry, B., & Dockett, S. (2008). *Voices of children in starting school.* www.transitiontoschool.net/uploads/2/9/6/5/29654941/voices_of_children_in_starting_school_-_bob_perry_and_sue_dockett.pdf

Perry, B., & Dockett, S. (2011). "How 'bout we have a celebration?" Advice from children on starting school. *European Early Childhood Education Research Journal, 19*(3), 375–388. https://doi.org/10.1080/1350293X.2011.597969

Peters, S. (2003). "I didn't expect that I would get tons of friends ... more each day". Children's experiences of friendships during the transition to school. *Early Years, 23*, 45–53. https://doi.org/10.1080/0957514032000045564

Ponizovsky-Bergelson, Y., Dayan, Y., Wahle, N., & Roer-Strier, D. (2019). A qualitative interview with young children: What encourages or inhibits young children's participation? *International Journal of Qualitative Methods, 18*. https://doi.org/10.1177/1609406919840516

Qvortrup, J. (1994). Childhood matters: An introduction. In J. Qvortrup, M. Bardy, G. Sgritta, & H. Wintersberger (Eds.), *Childhood matters: Social theory, practice and politics* (pp. 1–24). Aldershot: Avebury.

Rinaldi, C. (2005). *In dialogue with Reggio Emilia: Listening, researching and learning.* London: Routledge.

Salmi, S., & Kumpulainen, K. (2019). Children's experiencing of their transition from preschool to first grade: A visual narrative study. *Learning, Culture and Social Interaction, 20*, 58–67. https://doi.org/10.1016/j.lcsi.2017.10.007

Sandberg, G. (2017). Different children's perspectives on their learning environment. *European Journal of Special Needs Education, 32*(2), 191–203. https://doi.org/10.1080/08856257.2016.1216633

Smith, D. (2010). *Early childhood readiness: The status of early childhood programs in one of Jamaica's educational regions.* Unpublished PhD dissertation, Fielding Graduate University, Santa Barbara, CA.

Sumsion, J., & Wong, S. (2011). Interrogating "belonging" in belonging, being and becoming: The early years learning framework for Australia. *Contemporary Issues in Early Childhood, 12*(1), 28–45. https://doi.org/10.2304/ciec.2011.12.1.28

Tatlow-Golden, M., O'Farrelly, C., Booth, A., & Doyle, O. (2017). "Bursting" to go and other experiences: Children's views on using the toilet in the first school year. *The Journal of School Nursing, 33*, 214–222. https://doi.org/10.1177/1059840516646422

United Nations. (1989). *The United Nations convention on the rights of the child.* New York, United Nations. www.ohchr.org/EN/ProfessionalInterest/Pages/CRC.aspx

White, G., & Sharp, C. (2007). "It is different . . . because you are getting older and growing up". How children make sense of the transition to Year 1. *European Early Childhood Education Research Journal*, *15*(1), 87–102. https://doi.org/10.1080/13502930601161882

Wong, M. (2015). Voices of children, parents and teachers: How children cope with stress during school transition. *Early Child Development and Care*, *185*, 658–678. https://doi.org/10.1080/03004430.2014.948872

Yeo, L. S., & Clarke, C. (2005). Starting school – A Singapore story told by children. *Australasian Journal of Early Childhood*, *30*(3), 1–8. https://doi.org/10.1177/183693910503000302

7 Generating and analysing data for the evaluation of transition to school programs – perspectives of adults

Sue Dockett and Bob Perry

Introduction

Informal evaluations of transition programs have occurred over many years as educators have had quick conversations with family members about how they thought their children had made the transition, discussions with other educators about how a specific activity had worked well or had not worked as well as expected, and conversations about how children seemed to *have settled* into school. Families too have shared their stories of starting school, sometimes as they have gathered at the school gate. While a useful starting point, there is much more that adult perspectives can contribute to informing decisions about the worth and merit of transition programs.

We begin this chapter with a reminder of the potential adult stakeholders in transition to school programs and some of the ways they might be involved in the evaluation of programs. These range from being involved in consultations to the collaborative inquiry and reflection processes reported in Chapter 7A. We provide some examples of how adult perspectives may be accessed, documented, and analysed as part of needs analyses, process, and outcome evaluations. As with strategies involving children, we acknowledge the potential strengths, as well as challenges, of participatory evaluation involving a range of stakeholders. Ethical considerations are highlighted.

Stakeholders and their involvement in evaluation of transition programs

Chapter 2 identified stakeholders in transition to school programs as anyone who has an active interest in the processes and outcomes of transition to school. Potential stakeholders include children, families, ECEC and school educators, school-age care providers, other school personnel, Elders and other community leaders, health and other community professionals, and community members as well as others who have interest or involvement in the transition. Some of these people – such as the bus driver, crossing supervisor, local librarian, or school-age care educators – might be involved in some aspects of the evaluation; the participation of others – including educators, interpreters, liaison officers, and family members – may be more extensive.

DOI: 10.4324/9781003055112-12

Why involve so many people in evaluation of transition programs? The simple answer is that all of the people noted, and possibly more in different settings, have an interest in transition to school and contribute in some way to what happens in transition. For some children and families, the first person they see when they visit the school is the crossing supervisor; some families will rely on translated information or seek clarification through interpreters; liaison officers or outreach personnel may have existing strong and trusting relationships with families; information about school might be gleaned from story time at the library; and extended family/community members will probably want to share stories about school. Much can be gained when there are considered and consistent messages coming from these people and a sense of all working together to support effective transitions. In order to know what these messages are and what is expected of the transition as well as what different people are doing to promote this, we need to be willing to seek out and listen to their perspectives.

Another reason for involving a range of people recognises that the transition to school is not just a transition for children. Rather, processes of continuity and change affect all involved. As examples, the transition to being the parent of a school child involves a raft of changes, as well as levels of continuity in family life (Griebel & Niesel, 2009; Griebel et al., 2017; Miller, 2015); and educators experience both continuity and change as they engage with new groups of children and families (Dockett & Perry, 2014). Of interest is that when asked to think about their perspectives of transition, most educators reflect on what has happened – or should happen – for children rather than considering the changes they make themselves or the changes experienced by families (Barblett et al., 2011; Hustedt et al., 2018; Ohle & Harvey, 2019). Yet these changes for adults can have a major impact on the transition experiences of children.

Studies from many countries including Australia (Dockett & Perry, 2004), Germany (Arndt et al., 2013), South Africa (Margetts & Phatudi, 2013), Iceland (Einarsdóttir, 2006), and Portugal (Correia & Marques-Pinto, 2016) indicate that different groups of adults have different perspectives of transition and different ideas about what is needed to support optimal transitions. In general, these studies report educators' focus on the importance of children's social and emotional skills in making an effective transition to school. While parents across these studies considered these skills important, they tended to prioritise children's acquisition of knowledge and academic skills.

Other studies report both differences and similarities among groups of ECEC and school educators, often dependent on context. For example, some studies have reported a focus on the development of children's social-emotional skills and strategies from ECEC educators, compared with a focus on academic skills from school educators (Chan, 2012; Einarsdóttir, 2006; Lin, Lawrence, & Gorrell, 2003). Others suggest that all educators emphasise the importance of children's developing academic skills (Gill, Winters, & Friedman, 2006) and still others indicate that educators regard both academic and non-academic skills as necessary contributors to effective transition to school experiences (Hustedt et al., 2018). This range of evidence indicates that there is no one set of perspectives or beliefs that can be attributed to a whole group of people. Rather, it reiterates the importance of foregoing assumptions and seeking input from a wide range of stakeholders in each context. The importance of this is noted in Chapter 7A, where clarifying the perspectives and expectations of both ECEC and school educators was critical to developing a collaborative approach to transition.

Recall that we defined transitions as a process of relationship building (Chapter 2), based on mutual trust and respect. Sharing a focus on a positive start to school provides opportunities to build that trust and respect and to carry that throughout later school years. Seeking multiple perspectives also affords opportunities to build and strengthen relationships with other professionals, heighten community awareness around the importance of transition, and promote advocacy for both families and the provision of early childhood (ECEC) education. As one example of community awareness and support, we have been delighted to be associated with the Wollongong Transition to School picnic for more than 15 years. The event is managed by Big Fat Smile and Wollongong City Council (www.transitiontoschool.com.au), with support from the local organisations, businesses, and community as they recognise and celebrate the transition to school (Kirk-Downey & Hinton, 2014; Kirk-Downey & Perry, 2006).

Engaging with adults

Participatory evaluation requires the involvement of stakeholders in decision-making throughout the evaluation process, with responsibility for the evaluation resting with those stakeholders rather than external evaluators (Coghlan, 2011). This does not imply that all stakeholders need necessarily be involved in all – or the same – aspects of the evaluation or that there is no place for external evaluators, whose many roles may include partner, facilitator, mentor, or provocateur. The same range of engagement in evaluation outlined in Chapter 6 as relevant for children – consultation, participation, and self-initiation (Lansdown, 2005) – is applicable for adult stakeholders.

Consultation

Consulting adults about transition programs and practices can take many forms. Common methods include surveys and questionnaires, conversations, interviews, and rating scales. Consultation can form an integral part of a needs analysis, seeking information about existing transition programs and practices and identifying any gaps, as well as building a picture of what is perceived as needed in a particular context. Consultation can also play an important role in process evaluations, highlighting participants' views on the ways a program or practices are implemented, and in outcome evaluations as individuals and groups identify what has changed for them and/or their children as a result of the transition program.

One of the challenges associated with consultation is that once stakeholders have shared their perspectives, they expect that these will be acted upon. For example, surveying family members about *What they would like to know about school* can be valuable if responses are incorporated into the information subsequently provided. However, if participants feel that their views have not been responded to or taken seriously they are likely to feel disengaged from the process. Effective communication strategies will be needed to promote consultation and to respond to information received.

At its best, consultation seeks information from those involved in or impacted by policy and practice. Examples could include seeking parent perspectives of the value and timing of transition information sessions, educators identifying appropriate timing and content for reciprocal transition visits, seeking input about the perceived purposes and potential benefits of transition, or identifying consequences of the transition program.

Example: Consulting parents

As one element of consultation with families, educators set up a noticeboard near the first-year-of-school classroom inviting family members to respond to captions such as:

- What do you want to know?
- What does your child want to know?
- What have you heard?
- What are you looking forward to?
- With my child starting school the hardest thing will be . . .
- Contact method – what works for you?

Parents and children passed the noticeboard each time they visited the school and were invited to leave comments, ask questions, or raise issues. Contributions could be anonymous. Markers and sticky notes were provided. Several children posted drawings, and parents posed comments/questions such as:

- What happens in science?
- Ally wants to make her idea: a circle round marble run.
- Email works best for me.
- Prefer talking.
- What do they need to know?
- Letting go.
- Where do they go?

The comments provided were used as the basis for an information session and follow-up discussions with families.

Consultations such as these offer opportunities for people to choose whether they wish to participate and, should they choose to do so, how much or how

Evaluation of programs – perspectives of adults 145

Figure 7.1 Consultation noticeboard.

little they contribute. They also allow participants to be anonymous, although seeing someone post a note on a noticeboard may negate this.

Consulting the various adult stakeholders can contribute to needs analyses, as well as process and outcome evaluations. In the following example, consultation provided impetus for evaluating the processes around Transition to School Statements and led to changes in practice.

Example: Evaluating processes

The introduction of Transition to School Statements in one community was greeted by families and educators with uncertainty. In efforts to understand the cause of the uncertainty, the ECEC management organisation evaluated the processes of developing, sharing, and using statements. Interviews were held with ECEC educators soon after they completed the statements, seeking information about how they had developed them, what had worked well, and any challenges they had identified. They were also asked about how the recorded information matched their broad knowledge of individual children, how they felt about the information they were sharing, and how they felt families had responded. A group of parents was asked similar questions. Children were also asked about the statements and what information they felt should be shared as they started school.

Analysis of responses indicated that several parents and educators were unsure of the purpose of the statements, with some specifically referring to them as *reports*. In the main, children were excited about starting school and positive about the idea of sharing some information with their new teachers. From these data, the organisation facilitated some professional learning sessions for educators to work through the statements and their purposes, as well as some visits to other ECEC settings where transition statements had been used for some time and where educators had established strategies for their development and sharing. School educators who would be receiving the statements were also invited to these sessions to promote their understanding of the processes involved. Parents were invited to participate in relevant sessions, and a series of parent information leaflets about the statements was developed. As a result of the evaluation, educators engaged in more regular conversations with children and families about their observations and the ways they might record these in the transition statements.

Participatory evaluation

Using Lansdown's (2005) categorisation (see also Chapter 6), participatory and self-initiated processes move beyond consultation, engaging stakeholders in defining the evaluation focus, implementing the evaluative processes, and reporting the results. Participatory evaluation may involve collaboration between external and internal participants as they seek to understand both professional and practical knowledge. A more specific focus on understanding practice and supporting change at a local level can come from participatory action research (PAR; see Chapter 4).

The following example refers to processes of practitioner inquiry, which is sometimes equated with action research and/or reflection (see Chapter 4). Baumfield, Hall, and Wall (2013, pp. 4–5) have positioned practitioner inquiry between these processes, arguing that "practitioner inquiry can be a step in a process that begins with reflection and leads to sustained action research . . . or as the trigger to further development through reflection or action research".

Example: Practitioner inquiry

In a statewide project, South Australian educators were supported to use processes of practitioner inquiry (Reid, 2004) to evaluate their approaches to transition and the first year of school. Local professional learning networks consisting of ECEC and school educators were encouraged to generate inquiry questions that challenged them to think critically about their practice and underlying assumptions. Examples of inquiry questions included:

- How can we improve continuity in transition through strengthened teacher relationships?
- How do we know if we have provided quality transition, incorporating community partnerships, with students, parents, educators, and interagency staff?

- How can curriculum/behavioural expectations in school support early childhood experience? What assumptions do we make of the child, their family experiences, and their ability to adapt?

The professional learning networks were supported at the state level to include the perspectives of multiple stakeholders in their inquiry processes and to use their results to ensure that pedagogy and practice supported the positive transition experiences for children and families.

Participatory evaluation of transition programs is often conducted by educators. However, as evident in the following example, parents also can make important contributions to the evaluation of transition programs and practices.

Example: Parent-initiated questionnaire

A group of parents in one community were keen to have their children participate in an orientation program at the local school but very disappointed when they felt that this program did not help their children form a positive view of school. The program involved the children and parents attending the school for one morning. This time was spent in the first-year-of-school classroom with the existing class and teacher. The morning started well, as the children were excited to meet each other and parents got to see the classroom. However, with 25 current school children and 20 visiting children, as well as many parents, the classroom soon became very crowded, hot, and noisy. Several children were visibly upset, and they and their parents left the session early. In response, a group of parents worked with the teacher to develop a brief written questionnaire and circulate this among families. The questionnaire invited parents to nominate the positive and/or negative aspects of the program for them and their children and to suggest alternative practices. The parents and teacher collated responses and shared these with the school executive. As a result of the feedback from the survey, future transition practices were changed.

Generating data for the evaluation of transition programs

Some broad measures for evaluating transition to school practices have been identified (Department for Education and Child Development, South Australia, 2014; Dockett & Perry, 2006; KidsMatter, 2013; Nolan et al., 2012; NSW Department of Education, 2020; Pianta & Kraft-Sayre, 2003; Queensland Department of Education, 2020). Typically, these include collaboration between the stakeholders in the transition process: children, families, educators, and communities. Strategies to generate data about transition programs and practices that can inform these broad measures include questionnaires seeking information about specific transition activities, their usefulness and use; interviews with those who participated in the transition, including children; contact logs, to track contact, those contacted, topics discussed; the planned – and actual – follow-up; and a transitions menu, identifying the options for transitions practices, as well as those implemented and those responsible for implementing these.

Building on the publication of the *Guidelines for Effective Transition to School* (Dockett & Perry, 2001), and the *Indicators of Progress* tool (Dockett & Perry, 2006), the *Peridot Education Transition Reflection Instrument* outlined in Chapter 8 provides an example of a comprehensive rating scale for evaluating programs. In the following discussion, we focus on some specific strategies that provide evidence to feed into this and other measures. While rating scales are valuable tools for evaluating programs, we stress the important of evidence to support these ratings.

Identifying the program theory – the mechanism for change – is integral to evaluating transition programs. Chapter 4 shared an example, suggesting that a series of visits might contribute to building a sense of belonging and familiarity with school based on trusting and respectful relationships (the proposed mechanism for change). In the following discussion, we consider the methods that might be used to access adult perspectives of and/or how activities – such as school visits – contribute to the identified mechanism for change and the anticipated outcome of an effective transition to school.

Questionnaires, such as the one noted in what follows, can be a useful method for seeking input about participation and the perceived usefulness of transition practices and programs, contributing to outcome evaluations. As noted in Chapter 7A, they can also be used as starting points for discussions about what might be taken for granted. In this example, Boyle notes that a questionnaire helped to identify sources of tension as educators realised how their different practice traditions contributed to different perspectives about transition and what was important to include in transition programs. Establishing this early was critical to building shared understandings and common goals for the transition program.

Table 7.1 provides an excerpt from a questionnaire that was distributed to educators in both ECEC and school contexts and, with relevant modifications, to parents of children starting school (Dockett & Perry, 2006). It was based on a questionnaire developed by Pianta and Kraft-Sayre (2003) and has been modified for use in a range of contexts (see, for example, Einarsdóttir, Perry, & Dockett, 2008). It formed one aspect of an outcome evaluation, seeking input from participants after relevant transition programs had been completed.

Rating scales seek responses to closed survey questions. This questionnaire included a rating scale where respondents were asked to rate specific transition practices as *very*, *somewhat*, or *not useful*. As another example, the 2010 evaluation of the *Transition: A Positive Start to School Initiative* in Victoria (SuccessWorks, 2010) asked respondents to rate their perceptions of the initiative on a scale of 1 to 5, labelled *very ineffective*, *ineffective*, *neither effective nor ineffective*, *effective*, and *very effective*.

Several standardised *rating scales* have been used in evaluations of transition experiences. Mostly, these involve adults rating children's adjustment to school, which then contribute to assessments of the effectiveness of transition. Examples include the *Social Skills Rating System* (Gresham & Elliott, 1990); the *Student–Teacher Relationship Scale* (Pianta, 1992, 2001), and the *Teacher Rating Scale for School Adjustment* (Birch & Ladd, 1997). Analysis of data from these scales derives from established procedures and interpretations. Using these and other standardised rating scales may require specific expertise and may incur costs to access the measures. While these established measures are likely to provide in-depth information about some aspects of transition, focusing only on adult perspectives, particularly only on those of educators, is unlikely to yield information about child or family perspectives.

Data from self-developed questionnaires, such as that in Table 7.1, can be analysed using frequency counts – for example, indicating how many people from different groups participated in the different transition practices and, of those, how many found the practice to be useful – as well as more sophisticated analysis of inter-group patterns. For example, analysis of the full questionnaire utilised Chi-square analysis of group responses and indicated significant levels of difference among teachers and parents around the importance of children's

Table 7.1 Questionnaire on the usefulness of transition practices (ECEC educators).

The following activities relate to helping children make the transition to school. For each activity, please indicate whether you participated in the activity with children who had not yet started school. If you did participate in the activity, please indicate whether you found the activity to be *very useful*, *somewhat useful*, or *not useful* for children and families by ticking the appropriate box.

Transition activities	Did you participate?	Very useful	Somewhat useful	Not useful
Children who had not yet started school visited a first-year-of-school classroom				
Children who had not yet started school visited the first-year-of-school classroom they are expected to attend when they start school				
I visited a first-year-of-school classroom				
A first-year-of-school teacher visited my ECEC setting				
Primary schoolchildren visited my ECEC setting				
Children who had not yet started school participated in orientation to school visits				
Parents visited the school to attend an information session about school				
Children who had not yet started school participated in a schoolwide event, such as assembly				

academic preparation for school (Dockett & Perry, 2004). However, such analysis does require a substantial number of respondents from each group in order to make comparisons. To generalise results further than the respondent group, it is also necessary to show how participants form a representative sample of the targeted population. Despite these challenges, these data and their analysis make valuable contributions to the evaluation of transition programs.

At the same time, it is important to recognise what responses such as these do not tell us. For example, they do not indicate why a practice was or was not useful, what could be done to make practices more useful for respondents, or why they did or did not take part in the nominated practices. Some follow-up open-ended questions within the questionnaire can be used to seek this information, or such questions could be asked in follow-up interviews with participants.

Sometimes, it is convenient for all involved to create and distribute a questionnaire electronically. While this does offer some ease of circulation and analysis, as many programs perform some basic statistical processes such as frequency counts, it may also raise some challenges. For example, some organisations are not supportive of staff using programs that are hosted overseas or where data are stored on overseas servers; some potential participants may not have easy or regular internet access; and some may not have the required literacy skills to complete the questionnaire. As a result, response rates may be low and not necessarily representative. In several of our studies, both educators and parents have indicated that they would rather have a conversation than complete an online questionnaire.

The apparent simplicity of many questionnaires and surveys often belies the complex elements of their development. Constructing a survey or questionnaire that generates useful data and that people are willing to complete can be a challenging task. For example, the number and nature of questions asked can influence people's responses as well as their willingness to complete the entire process, and questions that seem intrusive or irrelevant are unlikely to be answered. Following simple rules such as only asking questions that are relevant, providing a balance of open-ended as well as closed questions, and indicating how long completing the questionnaire might take can help make the process manageable for all. Testing the questionnaire out with a few people who can provide critical feedback is always a good idea before distributing it widely. These considerations come on top of the ethical issues that apply to all data generation, such as clarity around the source and purpose of the questionnaire, how information will be stored, and issues of confidentiality and voluntary participation. These issues are discussed in more detail later in the chapter, as well as in a range of research texts and guidelines (see, for example, Diem, 2004; Fink, 2002; Harlacher, 2016).

Adults may prefer to engage in *conversations and/or interviews* rather than complete a questionnaire. Depending on the context, the same questions can be asked, but in a face-to-face interaction and with opportunities to follow up issues or concerns. In many of our projects, we tend to rely on informal or conversational interviews, where we can ask an opening question, such as "What has been your experience of the transition to school?" and invite people to tell their story. Follow-up questions can focus on the experiences of other members of the family, perceptions of what worked or did not work, and why this might have been. While the aim of conversational interviews is to find out about transition, it is also important that the interaction not feel like an interrogation but is perceived as an opportunity for participants to tell their story and for the interviewer to listen. Sometimes the inclusion of artefacts – such as a photo or drawing – can act as a prompt for conversations as well as contribute to a relaxed atmosphere, as in the following example.

Example: Photo elicitation

Miller (2016) used photographs as prompts in her conversations with families about their transition activities. She asked participating parents to photograph activities that *might help their children at school* over the period of a week. Families had control over what images were taken and retained. Cameras were provided and collected after that period. Prints of the photos were used as prompts for discussion in follow-up interviews.

The location of conversations and interviews is important; people are unlikely to share concerns in a public space where they can be overheard or in locations where they do not feel comfortable. Sometimes people will be more likely to engage in a conversation in a neutral location, such as a coffee shop or community space. While conversations and interviews can be informal, if the data are to contribute to the evaluation, they must be documented in some way. With permission, the interactions can be recorded in notes or electronically. These data will need to be stored securely and any transcriptions de-identified to maintain confidentiality. With permission, the following conversation was recorded electronically and transcribed for analysis.

Example: Conversational interview

Interviewer: How will you know if the transition program has been effective?

Parent: I think that . . . I think that if Lulu settles in with a minimum of disruption, I think that it will have been effective for her . . . I am not expecting anything, I would not expect anything less of her, with her personality and how familiar she is with the school, so it will probably have been effective if it's not disruptive.

Interviewer: What about for you, how will you know if the transition program has been effective for you?

Parent: For me . . . I would like to hear something from the teachers in the first few weeks . . . to know whether or not the children have settled. I will expect to know, just to know if they have settled in well, and, communication from the teachers would

152 Sue Dockett and Bob Perry

	be a good start. Just to ensure that the teacher knows the kids . . .
Interviewer:	Can you tell me some more about knowing the kids?
Parent:	The kids come from different preschools, so there's a lot the teachers will need to do to get to know about the kids and find out different relationships, and how they work. It will be quite a difficult thing for them to do over the transition period.
Interviewer:	You said you would like to have communication. How would you expect that to come?
Parent:	I think the teachers will use [an online program]. They didn't have any communication strategies when my son started school, and it meant that we weren't aware of what was happening in the classrooms. It would be nice to have a little bit more understanding of what was going on in the classroom, especially in those first months, when you are kind of unsure how your child is doing at school.

Sometimes, adults will be interested in participating in group conversations or interviews. These can follow the structure of focus groups (Smithson, 2008) or more informal group conversations. For example, the conversations within a transition network about a specific topic might constitute an informal group conversation. Documenting group events (with permission) can include video- or audio-recording as well as field notes or involve members of the group creating their own documentation, such as that in Figure 7.2, which records a group

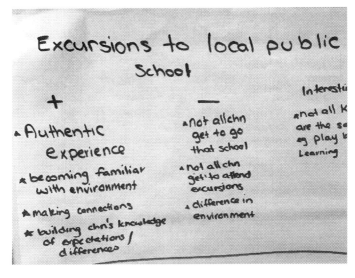

Figure 7.2 ECEC educators' brainstorming.

Evaluation of programs – perspectives of adults 153

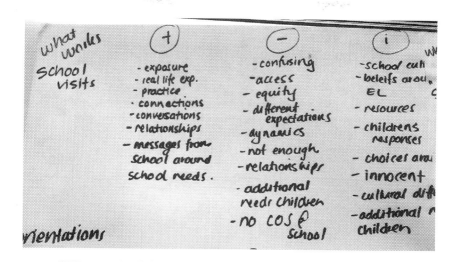

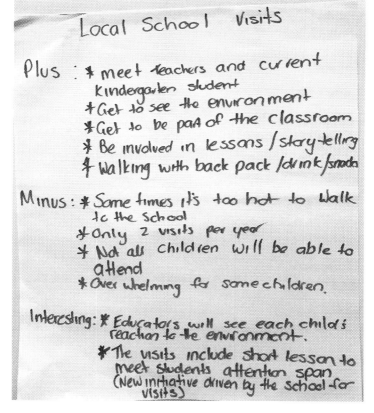

Figure 7.2 (Continued)

brainstorming session organised using the PMI procedure (de Bono, 1988) to consider school visits made by children and their ECEC educators as part of transition programs. In this example, small groups of educators explored and documented the plusses (P) or positive aspects, the minuses (M) or negative aspects, and the interesting (I) aspects of school visits.

Analysis of narrative data can take several forms. All begin with being familiar with the data, so it is critical that they be read carefully. From this, it may be possible to discern particular words or phrases that occur across the data or to identify common themes. Content analysis (Miles & Huberman, 1994) involves breaking up the text into units of meaning. This may involve focusing on specific words or phrases or synonyms of these. Grouping these together helps to condense them into codes. For example, across the three group reports listed, some similarities can be seen, and some possible groupings and codes that form descriptive labels are noted in Table 7.2. Several codes that seem to belong together can then be

Table 7.2 Sorting data into codes and categories.

Meaning units	Code	Category
Authentic experience	Experiencing school	Experiencing school
Real-life experience		
Be involved in lessons/storytelling		
Get to see the environment	Familiarity with the environment	Experiencing school
Becoming familiar with the environment		
Practice		
Get to be part of the classroom		
Building children's knowledge of expectations/differences	Differences in the environment	Experiencing school
Differences in environment		
Different expectations		
Cultural differences		
School culture		
Not all children will be able to attend	Access	Access
Not all children get to attend excursions		
Access, equity		
Not all children go to that school		
Overwhelming for some	Children's reactions	Children's reactions
Educators will see each child's reaction to the environment		
Meet teachers and current kindergarten students	Relationships	Relationships
Making connections		
Conversations		
Relationships		

sorted into categories. Categories are made up of codes that relate to the same or similar issues. These can also be labelled. With rich and detailed data, it may be possible to coalesce categories into themes (Taylor-Powell & Renner, 2003).

Another approach to analysis applies an existing coding framework to data. As an example, we asked the same question – "What are the first five things that come to mind when you think of children starting school?" – to different groups of educators in 1999 and 2015. To enable comparisons across the groups, we used the same coding framework that had been established for the earlier study (see also Chapter 6). This identified eight categories of responses:

Adjustment: social adjustment to the school context, including interpersonal and organisational adjustment

Disposition: children's attitudes towards or feelings about school or learning

Educational environment: concern about the nature of the school environment

Family issues: issues related to family functioning or involvement with the school

Knowledge: ideas, facts, or concepts that needed to be known in order to enter school

Physical: physical attributes, needs or characteristics of children, including issues about safety, health, and age

Rules: fitting in with the school and school expectations

Skills: small units of action that could be observed or inferred from observable behaviour

Mapping responses across the categories resulted in Figure 7.3 (Dockett, Perry, & Davies, 2015), suggesting a shift in emphasis over this 15-year period.

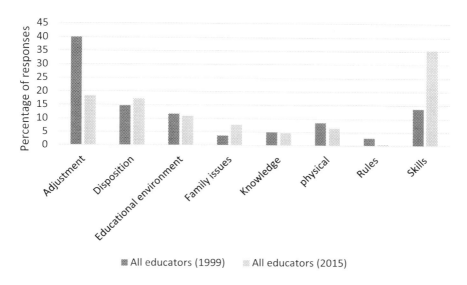

Figure 7.3 Comparison of educator responses over time.

Contact logs document contacts and interactions relevant to transition. We have seen these used effectively by families – particularly those whose children have special education needs – as they make decisions about which school might be most appropriate for their children and experience the transition opportunities available. Parents using these have reported that they help them keep track of people they have spoken with, their contact details, and the topics discussed. Table 7.3 shows one example of a contact log developed by parents.

Table 7.3 Contact log.

Date	Talked with	Where	Topic discussed	Outcome	Follow-up

Hopps (2014) has used logs to explore the nature and type of communication among educators around transitions. Figure 7.4 provides an example. Data from the logs can inform discussions among educators about the most effective forms of communication and strategies to promote these. Analysis can identify preferred modes of communication, as well as the regularity and perceived value of these. When different partners in transition programs complete similar logs, direct comparisons can be made.

Contact logs can also be used by educators to note which children and/or families have participated in specific transition practices and any specific responses or issues relevant to that involvement. For example, it may become clear that several children/families participated in all transition activities, while others participated in only a few. It may also indicate that some children/families starting school have not participated in any transition activities. Knowing this can help educators target information to support the transition rather than assuming that all children and families have had similar experiences.

A range of *creative processes* can also be used to record data from adults. Some – albeit not many in our experiences – are happy to draw about their experiences; others have referred to photographs or other visual images related to their

Communication Diary Log

Preschool _____ Name of communicator _____ Start date _____ Finish date _____

Date	SOURCE			TOPIC	CHANNEL					LENGTH	FEEDBACK		EVALUATION
	Person	School	Sent	Received		Face to face	Phone	Email	Paper Based	Other		One way	Two way	

Figure 7.4 Communication Diary Log (Hopps, 2014, p. 395).

Evaluation of programs – perspectives of adults 157

experiences. For example, McLeod and Anderson (2020) invited their participants to select one image from a set of stimulus cards that reflected the understandings they had gained from the project. Working in pairs, each participant discussed how they and their practice had changed while the other recorded their comments. Analysis of the comments contributed to the evaluation.

In a similar way, we have invited participants across several projects to consider the image on the *Transition to School: Position Statement* (Educational Transitions and Change (ETC) Research Group, 2011) (Figure 7.5) to reflect on their experiences of transition. The task is an open-ended one and usually involves choosing one of the figures from the image – or one that is missing – and describing the experiences of that person as they make the transition to school (see also Chapter 3A).

Observation can be an overlooked method for documenting information about transition. While educators are often quite skilled in observing children's actions and interactions, these skills may not be applied in contexts involving adults. Yet much may be gleaned from observing others and from having others observe our own practice. Observations can provide clues as to the levels of comfort people feel in different environments and can also highlight changes in actions over time. They can also help to identify how information shared or understandings generated through the transition program are applied in practice. For example, indicating whether people know where to go to access specific support or resources or preferred communication strategies.

Many *documents* are produced and/or completed during transition programs. These include notices advertising the program, documentation about specific practices, letters to families, information packs for ECEC settings, schools, and/

Figure 7.5 Transition to School: Position Statement image.
Source: Image by Bernard Caleo. Copyright Sue Dockett and Bob Perry.

or families, social storybooks for children, school-based forms, information provided by ECEC settings and other organisations, as well as transition to school statements. Further, there may be organisational or systemwide policies or resources that are relevant to transition. Analysis of these can indicate prevailing conceptions of the transition to school and its purpose and intended outcomes (Hard, Lee, & Dockett, 2018).

Many other methods can be used to generate evaluation data from adults. They include journal keeping, photographic records, and creative expressions. It is important not only to consider how to generate data but also to consider why these have been generated and how they will be analysed. Before data can be analysed, it is necessary to consider what counts as data. Is it images, written word or spoken words, numerical records, or documents? It can be all of these. The images shared by participants, what is said in conversations or interviews and written on questionnaire responses and tabulations of involvement can all count as data. What is important is that these data accurately reflect what participants choose to share. In quantitative analysis, the terms *reliability* and *validity* are used to refer to the consistency and accuracy of the data (Cohen, Manion, & Morrison, 2018). As noted in Chapter 6, qualitative analyses focus on the trustworthiness of data, as evidenced by credibility, dependability, and transferability (Guba & Lincoln, 1989).

Ethical considerations

The same principles for ethical engagement noted in Chapters 4 and 6 are relevant in seeking adult perspectives of transition to school. While educators may have a professional responsibility to evaluate their practice, the notion of voluntary, informed participation remains central to ethical practice. So too do the principles of respect for those involved and commitments to confidentiality.

Power relations exist within and about schools and ECEC settings (Barnett & Camfield, 2016). These relations may be heightened when parents believe that their decisions about participating in an evaluation, as well as the information they contribute, could influence their children's experiences. It is quite likely that some parents will feel uncomfortable sharing their experiences with their child's teacher or teacher's colleague, especially if these are negative. It may even be that some parents prefer to gloss over concerns rather than risk rocking the boat. It is also possible that some educators will be hesitant to be seen to criticise their colleagues or will feel uncomfortable questioning something that has been taken for granted for some time.

Not all adults will choose to participate in evaluations, and of those who do, it is likely that some will choose to participate in some aspects rather than all. For example, questionnaire response rates can be quite low, and among those responding, it is likely that some respondents will choose to answer some but not all questions. Despite these challenges, it is important that participation in an evaluation is open to all involved and that participation choices are available and respected. Reaching out to all potential participants will take time and may involve offering several different methods for contributing information. It may also require the involvement of trusted others – such as interpreters, community professionals, other parents/family members, and educators or external members of the evaluation team – in data collection processes. While respecting the right of adults to choose participation, it is important to offer viable and realistic choices and to respect the choices made. Knowing what constitute viable and realistic choices will be enhanced by the involvement of a range of people in the evaluation planning and implementation.

As well as considering who invites people to contribute to the evaluation, we have noted the importance of location – such as where to conduct an interview or conversation. Issues of timing and method also are important. For example, it is usually not appropriate to engage in an informal interview as parents are rushing to get to work in the morning or when they have just collected children from school and both parents and children just want to get home. The method used also impacts on participation: a lengthy or poorly designed questionnaire, an interview that includes intrusive questions, or a task that does not make sense is unlikely to generate a lot of helpful responses.

Ethical principles apply to the generation of data, as well as the analysis and reporting of these. Issues of confidentiality are paramount, particularly as it is possible that the evaluation may access sensitive information. Even when information may not be considered sensitive, it can be disconcerting for someone to see comments or images shared in an individual conversation highlighted in a report, displayed on a poster, or magnified many times in a presentation. Respecting confidentiality requires the careful management of data and their reporting, as well as care to avoid possible harm or discomfort.

Conclusion

The focus in this chapter on generating and analysing data from adults in the evaluation of transition to school programs is a reminder that the transition to school does not only involve or impact upon those children starting school; it also involves many adults. As noted in Chapter 7A, the beliefs and expectations of adults, as well as their actions and interactions, have a substantial impact on what happens during the transition.

In this chapter, we have described several methods for accessing the perspectives of adults, some of the ways in which these data may be analysed, and some of the ethical considerations that need to underpin the evaluation. In the following chapters, we consider how these data might be used in reporting the evaluation and in prompting changes to transition programs and practices.

7A Professional relationships and spaces as children start school

Tess Boyle

Introduction

Generation of data about transition to school programs through the many different methods outlined in Chapter 7 is necessary but not sufficient when evaluating such programs. Analysis of these data and by whom this analysis is undertaken are critical and sometimes quite fraught challenges for early childhood education communities. In this chapter, I report on my work with the Building Bridges Professional Learning Community (BBPLC) which was established to investigate shared concerns about transitions to school practices, including the analysis of data around the effectiveness of transition to school programs. The BBPLC provides an example of a long-term cross-sectorial approach establishing professional relationships and spaces around transition to school.

Site

The BBPLC is located in the Australian state of New South Wales. In this state, different "practice traditions" (Kemmis, Wilkinson et al., 2014, p. 31) influence policies and practices in the pre-compulsory and compulsory school sectors. Identified as "two worlds" (Dunlop, 2007, p. 165), these sectors have fundamentally different philosophical foundations. Disparities between them are most evident as children transition from one to the other. Efforts to establish continuity of learning during this critical time are often challenged by the physical dislocation and diversity of sites across the sectors. In contrast, the BBPLC is ideally situated, as almost all of the children who attend the Long Day Care Centre (LDC) at the site transition to the co-located primary school. Knowing the two worlds at this site are separated by no more than a concrete pathway, it is illogical to contemplate that before the establishment of the BBPLC, interactions between them were limited to infrequent "functional linkages" (Boyle & Petriwskyj, 2014, p. 393). Motivated by shared concerns about missed opportunities to enhance continuity and alignment and tensions about divergent practices, the BBPLC was formed as a communicative space (Habermas, 1984, 1987) to negotiate shared understandings of transitions practices and the conditions shaping them (Kemmis, Wilkinson et al., 2014).

DOI: 10.4324/9781003055112-13

Theoretical framework

Building on an established professional practice at the site, the BBPLC followed the inclusive principles of a learning community (Dufour et al., 2010). Mindful of existing tensions at the site, including asymmetrical power relations, the first action of the BBPLC was to negotiate a set of protocols (norms) to clarify expectations, promote open dialogue, support professional relationships, and guide the collective efforts of the group. This stance aligned with and was augmented by a critical participatory action research (Kemmis, McTaggart, & Nixon, 2014) approach. Informed by critical theory (Habermas, 1984, 1987) and the theory of practice architectures (Kemmis, Wilkinson et al., 2014), this approach acknowledges that participants come to the research with concerns and a commitment to take action based on their critical views of and shared concerns about current practice. Further, it highlights the capacity of communicative spaces to change practices by establishing shared understandings of practices and the conditions shaping them. In the case of the BBPLC, a shared concern about current transition to school practices generated a collective commitment to change. This commitment, while initially tentative, was forged over time and, in time, became a critical enabling condition of the group.

Evidence and analysis

The BBPLC was established in 2012 and continues to meet regularly. It has survived the rigours of time and fluctuating membership – a testament to the collective commitment of its members and changed conditions at the site. The information that follows is a snapshot of the actions and analysis undertaken by the BBPLC in a particular year. As such, it provides empirical evidence of a long-term cross-sectorial approach to changing practices and the conditions holding them in place.

In this snapshot, the participants of the BBPLC included four early years teachers: two from the preschool room in the LDC and two from the kindergarten (first-year-of-school) room in the primary school. Four executive staff also were involved: the director of the LDC, the principal and assistant principal of the primary school, and an assistant director of the systemic authority governing the school. All were directly involved in transition to school practices and policies. The author, who has a long-term association with the systemic authority and shared the concerns of the group, was invited to join the research in the role of "critical friend" (Kemmis, McTaggart et al., 2014, p. 189). Consistent with the collaborative nature of the approach, the members of the BBPLC negotiated the cycles of action, evidence to be gathered, and decisions about how it would be used. For want of a better organisational structure, the cycles of action mirrored the four school terms. The analysis was an iterative and generative approach, as evidence gathered in one cycle informed the actions of the next. Table 7A.1 provides an overview of the evidence gathered across the four cycles in this particular year.

162 Tess Boyle

Table 7A.1 Evidence gathered.

Cycle 1 22.01–24.04	Research Journal Survey questionnaire Meeting transcripts (2 hours 25 minutes) Interview transcripts (7 hours 8 minutes)
Cycle 2 29.04–28.06	Research Journal Meeting transcripts (9 hours 46 minutes)
Cycle 3 15.07–20.09	Research Journal Meeting transcripts (6 hours 51 minutes)
Cycle 4 08.10–20.12	Research Journal Survey questionnaire Meeting transcripts (5 hours 20 minutes) Interview transcripts (5 hours 8 minutes)

Figure 7A.1 Collated response to Q2 of the Cycle 1 survey questionnaire

In cycle one, a survey questionnaire was developed using Qualtrics™. Its purpose was to gather information about the BBPLC members' qualifications, experience, aspirations, and expectations. Figure 7A.1 illustrates a Wordle™ compilation of the responses to Question 2 "What do you hope to achieve by participating in the BBPLC?" This image provided a stimulus for a conversation at the cycle two BBPLC meeting about the aspirations of the group and the formation of a collective aim. The opportunity to engage in a sustained, informed, and robust conversation about this response revealed two significant outcomes. First, solidarity around the commitment to establishing shared understandings and second, the importance of negotiating these from the perspective of both worlds.

The BBPLC members set the meeting agendas, and, at their request, a pre-reading for discussion was included for each meeting. Audio-recordings of the meetings were transcribed, validated, thematically analysed, and presented to the group for discussion and elaboration of points of interest. These discussions informed the design of subsequent cycles of action. The inclusion of semi-structured interviews (Kvale, 2007) in cycles 1 and 4 was an unexpected addition to the schedule. Their purpose was to provide an opportunity to speak confidentially about lived experiences (Flick, 2009) and raise matters of concern/interest beyond the gaze of the group. The online questionnaire survey responses informed the interview questions; transcripts of these interviews were thematically analysed and key themes presented to the group at the subsequent meeting for discussion. This interview evidence revealed tensions about practices and the conditions at the site. Discussing the collated results in the ensuing meeting provided an opportunity to activate engagement with "unwelcome truths" (Mockler & Groundwater-Smith, 2015, p. 603).

Changing practices

A source of tension uncovered by the interview evidence related to practices associated with gathering information about the children commencing school. A *Ready for School* checklist, developed by the first-year-of-school teachers, was comprised of questions about literacy and numeracy and social, emotional, and fine/gross motor skills. A checklist was completed for each child commencing school the following year. The assessment was informed by the teacher's observations of the child and a conversation with the preschool room teacher. Discussions about the checklist within the BBPLC revealed fundamental differences in and a lack of knowledge of philosophies informing teaching/learning, curriculum/learning frameworks, assessment, and outcomes resulting in incongruent expectations of children (Dockett & Perry, 2007). The practice, undertaken with the best of intentions, exemplifies a hierarchical approach to transition to school that positions the pre-compulsory sector as the *sender* and the school sector as the *receiver*. The lack of alignment between the outcomes mandated by the LDC's nationally endorsed learning framework (Department of Education, Skills and Employment, 2019) and those of the school's state-endorsed curriculum (New South Wales Education Standards Authority, n.d.) was identified as a constraining condition influencing illogical practices and tensions at the site. Responding to this finding, the BBPLC negotiated a shared goal *to define and develop transitions statements*. Achieving this goal required their collective commitment to negotiate new understandings and relationships, review current practices, and engage in professional learning (Boyle & Grieshaber, 2017).

Sectoral differences were identified as a source of contrary practices and divergent understandings. These differences included structural elements, such as physical environments and resources. However, it was considerations of practice, in particular the philosophies that inform them, that produced critical and generative conversations. Within the dialogic space provided by the BBPLC, members pushed boundaries, took risks to defend their philosophical stance, and articulated how deeply held beliefs influenced their practices. New understandings of each other's world and the conditions shaping different practices led to the realisation that both worlds are important and that neither should be compromised or privileged. This new and shared understanding laid the foundations for new conditions to emerge at the site. Under these conditions, the members of the BBPLC worked together to design and develop mutually respectful and relevant transition to school statements. The collective analysis of and sustained conversations about the evidence generated by the BBPLC led to transformative changes to transition to school practices and professional relationships. The LDC continues to use the statements to communicate learning outcomes to parents, and the school uses them as part of its enrolment policy and practices.

Conclusion

This research captures the lived experiences of a particular group of people in a specific site and point in time. The findings serve the purpose of sharing a story with an appropriate audience so that they may learn something from it – in much the same way one might learn from history and the experiences of others. Stake (1995) describes this transference of meaning as a "naturalistic generalisation" (p. 85). For the author, a key learning from the BBPLC was that while the recognition and acceptance of different practice traditions at this site did not magically resolve cross-sectoral tensions, it did facilitate acceptance of and respect for immutable differences. Acknowledging that transitions practices are not universal, the responsive site-specific approach adopted by the BBPLC is consistent with contemporary considerations that account for the ways different structural, developmental, and contextual continuities influence the lived experience of transitioning to school (Boyle, Petriwskyj, & Grieshaber, 2018; Dockett & Einarsdóttir, 2017).

References

Arndt, A. K., Rothe, A., Urban, M., & Werning, R. (2013). Supporting and stimulating the learning of socioeconomically disadvantaged children – Perspectives of parents and educators in the transition from preschool to primary school. *European Early Childhood Education Research Journal, 21*, 23–38. https://doi.org/10.1080/1350293X.2012.760336

Barblett, L., Barratt-Pugh, C., Kilgallon, P., & Maloney, C. (2011). Transition from long day care to kindergarten: Continuity or not? *Australasian Journal of Early Childhood, 36*(2), 42–50. https://doi.org/10.1177/183693911103600207

Barnett, C., & Camfield, L. (2016). Ethics in evaluation. *Journal of Development Effectiveness, 8*(4), 528–534. https://doi.org/10.1080/19439342.2016.1244554

Baumfield, V., Hall, E., & Wall, K. (2013). *Action research in education: Learning through practitioner enquiry* (2nd ed.). London: SAGE. https://doi.org/10.4135/9781526402240

Birch, S., & Ladd, G. (1997). The teacher-child relationship and children's early school adjustment. *Journal of School Psychology, 35*(1), 61–79. https://doi.org/10.1016/S0022-4405(96)00029-5

Boyle, T., & Grieshaber, S. (2017). Linking learning: Developing cross-sector policies for transitions to school. In R. Maclean (Ed.), *Life in schools and classrooms: Past, present and future* (pp. 369–384). Singapore: Springer. https://doi.org/10.1007/978-981-10-3654-5_23

Boyle, T., & Petriwskyj, A. (2014). Transitions to school: Reframing professional relationships. *Early Years: An International Research Journal*, 34(4), 392–404. https://doi.org/10.1080/09575146.2014.953042

Boyle, T., Petriwskyj, A., & Grieshaber, S. (2018). Reframing transitions to school as continuity practices: The role of practice architectures. *Australian Education Researcher*, 45, 419–434. https://doi.org/10.1007/s13384-018-0272-0

Chan, W. (2012). Expectations for the transition from kindergarten to primary school amongst teachers, parents and children. *Early Child Development and Care*, 182(5), 639–664. https://doi.org/10.1080/03004430.2011.569543

Coghlan, A. (2011). Participatory evaluation. In S. Mathison (Ed.), *Encyclopedia of evaluation* (pp. 292–296). Thousand Oaks, CA: Sage. https://doi.org/10.4135/9781412950558

Cohen, L., Manion, L., & Morrison, K. (2018). *Research methods in education* (8th ed.). London: Routledge.

Correia, K., & Marques-Pinto, A. (2016). Adaptation in the transition to school: Perspectives of parents, preschool and primary school teachers. *Educational Research*, 58(3), 247–264. https://doi.org/10.1080/00131881.2016.1200255

de Bono, E. (1988). *De Bono's thinking course*. London: BBC Books.

Department for Education and Child Development, South Australia. (2014). *Transition to school rubric*. www.beachroadpartnership.sa.edu.au/wp-content/uploads/2013/03/Transition-to-school-rubric.pdf

Diem, K. (2004). *A step-by-step guide to developing effective questionnaires and survey procedures for program evaluation and research*. New Brunswick, NJ: Rutgers Cooperative Research & Extension. http://fs.cahnrs.wsu.edu/wp-content/uploads/2015/09/A-Step-By-Step-Guide-to-Developing-Effective-Questionnaires.pdf

Dockett, S., & Einarsdóttir, J. (2017). Continuity and change as children start school. In N. Ballam, B. Perry, & A. Garpelin (Eds.), *Pedagogies of educational transitions. European and antipodean research* (pp. 133–150). Dordrecht: Springer. https://doi.org/10.1007/978-3-319-43118-5_9

Dockett, S., & Perry, B. (2001). Starting school: Effective transitions. *Early Childhood Research and Practice*, 3(2). www.ecrp.illinois.edu/v3n2/dockett.html

Dockett, S., & Perry, B. (2004). What makes a successful transition to school? Views of Australian parents and teachers. *International Journal of Early Years Education*, 12, 217–230. https://doi.org/10.1080/0966 976042000268690.

Dockett, S., & Perry, B. (2006). *Starting school: A handbook for early childhood educators*. Sydney: Pademelon Press.

Dockett, S., & Perry, B. (2007). *Transitions to school: Perceptions, expectations and experiences*. Sydney: University of New South Wales Press.

Dockett, S., & Perry, B. (2014). *Continuity of learning: A resource to support effective transition to school and school age care*. Canberra, ACT: Australian Government Department of Education. https://docs.education.gov.au/system/files/doc/other/pdf_with_bookmarking_-_continuity_of_learning-_30_october_2014_1_0.pdf

References – Chapters 7 and 7A

Dockett, S., Perry, B., & Davies, J. (2015). *Starting school: Connecting policy and practice*. Presentation at the Pedagogies of Educational Transition international conference. Canberra, February.

Dufour, R., Dufour, R., Eaker, R., & Many, T. (2010). *Learning by doing: A handbook for professional learning communities at work*. Bloomington, IL: Solution Tree Press.

Dunlop, A.-W. (2007). Bridging research, policy and practice. In A.-W. Dunlop & H. Fabian (Eds.), *Informing transitions in the early years: Research, policy and practice* (pp. 151–168). Berkshire: Open University Press.

Educational Transitions and Change (ETC) Research Group. (2011). *Transition to school: Position Statement*. https://arts-ed.csu.edu.au/education/transitions/publications/Position-Statement.pdf

Einarsdóttir, J. (2006). From the pre-school to primary school: When different contexts meet. *Scandinavian Journal of Educational Research, 50*(2), 165–184. https://doi.org/10.1080/00313830600575965

Einarsdóttir, J., Perry, B., & Dockett, S. (2008). Transition to school practices: Comparisons from Iceland and Australia. *Early Years, 28*(1), 47–60. https://doi.org/10.1080/09575140801924689

Fink, A. (2002). *The survey kit* (2nd ed.). London: SAGE.

Flick, U. (2009). *An introduction to qualitative research* (4th ed.). London: SAGE.

Gill, S., Winters, D., & Friedman, D. (2006). Educators' views of pre-kindergarten and kindergarten readiness and transition practices. *Contemporary Issues in Early Childhood, 7*(3), 213–227. https://doi.org/10.2304/ciec.2006.7.3.213

Gresham, F. M., & Elliott, S. N. (1990). *Social skills rating system*. Circle Pines, MN: American Guidance Service.

Griebel, W., & Niesel, R. (2009). A developmental psychology perspective in Germany: Co-construction of transitions between family and education system by the child, parents and pedagogues. *Early Years, 29*(1), 59–68. https://doi.org/10.1080/09575140802652230

Griebel, W., Wildgruber, A., Schuster, A., & Radan, J. (2017). Transition to being parents of a school-child: Parental perspective on coping of parents and child nine months after school start. In S. Dockett, W. Griebel, & B. Perry (Eds.), *Families and transition to school* (pp. 21–36). Cham, Switzerland: Springer. https://doi.org/10.1007/978-3-319-58329-7_2

Guba, E. G., & Lincoln, Y. (1989). *Fourth generation evaluation*. Newbury Park, CA: SAGE.

Habermas, J. (1984). *The theory of communicative action: Volume 1 – Reason and rationalisation of society* (T. McCarthy, Trans.). Boston, MA: Beacon.

Habermas, J. (1987). *The theory of communicative action: Volume 2 – Lifeworld and system: A critique of functionalist reason* (T. McCarthy, Trans.). Boston, MA: Beacon.

Hard, N., Lee, P., & Dockett, S. (2018). Mapping the policy landscape of Australian early childhood education policy through document analysis. *Australasian Journal of Early Childhood, 43*(2), 4–13. https://doi.org/10.23965/AJEC.43.2.01

Harlacher, J. (2016). *An educator's guide to questionnaire development* (REL 2016–108). Washington, DC: U.S. Department of Education, Institute of Education Sciences, National Center for Education Evaluation and Regional Assistance, Regional Educational Laboratory Central. http://ies.ed.gov/ncee/edlabs

Hopps, K. (2014). *Intersetting communication and the transition to school.* Unpublished PhD thesis, Charles Sturt University. https://researchoutput.csu.edu.au/en/publications/intersetting-communication-and-the-transition-to-school-3

Hustedt, J., Buell, M., Hallam, R., & Pinder, W. (2018). While kindergarten has changed, some beliefs stay the same: Kindergarten teachers' beliefs about readiness. *Journal of Research in Childhood Education, 32*(1), 52–66. https://doi.org/10.1080/02568543.2017.1393031

Kemmis, S., McTaggart, R., & Nixon, R. (2014). *The action research planner: Doing critical participatory action research.* Singapore: Springer. https://doi.org/10.1007/978-981-4560-67-2

Kemmis, S., Wilkinson, J., Edwards-Groves, C., Hardy, I., Grootenboer, P., & Bristol, L. (2014). *Changing practices, changing education.* Singapore: Springer. https://doi.org/10.1007/978-981-4560-47-4

KidsMatter. (2013). *Transition matters: A resource for starting school for early childhood educators and school staff.* https://talkingtransitionblog.files.wordpress.com/2018/06/kmp20130228_transitionmatters_0.pdf

Kirk-Downey, T., & Hinton, S. (2014). The Wollongong transition to school experience: A big step for children, families and the community. In B. Perry, S. Dockett, & A. Petriwskyj (Eds.), *Transitions to schools – International research, policy and practice* (pp. 229–247). Dordrecht: Springer. https://doi.org/10.1007/978-94-007-7350-9_17

Kirk-Downey, T., & Perry, B. (2006). Making transition to school a community event: The Wollongong experience. *International Journal of Transitions in Childhood, 2,* 40–49.

Kvale, S. (2007). *Doing interviews.* London: SAGE.

Lansdown, G. (2005). *Can you hear me? The rights of young children to participate in decisions affecting them.* Working paper No. 36. The Hague: Bernard van Leer Foundation.

Lin, H., Lawrence, F., & Gorrell, J. (2003). Kindergarten teachers' views of children's readiness for school. *Early Childhood Research Quarterly, 18,* 225–237. https://doi.org/10.1016/S0885-2006(03)00028-0

Margetts, K., & Phatudi, N. (2013). Transition of children from preschool and home contexts to Grade 1 in two township primary schools in South Africa. *European Early Childhood Education Research Journal, 21,* 39–52. https://doi.org/10.1080/1350293X.2012.760341

McLeod, N., & Anderson, B. (2020). Towards an understanding of "school" readiness: Collective interpretations and priorities. *Educational Action Research, 28*(5), 723–741. https://doi.org/10.1080/09650792.2019.1654902

Miles, M., & Huberman, A. (1994). *Qualitative data analysis: An expanded sourcebook* (2nd ed.). Thousand Oaks, CA: SAGE.

Miller, K. (2015). The transition to kindergarten: How families from lower-income backgrounds experienced the first year. *Early Childhood Education Journal, 43*(3), 213–221. https://doi.org/10.1007/s106453-014-0650-9

Miller, K. (2016). Learning about children's school preparation through photographs: The use of photo elicitation interviews with low-income families. *Journal of Early Childhood Research, 14*(3), 261–279. https://doi.org/10.1177/1476718X14555703

Mockler, N., & Groundwater-Smith, S. (2015). Seeking for the unwelcome truths: Beyond celebration in inquiry-based teacher professional learning. *Teachers and Teaching*, 21(5), 603–614. https://doi.org/10.1080/13540602.2014.995480

New South Wales Education Standards Authority [NESA]. (n.d.). *New South Wales curriculum and syllabuses.* https://educationstandards.nsw.edu.au/wps/portal/nesa/k-10/understanding-the-curriculum/curriculum-syllabuses-NSW

Nolan, A., West, S., Schroder, C., Barber, L., Symes, L., Sayers, M., McDonald, M., Kellett, E., O'Connor, M., McCartin, J., Hunt, J., Aitken, J., & Scott, C. (2012). *Outcomes and indicators of a positive start to school: Development of framework and tools.* Melbourne: Department of Education and Early Childhood Development. www.education.vic.gov.au/Documents/about/research/outcomesandindicators.pdf

NSW Department of Education. (2020). *Strong and successful start to school: Transition assessment and planning tool.* https://education.nsw.gov.au/content/dam/main-education/teaching-and-learning/curriculum/early-learning/media/documents/transition-assessment-planning-tool.DOCX

Ohle, K., & Harvey, H. (2019). Educators' perceptions of school readiness within the context of a kindergarten entry assessment in Alaska. *Early Child Development and Care*, 189(11), 1859–1873. https://doi.org/10.1080/03004430.2017.1417855

Pianta, R. C. (1992). *Student-teacher relationships scale.* https://curry.virginia.edu/sites/default/files/uploads/resourceLibrary/STRS-SF.pdf

Pianta, R. C. (2001). *Student-teacher relationship scale: Professional manual.* Odessa, FL: Psychological Assessment Resources.

Pianta, R. C., & Kraft-Sayre, M. (2003). *Successful kindergarten transition: Your guide to connecting children, families, & schools.* Baltimore, MD: Paul H Brookes.

Queensland Department of Education. (2020). *Supporting successful transitions: School decision-making tool.* https://earlychildhood.qld.gov.au/earlyYears/Documents/transition-to-school-decision-making-tool.pdf

Reid, A. (2004). *Towards a culture of inquiry in DECS.* Occasional Paper Series, No 1. Adelaide: Department of Education and Children's Services.

Smithson, J. (2008). Focus groups. In P. Alasuurtari, L. Bickman, & J. Brannen (Eds.), *The SAGE handbook of social research methods* (pp. 356–371). London: SAGE. https://doi.org/10.4135/9781446212165.n21

Stake, R. E. (1995). *The art of case study research.* Thousand Oaks, CA: SAGE.

SuccessWorks. (2010). *Evaluation of transition: A positive start to school initiative.* www.education.vic.gov.au/Documents/about/research/evaluationtrans.pdf

Taylor-Powell, E., & Renner, M. (2003). *Analyzing qualitative data.* Madison, WI: University of Wisconsin Extension. http://learningstore.uwex.edu/assets/pdfs/g3658-12.pdf

8 Development and use of a rubric framework for the evaluation of transition to school programs

Sue Dockett and Bob Perry

Introduction

Many formal instruments have been used recently in Australian education systems and research projects to assist in the evaluation of transition to school programs (Department for Education and Child Development, South Australia, 2014; KidsMatter, 2013; NSW Department of Education, 2020; Queensland Department of Education, 2020b; West et al., 2012). Chapters 3A and 8A in this book provide international examples. In this chapter, we introduce an instrument which has been developed over a period of more than 20 years and has been used in various guises in both research and practice in several jurisdictions. Many of the features of this instrument have been incorporated into the systemwide instruments and approaches cited.

Many of these instruments utilise a rubric design. In its broadest terms, a rubric is defined as "a type of matrix that provides scaled levels of achievement or understanding for a set of criteria or dimensions of quality for a given type of performance" (Allen & Tanner, 2006, p. 197). While both rubrics and scoring checklists are built from criteria which have been determined to indicate achievement or understanding, "a 'full rubric' is distinguished from the scoring checklist by its more extensive definition and description of the criteria or dimensions of quality that characterize each level of accomplishment" (Allen & Tanner, 2006, p. 197), not just whether the criteria are perceived to be present. Further, "the performance criteria in a rubric identify the dimensions of the performance or product that is being taught and assessed" (Tierney & Simon, 2004, p. 1).

Most often, rubrics are used in education to provide judgements on the quality of learning in a specific area or topic. Their virtues have been extolled in terms of assisting learners to be aware of the criteria required for learning at several levels, usually ranging from mediocre or less through to expert knowledge or understanding of the learning contained in the criteria. As well, there is a planning dimension present in every rubric, encouraging learners to reach for a higher level than they might otherwise have done and providing them with some guidance as to how to do this. However, rubrics are not without their potential downsides. Mostly, these perceived deficiencies of rubrics arise in their

DOI: 10.4324/9781003055112-14

construction and, in particular, in the construction of the descriptions of the different levels of performance criteria (Tierney & Simon, 2004). However, another potential deficiency occurs in the ways in which judgements are made about the level of performance on each criteria. Not only should there be consistency in judgement across a given cohort or in a specific context – the so-called *norming process* (Schoepp, Danaher, & Ater Kranov, 2018) – but the perennial evaluation question "On what evidence is the judgement being made?" needs to be considered. A rubric does not specify what evidence is required nor how such evidence might be gathered. Earlier chapters in this book have provided input to these important components of any assessment or evaluation.

Rubrics have also been used to assist in the evaluation of educational and other programs, with similar virtues and deficiencies extolled. For example, Dickinson and Adams (2017, p. 114) suggest that

> When evaluation criteria and rubrics are established at the start of a project and its evaluation, it is clear to staff and stakeholders what high quality interventions . . . and successful outcomes . . . will look like . . .
>
> Rubrics help stakeholders to articulate the criteria (or vital features) they are looking for and make those features explicit to those engaged in programme implementation. This avoids the gap between what the evaluator knows and what the stakeholders know . . .
>
> Rubrics allow the communication of specific goals or intentions to key stakeholders so that everyone knows what is expected and what behaviour or characteristics constitute the different levels of performance. Evaluand strengths and weaknesses can be highlighted through the use of rubrics which allows for changes to be made to what is being implemented.

In this chapter, we trace the development and implementation of one such rubric-based instrument used to help measure the efficacy of transition to school programs.

History of the Peridot Education Transition Reflection Instrument

The genesis of the *Peridot Education Transition Reflection Instrument* begins in our early work with transition to school which was based in New South Wales in the late 1990s and early 2000s. As part of the *Starting School Research Project* (Dockett & Perry, 1999, 2001, 2002, 2003a, 2003b, 2004; Dockett, Perry, & Howard, 2004; Dockett, Perry, & Nicolson, 2002; Perry, Dockett, & Howard, 2000; Perry, Dockett, & Tracey, 1998), a set of guidelines for effective transitions was developed and used. These have already been introduced in Chapter 3. Taking inspiration from the *Toronto First Duty Project* (Corter et al., 2007), for each of the ten guidelines, essential elements were identified in a workshop process involving a range of stakeholders. Four levels of performance were described, thus forming a rubric against which the effectiveness of transition programs could be measured. This rubric was used in several subsequent research projects, including one considering transition to school for Aboriginal and Torres Strait Islander children and families (Dockett, Mason, & Perry, 2006; Dockett et al., 2007; Perry et al., 2007) and another investigating transition from primary to secondary school (Perry et al., 2006; Whitton & Perry, 2005).

Indicators of Progress

The initial publication of the complete rubric, titled *Indicators of Progress* occurred in Dockett and Perry (2006) as part of advice to educators about the planning, implementation, and evaluation of transition to school programs. The *Indicators of Progress* is a large document in which each of the ten guidelines is represented by between two and six elements (40 in total), and against each of these elements are statements indicating four levels of progress. It is not necessary to reproduce the entire document here, but we do provide an example derived from Dockett and Perry (2006, pp. 84–85). The entire document is available over 35 pages in Dockett and Perry (2006, pp. 164–198)!

The first of the ten guidelines is *Effective transition programs establish positive relationships between children, parents, and educators.* Identified elements for this guideline were:

- building relationships between children;
- building relationships between children and school community members;
- building relationships between families and schools;
- building relationships between school staff and staff in prior-to-school settings; and
- building relationships in the broader community.

Through an exhaustive consultation process with key stakeholders in the *Starting School Research Project*, four levels of practice were determined for each of these elements. Table 8.1 provides a shortened version of the result for the first element (derived from Dockett & Perry, 2006, p. 85).

The *Indicators of Progress* were designed to assist transition teams to:

- identify starting points and goals against each of the identified elements;
- reflect on progress towards the goals;
- evaluate transition programs; and
- engage in conversations and planning around the effectiveness of transition to school programs.

"Essentially, the *Indicators of Progress* are a tool to assist in planning, evaluation and reporting of transition programs. They are based on collaboration between all involved in transition, and will look different in different contexts" (Dockett & Perry, 2006, p. 163).

Table 8.1 Framework for the first key element for the Guideline *Effective transition programs establish positive relationships between children, parents and educators* (Level 4 highest).

Key elements	Level 1	Level 2	Level 3	Level 4
building relationships between children	Children have limited acquaintance with others starting school and/or children at school. Transition programs provide limited opportunities for children to interact in self-initiated or play situations. There are no strategies for promoting interaction between children who do not access prior-to-school services.	Children have opportunities to engage in a range of positive social interactions with children attending school or with whom they will attend school. There are opportunities within transition programs for children to be with friends and to make friends.	Children starting school know and interact positively with each other. Children already at school interact positively with children about to start school. Children who have similar interests or backgrounds are grouped in ways to promote interactions. Adults model strategies for initiating and maintaining positive relationships. Siblings, other family members, and children from other grades are welcome participants in transition programs.	Children have opportunities to develop confident relationships with other children in prior-to-school, school, or community settings. Strategies are in place to promote positive interactions among children who do not access prior-to-school services. Adults actively support the positive relationships among children. Transition to school programs are recognised as a resource by broader community.

While the *Indicators of Progress* became a very useful tool for the *Starting School Research Project* team, 35 pages of detailed documentation against 40 key elements, let alone the masses of data generation, analysis, and interpretation, were less useful to busy practitioners in the field. Some attempts were made to make them more accessible but their main impacts on the field were to show the relevance of the rubric-based approach to the evaluation of transition to school programs, emphasise the importance of collaborative development of transition to school programs and their evaluation, and point to future directions.

The Transition to School: Position Statement

In 2010, the authors hosted a meeting of leading transition to school researchers from across the world, as well as early childhood educators and policy makers which changed the way in which transition to school was perceived by many. Two important products came from this meeting. The first (Perry, Dockett, & Petriwskyj, 2014) recorded the proceedings of the meeting, the papers presented, and the innovations derived. The second (Educational Transitions and Change (ETC) Research Group, 2011) presented a reconceptualisation of transition to school from social justice, rights-based, and strengths-based foundations. This *Transition to School: Position Statement* has been mentioned several times already in this book (Chapters 3, 5, and 7). For the purposes of this chapter, we are particularly interested in the *Position Statement's* reconceptualisation of transition to school into four elements: opportunities, aspirations, expectations, and entitlements (Dockett & Perry, 2014). Adoption of these four elements as alternatives to the ten guidelines previously used in the *Indicators of Practice* not only provided a refreshing and innovative way to consider the evaluation and planning of transition to school programs but also eventually resulted in a much more practical and useful instrument.

Developments in Queensland

Soon after the 2010 international meeting, the Darling Downs South West Region of the Queensland Department of Education and Training implemented its *Great Start Great Futures Early Years Transition Project* from 2013–2015 (for some information on the project and its foundations, see Darling Downs South West, 2014; Hand, 2014). The project supported schools in leading relationships, processes, and pedagogy across the early childhood years through effective transition to school programs. It emphasised the need for schools to be *ready* for children as they start school and the importance of the principal of the school in this endeavour.

The five pillars on which the project was built were:

- purposeful use of data;
- collaborative leadership;
- inclusive leadership;
- procedural leadership; and
- pedagogical leadership (Hand, 2014).

For each of these pillars, four levels of action, with examples, were devised, allowing the development of an evaluation matrix to test the impact of the project. While this matrix served a useful purpose within the *Great Start Great Futures Early Years Transition Project*, its major impact was that it provided a model for work which was being undertaken in the central office of the Queensland Department of Education and Training. The impact of the Darling

174 Sue Dockett and Bob Perry

Downs South West project has been acknowledged in the major product of the central office work: *Supporting Successful Transitions: School Decision-Making Tool* (Queensland Department of Education, 2020b). This tool has been used in Queensland schools since 2016, was reviewed in 2020, and forms one of the key components of the statewide approach to transitions (Queensland Department of Education, 2020a). The *School Decision-Making Tool*

> . . . provides a framework for school reflection on current transition practices. It also provides scope to identify opportunities to plan and implement targeted, evidence-based actions to maximise the school's readiness to meet the needs of all children and families. It is designed to assist schools in strengthening their approach to transition and their selection of transition-to-school strategies.
> (Queensland Department of Education, 2020b, p. 2)

The decision-making tool is based on the principles supporting the statewide approach to transition and five action areas:

- respect for diversity;
- effective use of data;
- responsive environments;
- effective pedagogy and practice; and
- reciprocal relationships

to guide reflection and planning. Further support is provided through "a reflecting-on-transition matrix developed to illustrate growth in the complexity and interrelatedness of transition practice" (Queensland Department of Education, 2020b, p. 3) and which "describes a range of behaviours across three levels of decision-making (school-centred, consultative, and collaborative) that inform the transition practices enacted by a school" (Queensland Department of Education, 2020b, p. 10).

To illustrate the content of the *School Decision-Making* matrix, we reproduce material from one action area *reciprocal relationships* in Table 8.2 and then comment on its contents.

The document from which the material in Table 8.2 is drawn is entitled *Successful Transitions: **School** Decision-Making Tool* (our emphasis). It is designed to help schools make decisions about their transition to school programs. While this approach can be very helpful, it does emphasise an overall leadership role for schools, which we and many of our colleagues have questioned (Dockett, 2018; Flottman, McKernan, & Tayler, 2011; Rogers, Dockett, & Perry, 2017). In spite of this seeming emphasis, the tool has been used effectively by professional partnerships of school and early childhood (ECEC) educators throughout Queensland in programs such as *Step Up into Education* (Queensland Department of Education, 2021). It has assisted many educators in schools and ECEC settings to focus on important challenges and achievements in transition to school and to stimulate movement towards more collaborative approaches.

Rubrics for evaluation of programs 175

Table 8.2 Action area *reciprocal relationships* from the *School Decision-Making* matrix (Queensland Department of Education, 2020b, pp. 12–13).

Action area	Focus	School-centred	Consultative	Collaborative
Reciprocal relationships	Communicating with service providers	• ECEC service providers have not been identified. • Communication is focused on gathering or giving information for administrative purposes.	• Service providers are provided with information about the school to share with families. • School personnel visit local service providers.	• School and service providers meet regularly to discuss practice and determine transition strategies. • School staff and service providers share professional development. • Common practices are shared, e.g. behaviour management and parent engagement.
	Involving families and children	• Relationships are developed when children start school. • Information about the child's previous experiences focus on service type and duration of participation.	• Information about the child and family is gathered through enrolment interviews. • The school requests a copy of the transition statement at interview.	• School prioritises times to meet with parents to discuss their children. • School facilitates parent education sessions for families with children of prior-to-school age. • Transition statements are used to inform discussions with families.
	Community participation	• Agencies are contacted once children have commenced school.	• Agencies are contacted prior to or following the orientation and interview. • Agencies are invited to provide professional development for school staff.	• School involves relevant agencies in discussions and planning for individual children. • Advice is sought from relevant agencies about strengths-based transition strategies for specific groups of children.

As with any rubric of the type illustrated by the *School Decision-Making* matrix, the decisions that are made can only be as sound as the quality of the data used to inform those decisions. The matrix is not, and is not claimed to be, a stand-alone document. While it does provide focus on the aims of local transition to school programs and a great deal of guidance about what questions might need to be asked and highlights possible transition to school strategies, any decisions to be made must be informed by the effective use of data – one of the key action areas. As with any evaluation of aspects of transition to school programs, including the Queensland *School Decision-Making Tool*, and those discussed in Chapters 3A and 8A of this book, appropriate data are needed to justify any decisions that are made.

In the remainder of this chapter, we consider the development of another rubric-based evaluation instrument which has been used by the authors over a number of years in both research and practice.

The Peridot Education Transition Reflection Instrument

The *Peridot Education Transition Reflection Instrument* is an adaptation of the *Indicators of Progress* (Dockett & Perry, 2006) discussed earlier in this chapter, utilising the *Transition to School: Position Statement* (ETC Research Group, 2011). It is discussed here as one way in which the findings of an evaluation of a transition to school program can be recorded and used for reflection on current programs and planning of future programs.

The *Peridot Education Transition Reflection Instrument* is built on the four constructs of the position statement: opportunities, aspirations, expectations, and entitlements for the major partners in transition to primary school: educators – both ECEC and school – children, families, and communities. The authors have previously analysed how each of these constructs can apply to the partners in a transition to school program (Dockett & Perry, 2015). As well as introducing alternative dimensions of quality, the *Peridot Education Transition Reflection Instrument* extends the earlier analysis to provide ways in which transition to school teams can reflect on progress that has been made in their transition to school programs over time and plan for future programs. Use of the instrument requires that there be a transition to school team consisting of, at least, representatives from the school and some of the ECEC settings from which children will move to the school.

The *Peridot Education Transition Reflection Instrument* consists of four tables linked to the four position statement constructs, which illustrate four levels of achievement for each of the four major partners. This set of tables allows evidence-informed decisions to be made for each of the constructs for each of the partners. The four tables are presented in Tables 8.3–8.6. Ways in which the instrument can be used are then discussed.

In each of Tables 8.3 through 8.6, a series of indicator statements demonstrates levels of progress for each construct and partner group. It is unlikely that any transition team would concentrate on all of these constructs for all of

Rubrics for evaluation of programs 177

Table 8.3 Peridot Education Transition Reflection Instrument: Opportunities.

	Level 1	Level 2	Level 3	Level 4
Children	There are limited opportunities for children to participate in or influence planned transition experiences.	There are opportunities for children to engage with and get to know members of the school community. Children have input to the transition program.	Children's strengths are recognised and utilised to facilitate relationship building and learning. Children are actively and meaningfully involved with members of the prior-to-school and school communities in planning starting school programs.	Children feel that they belong, that school is a place for them to learn, and that they can utilise their strengths to their full potential. Children have major roles in planning, implementation, and evaluation of starting school programs.
Families	There are limited opportunities for families to participate in or influence planned transition experiences.	Transition programs offer several opportunities for families to get to know school staff. Families have input in the transition program. Some families take the opportunity to share information through transition statements.	Families' strengths are recognised and utilised to facilitate relationship building and learning. Families are encouraged to provide substantial input into transition programs and to share information with school staff. Most families take the opportunity to share information through transition statements.	Families support their children's ongoing learning and development in partnership with educators. Family members work in collaboration with educators to plan, implement, and evaluate transition to school programs.
Educators	Staff in prior-to-school and school settings do not know each other, and there is little contact among them.	Staff in prior-to-school and school settings know their colleagues in different settings and have procedures for contacting them. Sharing of information about specific children (with parental consent) occurs regularly.	Educators in prior-to-school and school settings are aware of and respect the work of families and educators in different settings and the work of other professionals. Information sharing extends to curriculum approaches and frameworks.	Educators have strong and enduring partnerships with each other and other professionals and with children and families. These partnerships provide opportunities for working together and for effective learning.
Communities	Communities are not aware of or involved in transition to school programs.	There is limited involvement of communities in transition to school programs.	When invited, communities support transition to school programs.	Starting school is actively recognised as an important event in children's lives and is supported and celebrated by communities.

Table 8.4 Peridot Education Transition Reflection Instrument: Aspirations.

	Level 1	Level 2	Level 3	Level 4
Children	There is limited recognition or consideration of children's aspirations in transition to school programs.	That children have aspirations is recognised, but they are not used in planning and implementing transition programs.	Children's aspirations are recognised and used in planning and implementing transition to school programs.	There is strong recognition of children's agency and aspirations during the transition to school process and in the first year of school.
Families	There is limited recognition or consideration of families' aspirations in transition to school programs.	That families have aspirations for their children's education is recognised, but these aspirations are not used in planning and implementing transition to school programs.	Families' aspirations for their children are recognised and used in planning and implementing transition to school programs.	Families look forward to positive educational outcomes for their children – both social and academic – and supporting these outcomes in partnership with educators. Families believe that these aspirations are acted upon.
Educators	Children's "readiness for school" is the key element of transition programs.	Educators aspire to provide high-quality education to all children and to get to know children, their families, and other educators.	Educators combine their own aspirations with those of children and families to ensure excellent educational outcomes for all children.	Educators work towards professional partnerships that create strong and supportive educational environments for all children and result in excellent educational outcomes for all.
Communities	There is little expression of aspirations for children's education coming from the community.	Communities want the best for their children but do not overtly work with educators and families to help achieve this.	Communities have strong, positive educational aspirations for children and for education within the community.	Communities provide ongoing support and resources to promote and celebrate positive engagement with school and excellence in educational outcomes.

Rubrics for evaluation of programs 179

Table 8.5 *Peridot Education Transition Reflection Instrument*: Expectations.

	Level 1	Level 2	Level 3	Level 4
Children	Children have limited knowledge about school and what will happen during the transition to school program, other than what they have picked up informally.	Children expect that they will learn at school and spend some time playing with friends but do not know what to expect from the transition to school program.	Children have been consulted about the transition to school program and know what to expect. They have been able to share their expectations with educators.	Children start school expecting to learn, face challenges, be with friends, and have the support of adults in the school and families.
Families	Families have limited knowledge about school and what will happen during the transition to school program, other than what they have picked up informally.	Families expect that they will be informed about school and transition activities. Families expect that they will be treated with respect.	Families expect that their questions and concerns will be treated with respect and answered promptly. Families expect that they and their children will feel that they belong at the school.	Families expect their knowledge to be recognised and respected, to be listened to, and to be consulted as they contribute in partnership to their children's education.
Educators	Educators expect that the new group of children starting school will have similar knowledge, interests, and needs as last year's group. Prior-to-school educators expect to share written transition statements with families.	Educators expect that they will develop and implement a transition to school program for the new children. Educators expect respect from families, children and other educators. Educators expect that families will provide transition statements to the school, but little other information is sought or provided by educators.	Educators expect to build respectful relationships with children, families, other educators, and professionals. Educators have the resources they need to support excellent learning. School educators expect to use the transition statements provided by families in their planning. Educators use a variety of strategies to seek and respond to information concerning children's prior learning.	Educators expect professional recognition, support, and trust as they create positive environments for learning, teaching, and partnership. Educators expect to engage in dialogue about appropriate pedagogies to support continuity of learning as the children start school. Educators expect to provide excellent education for their children.
Communities	There is little evidence that the community has particular expectations for the education of its children.	Community members expect that they will have a role in children's education but also expect that the school will inform them of this.	Communities expect to play a proactive role in school education. Communities expect that educators will seek the opinion of the community about educational matters.	Communities expect that schools will attend to the well-being of all children and promote active citizenship, in partnership with the communities.

Table 8.6 Peridot Education Transition Reflection Instrument: Entitlements.

	Level 1	Level 2	Level 3	Level 4
Children	Children are positioned as recipients of transition – transition happens to them.	Children accept that their entitlements in education are what they receive.	Children are made aware of their entitlements to, and receive the benefits of, safe learning environments which demonstrate recognition and respect for their competencies, cultural heritages, and histories.	Children have access to equitable and excellent education that recognises and builds upon their strengths and aspirations.
Families	Families are positioned as recipients of transition programs. Their main role is to ensure children attend transition programs.	Transition programs recognise the transitions experienced by the family as well as the child.	Families are involved in responsive, respectful transition programs that respect their competencies, cultural heritages and histories.	Families acknowledge that their children are receiving equitable and excellent education and have a positive sense of their role within this.
Educators	Transition programs are generic. Educators have little time or few resources to devote to the development of responsive transition programs.	Educational settings prioritise transition, allocating appropriate resources to enable educators to engage with others and develop transition programs.	Educators from different settings access appropriate (sometimes shared) professional development that supports their roles in and understandings of transition.	Educators receive professional respect and the resources required, including ongoing professional learning, to provide excellent educational experiences.
Communities	Communities have access to limited information about transition programs.	Community members – including other professionals – respond positively to invitations to engage in transition programs and create appropriate transition programs for all involved.	Educators, community members, and other professionals collaborate to create responsive, respectful transition programs for all children and families that respect their competencies, cultural heritages, and histories.	Communities know that resources have been used to provide equitable and excellent education for all children.

the partner groups at the same time. It is much more likely that measures of progress and the data generation that would accompany these would focus on a small number of constructs and/or partner groups. For example, the focus may be on strategies relevant to the aspirations of children or the expectations of families and relevant data are generated for these. One of the dangers in evaluation is that too many aspects of the program are evaluated simultaneously, with resources for data generation, analysis, and interpretation becoming too stretched. It is likely to be more practical to evaluate smaller parts of the program well than to try to cover it all at the same time.

As well as being able to provide a *snapshot* of the transition to school program at any given time, the *Peridot Education Transition Reflection Instrument* also encourages transition to school teams to track progress towards effective transition to school programs by applying it several times as the program is adjusted using previous evaluation findings, with further aspects being introduced, implemented, and re-evaluated. Such a cycle could take years, allowing transition teams and their communities to map progress in the effectiveness of their transition to school programs over time. By using the instrument, with evidence derived from sound data generation and analysis, transition to school teams are encouraged to:

- identify their starting point – for example, how effective were certain constructs – opportunities, aspirations, expectations, entitlements – of the transition program for some of the key partners before the present iteration, say, 1 year ago;
- reflect on the effectiveness of actions targeted at the selected constructs and partner groups in the current iteration of the program, using data generated and analysed to provide relevant and usable evidence; and
- aspire to where they would like their transition to school program to be into the future, at its next iteration in, say, 1 year's time; that is, plan the next iteration of the program using the evidence gathered in the current evaluation.

In this way, transition to school teams can use the *Peridot Education Transition Reflection Instrument* to identify constructs and partner groups which might need to be targeted and to check that such targeting does not diminish gains that have already been made with other constructs and groups. An overall picture of the health and progress of transition to school in the community can be achieved, and increments in effectiveness can be celebrated.

Documenting progress – an example

There are many ways in which progress in the development, implementation, and evaluation of a transition to school program might be documented. Many of these have already been canvassed in this book, and Chapter 8A provides further exemplars. Stories might be written, tables collated, and pictures drawn.

182 *Sue Dockett and Bob Perry*

Chapter 3A introduces an example of a profile document – the *Paderborner Qualitätsstern* – which considers relationships among educators.

One way in which the findings of implementation of the *Peridot Education Transition Reflection Instrument* have been disseminated is through a visual progress profile. This technique has been adopted by many participants in research projects and evaluations we have conducted. Evidence-based measurement of the instrument levels attained in the transition to school program can be collated as a visual record of the progress being made in the constructs for the targeted partner group being considered.

For example, a transition team prioritising children's perspectives in transition may identify the construct of expectations as one of their key challenges. Processes against which to measure expectations about children are listed in the instrument (Table 8.5). Progress over time for the expectations for children can be demonstrated in a profile such as Figure 8.1.

To develop this profile, the transition to school team has used evidence derived from evaluation of their program to determine the levels shown in Figure 8.1. Some progress has been made, but the team want to do much more with the next iteration of the program – they want to move from Level 2 to Level 4. This provides planning aspiration for the team as they adjust the transition to school program in order to reach this goal.

Expectations						Starting point: 1 year ago
Level	1	2	3	4		Where we are now
Children						Where we plan to be in 1 year

Figure 8.1 Profile for expectations for children over time.

Another team have focussed particularly on families since the introduction of their transition to school program and are now able to display the profile of progress against all of the constructs for families in Figure 8.2. The judgements made in order to create this profile have been based on generated and analysed data, which can be included in a report to indicate the source of the judgements.

There are a number of interesting features of the profile in Figure 8.2. While the progression for the Aspirations and Expectations constructs is as one might

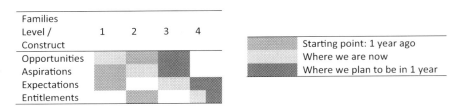

Figure 8.2 Complete profile across the four constructs for families.

hope, with the levels increasing over time, the other two constructs do not follow this pattern. With Opportunities, it would seem as though whatever was done in the current transition to school program may have resulted in the level for this construct going backwards from what was recorded in the previous year. This may be a result of some changes in measurement or interpretation in either or both years, or it may be that the transition team has taken their eyes off the ball in this aspect of their program, with the result that less has been achieved. In any case, the profile signals the need for further investigation. It would appear that the team is aware of this need, with their aspiration to be at Level 3 in the next iteration of the transition to school program. For the Entitlements construct, however, the message is much clearer. It would appear that Level 4 has been reached in the current transition to school program and that the aim is to at least maintain this level next year. It would be possible for local transition to school teams to aspire to something beyond Level 4 in any of the constructs and to create their own indicator(s) of this. If we consider the *Peridot Education Transition Reflection Instrument* as an ongoing work in progress, Level 4 is not necessarily the highest to which a team can aspire.

Use of the Peridot Education Transition Reflection Instrument

From the discussion, the *Peridot Education Transition Reflection Instrument* is able to demonstrate progress that transition teams have made in their transition to school programs over time. The instrument can highlight strong aspects of the programs and bring to the fore aspects which might need focussed attention. As well, it provides some guidance in planning by illustrating the general processes that may be needed for transition programs to progress through the levels in the selected constructs or participant groups. It focusses on these processes rather than specific activities or practices, reflecting our belief that these need to be chosen at the local level, recognising the local context and conditions.

While not all transition teams will choose to evaluate their entire transition to school programs using the *Peridot Education Transition Reflection Instrument*, some will, resulting in a complete profile across the four constructs and four major partner groups. We now illustrate this using profiles from two actual schools involved in one of our research projects. Firstly, we show the profiles (Figure 8.3), and then we offer some interpretations. Other interpretations are possible, and readers are invited to consider these alternatives themselves.

As we compare these two overall profiles, it would seem that School Community B sees itself further advanced on most aspects of their transition to school program than School Community A. Such a comparison would be quite inappropriate, however, given that we do know that context is a major factor in the effectiveness of transition to school programs and given what we do not know about the two contexts. There are some places in each school community's profile where little progress has been measured and/or expected. This may be because the transition teams have decided to focus on other constructs and

184 *Sue Dockett and Bob Perry*

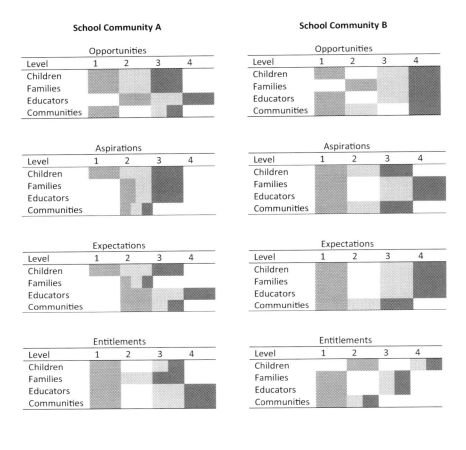

Figure 8.3 Complete profiles of two schools using the *Peridot Education Transition Reflection Instrument*.

groups, or it may be because the teams have not yet planned what they want to do. In other construct/group pairs, it appears that progress is planned to be achieved quite rapidly, especially in the profile of School Community B, with the exception of the Entitlements construct. While each school community reflected on their own profiles and aimed to progress through the levels, it may be that the communities would have benefited from studying each other's profiles in search of the stories underlying them and the messages for their own local communities. No doubt there are many other ways in which the profiles and the instrument overall can be used. The reader is challenged to consider some of these.

Conclusion

In this chapter, we have provided some examples of ways in which rubrics have been utilised in the evaluation of transition to school programs. Chapter 8A reports on a transition to school initiative in the Republic of Ireland and the evaluation of this initiative. It provides an example of a system wide evaluation of this initiative and shares some of the findings of the evaluation. While the details of the evaluation are relevant to the overall focus of this book and to Chapter 8, a key development reported is that of the Irish equivalent of transition to school statements used throughout Australia (see, for example, Hopps, 2014; NSW Department of Education, 2021; Queensland Department of Education, 2020c; Victorian Department of Education and Training, 2019). *Mo Scéal* (My Story) provides two alternative forms through which information might be transferred from prior-to-school settings to schools. *Mo Scéal* is designed to be completed collaboratively by educators, children, and families and was one of the key pillars in the transition to school initiative reported. In one of the forms of *Mo Scéal*, early childhood educators use a rubric to report on the key attributes of each child making the transition to school from their setting. Chapter 8A provides a picture into a systemwide evaluation which can be compared and contrasted with the local evaluation using the *Peridot Education Transition Reflection Instrument* described in this chapter.

8A *Mo Scéal* (My Story)
Evaluation of the transition to school initiative in Ireland

Mary Daly and Derek Grant

Introduction

The National Council for Curriculum and Assessment (NCCA) developed online reporting templates and support materials to promote a more positive and effective experience for young children and their parents in transitioning from preschool[1] to primary school. This developmental work took place between 2016 and 2018 as part of the NCCA's statutory role of advising the Minister for Education and Skills in relation to curriculum and assessment matters. The impetus for developing suitable online reporting templates, as part of a coordinated information-sharing process, came from *Literacy and Numeracy for Learning and Life: The National Strategy to Improve Literacy and Numeracy among Children and Young People 2011–2020* (Department of Education and Skills, 2011).

Literature review

In approaching this task, the NCCA commissioned three research reports to gain a greater understanding of transition and to determine current practice in relation to the transfer of information. The research considered socio-cultural theory and bioecological systems theory and consisted of (1) a review of literature, (O'Kane, 2016), (2) a paper on data transfer internationally (O'Kane and Murphy, 2016a), and (3) an audit of ten transfer documents in Ireland (O'Kane and Murphy, 2016b).

The main research findings confirmed that a positive transition is a "predictor of children's future success in terms of social, emotional and educational outcomes" (O'Kane, 2016, p. 13). The key messages from the research highlight that:

- children need to feel that they are welcome in their new school and to develop strong relationships;
- certain dispositions, skills, and knowledge are important and should be focused on in preschool – social and emotional skills, communication and language skills, positive learning dispositions – with less focus being placed on academic skills;

DOI: 10.4324/9781003055112-15

- greater alignment in curriculum and pedagogy between preschools and primary schools is vital. The research pinpoints the importance of interactive, playful learning;
- supporting transitions is a shared responsibility between children, families, communities, preschools, and primary schools. There has been a shift from a focus on a *school-ready child* to a *ready child*, *ready family*, and *ready school*;
- some children may need extra supports to help them transition well; for example, children living in disadvantaged circumstances, children for whom English is an additional language (EAL) and children with special educational needs (SEN); and
- the transfer of information on children's learning and development is important; the documentation should be positive in approach, and areas where children need extra support should be identified; parents and children should be included in a meaningful way.

In consideration of the research, the NCCA did two things: firstly, it developed two draft reporting templates based on *Aistear: the Early Childhood Curriculum Framework* (National Council for Curriculum and Assessment (NCCA), 2009). Secondly, it initiated a transition initiative which explored the key messages from the research and piloted the templates.

The preschool to primary school transition initiative

Implementation of the transition initiative

During 2017, the NCCA worked with a network of ten preschools and nine primary schools over a sustained period of time to help children experience a positive transition into primary school. The network represented both a geographical and contextual spread of schools and preschools. Each school partnered with a local feeder preschool, enabling teachers and practitioners to collaborate. Participation in the initiative was facilitated through workshops, visits to preschools and schools, and the provision of support materials. The initiative began with an introductory session followed by four workshops to share the learning from the research reports. Information was provided on the knowledge, skills, and dispositions that are important for children as they transition. The sessions also focused on planning for and undertaking transition activities along with suggestions and guidance on how to support continuity and progression in curriculum and pedagogy from preschool into primary school using *Aistear* (NCCA, 2009). Support around piloting the templates was also provided. As participants became secure and settled into the initiative, there were opportunities for cross-sectoral professional collaboration and building social capital.

Analysis of the transition initiative

The initiative was reviewed by an external academic to assess its benefits and consider the challenges. The evaluation considered:

- What benefits, if any, were associated with the initiative?
- What challenges, if any, were associated with the initiative?
- What changes to the draft reporting templates were needed?

Qualitative data were collected from practitioners and teachers through:

- Online questionnaires.
- Focus groups.
- Feedback at the end of each workshop.
- Follow-up interviews.

Qualitative data were collected from parents through:

- A hard-copy questionnaire.
- Focus groups.

Qualitative data were collected from children through:

- Their input in the templates, which showed the things they liked in pre-school, what they were looking forward to in school, and how they felt about the move.
- Teachers and practitioners eliciting children's views through annotated artwork.
- Video recordings of children in pairs and small groups.

Findings from the transition initiative

Overall, the initiative was deemed to be a very worthwhile, timely, and positive experience for all involved – for families, practitioners, teachers, and the NCCA (NCCA, 2018b). However, the evaluation also spotlighted challenges.

Benefits

The evaluation showed that participants thought that the building of cross-sectoral relationships was the greatest benefit. Many parents were surprised that preschools and schools were not in contact before the initiative. As one parent said, "It was something that should have happened years ago". Discovering that supporting transitions is a shared responsibility provided a stimulus for practitioners and teachers to work together to involve parents more, which was very positive. The mutual site visits were also deemed beneficial. One teacher commented, "I had never visited a preschool before so it was great to get an insight into how their day is planned. I especially enjoyed seeing how their room was laid out in different areas" (NCCA, 2018b, p. 29). Several participants felt, too, that it was a very good idea to have joint continuing professional development (CPD). Feedback showed that CPD on *Aistear* and the *Aistear Síolta Practice Guide* (NCCA, 2015) were central to professional learning in supporting curriculum alignment and play-based pedagogy.

Feedback on the reporting templates was very positive, too, from both parents and teachers, and practitioners welcomed the opportunity to share the valuable information they had. Parents really appreciated receiving the reports and made comments like, "I did not expect it to be so detailed . . . it was brilliant"; "It was evident they knew my child very well".

Finding out how children felt about the transition was a very important part of the initiative. The majority of children transitioned well. The opportunities to play and to be with friends and siblings were highlighted by them as being key in the transition. Most children adjusted well to school, but a small number expressed regret at leaving preschool: as one child said, "I feel happy and sad at the same time as I will miss my (preschool) teacher". Outward indicators of being a school-going child were important to children "I am very excited to be a big girl in my uniform"; "I have my school bag and lunch box with love hearts"; "I will be getting homework".

Challenges

While the fostering of relationships was the greatest positive outcome, it was also highlighted as being one of the greatest challenges. Communication was facilitated in local areas, in many cases for the first time, as only three of the ten preschools had any kind of existing relationship with their partner school. Building trust and working collaboratively took time, effort, and support. The evaluation also showed that a considerable amount of extra time and effort was needed to support the transition. This generated queries as to what extent the transition activities for children, the meetings between practitioners and teachers, extra contact with parents, along with the work on the reports would be manageable going forward without additional funding and without resource provision similar to that provided during the initiative.

Conclusion

The NCCA published the findings of the initiative in a Final Report (NCCA, 2018b), and the *Mo Scéal* reporting templates were published online in late 2018 (NCCA, 2018a). The reporting templates are available in two formats. In each format, only *Section 1: Practitioner* is different. Template 1 provides space for narrative descriptions based on *Aistear's* four themes,[2] while Template 2 provides ten statements based on *Aistear's* four themes, accompanied by a four-point rating scale. The participants in the initiative felt that it was important to offer both options. Sections 2, 3, and 4, which involve children and parents, are identical in each format. The website also provides information about important skills and dispositions for children, as well as information on transition activities, building relationships, and links to the research.

Currently, there is no requirement to use the reporting templates. However, the NCCA has met with key education stakeholders to inform them of the work on transition and facilitated a professional learning day on *Mo Scéal* for educators in initial teacher education (ITE) and early childhood care and education (ECCE). This was the first time these cross-sectoral institutions had been brought together for joint professional development.

First Five: A Whole-of-Government Strategy for Babies, Young Children and their Families 2019–2028 (Government of Ireland, 2018) includes a strong focus on supporting the transitions between preschools and schools. Therefore, it is envisaged that over the coming years, the NCCA will work with government departments and relevant partners to provide guidance and support processes for those focusing on this important transition.

Notes

1 The term *preschool* is used to refer to all education settings that provide the Early Childhood Care and Education Programme (ECCE). This is a universal entitlement to all children within the eligible age cohort (Department of Children and Youth Affairs, 2019).
2 The themes are *Well-being, Identity and Belonging, Communicating,* and *Exploring and Thinking.*

References

Allen, D., & Tanner, K. (2006). Rubrics: Tools for making learning goals and evaluation criteria explicit for both teachers and learners. *CBE – Life Sciences Education, 5,* 197–203. https://doi.org/10.1187/cbe.06-06-0168

Corter, C., Bertrand, J., Pelletier, J., Griffin, T., McKay, D., Patel, S., & Ioannone, P. (2007). *Toronto First Duty phase 1 final report.* Toronto, Canada: City of Toronto.

Darling Downs South West. (2014). *Community story: Great start, great futures.* www.aedc.gov.au/communities/community-stories/story/community-story-great-start-great-futures

Department for Education and Child Development, South Australia. (2014). *Transition to school rubric.* www.beachroadpartnership.sa.edu.au/wp-content/uploads/2013/03/Transition-to-school-rubric.pdf

Department of Children and Youth Affairs. (2019). *Early childhood care and education programme.* www.gov.ie/en/publication/2459ee-early-childhood-care-and-education-programme-ecce/?referrer=/viewdoc.asp/?docid=4354&ad=1

Department of Education and Skills (DES). (2011). *Literacy and numeracy for learning and life.* www.education.ie/en/Publications/Policy-Reports/lit_num_strategy_full.pdf

Dickinson, P., & Adams, J. (2017). Values in evaluation – The use of rubrics. *Evaluation and Program Planning, 65,* 113–116. https://doi.org/10.1016/j.evalprogplan.2017.07.005

Dockett, S. (2018). Transition to school: Professional collaborations. *Australian Educational Leader*, 40(2), 16–19.

Dockett, S., Mason, T., & Perry, B. (2006). Successful transition to school for Australian Aboriginal children. *Childhood Education*, 82(3), 139–144. https://doi.org/10.1080/00094056.2006.10521365

Dockett, S., & Perry, B. (1999). Starting school: What do the children say? *Early Child Development and Care*, 159, 107–119. https://doi.org/10.1080/0300443991590109

Dockett, S., & Perry, B. (Eds.). (2001). *Beginning school together: Sharing strengths*. Watson, ACT: Australian Early Childhood Association.

Dockett, S., & Perry, B. (2002). Who's ready for what? Young children starting school. *Contemporary Issues in Early Childhood*, 3(1), 67–89. https://doi.org/10.2304/ciec.2002.3.1.9

Dockett, S., & Perry, B. (2003a). Children's views and children's voices in starting school. *Australasian Journal of Early Childhood*, 28(1), 12–17. https://doi.org/10.1177/183693910302800104

Dockett, S., & Perry, B. (2003b). The transition to school: What's important? *Educational Leadership*, 60(7), 30–33.

Dockett, S., & Perry, B. (2004). What makes a successful transition to school? Views of Australian parents and teachers. *International Journal of Early Years Education*, 12, 217–230. https://doi.org/10.1080/0966 976042000268690

Dockett, S., & Perry, B. (2006). *Starting school: A handbook for early childhood educators*. Sydney: Pademelon Press.

Dockett, S., & Perry, B. (2014). Research to policy: Transition to school position statement. In B. Perry, S. Dockett, & A. Petriwskyj, (Eds.), *Transitions to school – International research, policy and practice* (pp. 277–294). Dordrecht: Springer. https://doi.org/10.1007/978-94-007-7350-9_20

Dockett, S., & Perry, B. (2015). Transition to school: Times of opportunity, expectation, aspiration and entitlement. In J. M. Iorio & W. Parnell (Eds.), *Rethinking readiness in early childhood education: Implications for policy and practice* (pp. 123–139). New York: Palgrave Macmillan. https://doi.org/10.1057/9781137485120_9

Dockett, S., Perry, B., & Howard, P. (2004). Young children starting school: A fine example of home-school partnership. In J. C. Lee, L. N. Lo, & A. Walker (Eds.), *Partnership and change: Towards school development* (pp. 223–237). Hong Kong: Chinese University of Hong Kong.

Dockett, S., Perry, B., Mason, T., Simpson, T., Howard, P., Whitton, D., Gilbert, S., Pearce, S., Sanagavarapu, P., Skattebol, J., & Woodrow, C. (2007). *Getting it together: Successful transition programs from prior-to-school to school for Aboriginal and Torres Strait Islander children*. Canberra: MCEETYA. www.curriculum.edu.au/verve/_resources/ATSI_Successful_Transition_programs_Report_Dec_2007.pdf

Dockett, S., Perry, B., & Nicolson, D. (2002). Social and personal transformation as children start school. *International Journal of Learning*, 9, 289–299.

Educational Transitions and Change (ETC) Research Group. (2011). *Transition to school: Position statement*. https://arts-ed.csu.edu.au/education/transitions/publications/Position-Statement.pdf

Flottman, R., McKernan, A., & Tayler, C. (2011). *Practice principle 2: Partnerships with professionals*. Melbourne: Melbourne Graduate School of Education. www.education.vic.gov.au/Documents/childhood/providers/edcare/pracpartner.pdf

Government of Ireland. (2018). *First Five: A whole-of-government strategy for babies, young children and their families 2019–2028*. https://assets.gov.ie/31184/62acc54f4bdf4405b74e53a4afb8e71b.pdf

Hand, R. (2014). *Great start, great futures: Engaging local partnerships in a framework for transition*. Paper presented to the 2014 ECA conference, Melbourne: 5–6 September. https://2019.ecaconference.com.au/wp-content/uploads/2014/09/Hand-Rebecca.pdf

Hopps, K. (2014). Preschool + school + communication = What for educator relationships? *Early Years, 34*(4), 405–419. https://doi.org/10.1080/09575146.2014.963032

KidsMatter. (2013). *Transition matters: A resource for starting school for early childhood educators and school staff*. https://talkingtransitionblog.files.wordpress.com/2018/06/kmp20130228_transitionmatters_0.pdf

National Council for Curriculum and Assessment (NCCA). (2009). *Aistear: the Early Childhood Curriculum Framework*. Dublin: NCCA. www.ncca.ie/en/Curriculum_and_Assessment/Early_Childhood_and_Primary_Education/Early_Childhood_Education/Framework_for_early_learning/

National Council for Curriculum and Assessment (NCCA). (2015). *Aistear Síolta practice guide*. www.aistearsiolta.ie

National Council for Curriculum and Assessment (NCCA). (2018a) *Mo Scéal preschool to primary transition*. www.ncca.ie/en/early-childhood/mo-scéal

National Council for Curriculum and Assessment (NCCA). (2018b) *Preschool to primary school transition initiative. Final report*. www.ncca.ie/media/3367/transitionpreschoolprimary_reportfinalfeb.pdf

NSW Department of Education. (2020). *Strong and successful start to school: Transition assessment and planning tool*. https://education.nsw.gov.au/content/dam/main-education/teaching-and-learning/curriculum/early-learning/media/documents/transition-assessment-planning-tool.DOCX

NSW Department of Education. (2021). *Transition to school statement*. https://education.nsw.gov.au/content/dam/main-education/early-childhood-education/working-in-early-childhood-education/media/documents/T2S-Statement-interactive-form-2018.pdf

O'Kane, M. (2016). *Transition from preschool to primary school*. Research Report No. 19. Dublin: National Council for Curriculum and Assessment. www.ncca.ie/media/2471/transition-research-report-no-19.pdf

O'Kane, M., & Murphy, R. (2016a). *Transition from preschool to primary school: Audit of policy in 14 jurisdictions*. Dublin: National Council for Curriculum and Assessment. www.ncca.ie/media/2468/transition-from-preschool-to-primary-school-audit-of-policy-in-14-jurisdictions.pdf

O'Kane, M., & Murphy, R. (2016b). *Supporting the transition from preschool to primary School: Audit of transfer documentation in Ireland*. Dublin: National Council for Curriculum and Assessment. www.ncca.ie/media/2469/transition-from-preschool-to-primary-school-audit-of-transfer-documentation-in-ireland.pdf

Perry, B., Dockett, S., & Howard, P. (2000). Starting school: Issues for children, parents and teachers. *Journal of Australian Research in Early Childhood Education, 7*(1), 41–53.

Perry, B., Dockett, S., Mason, T., & Simpson, T. (2007). Successful transitions from prior-to-school to school for Aboriginal and Torres Strait Islander children. *International Journal for Equity and Innovation in Early Childhood, 5*(1), 102–111.

Perry, B., Dockett, S., & Petriwskyj, A. (Eds.). (2014). *Transitions to school – International research, policy and practice*. Dordrecht: Springer. https://doi.org/10.1007/978-94-007-7350-9

Perry, B., Dockett, S., & Tracey, D. (1998). At preschool they read to you, at school you learn to read. *Australian Journal of Early Childhood*, 23(4), 6–11. https://doi.org/10.1177/183693919802300403

Perry, B., Dockett, S., Whitton, D., Vickers, M., Johnston, C., & Sidoti, C. (2006). *Sydney Region Transition Project final report*. Sydney: NSW Department of Education and Training.

Queensland Department of Education. (2020a). *Statewide approach to transitions*. https://earlychildhood.qld.gov.au/early-years/transition-to-school/supporting-successful-transitions/statewide-approach

Queensland Department of Education. (2020b). *Supporting successful transitions: School decision-making tool*. https://earlychildhood.qld.gov.au/earlyYears/Documents/transition-to-school-decision-making-tool.pdf

Queensland Department of Education. (2020c). *Transition statements*. https://earlychildhood.qld.gov.au/early-years/transition-to-school/transition-statements

Queensland Department of Education. (2021). *Step Up into Education*. https://education.qld.gov.au/schools-educators/ecec/step-up-into-education-schools

Rogers, S., Dockett, S., & Perry, B. (2017). Partnerships or relationships: The perspectives of families and educators. In S. Dockett, W. Griebel, & B. Perry (Eds.), *Families and transition to school* (pp. 243–257). Cham, Switzerland: Springer. https://doi.org/10.1007/978-3-319-58329-7_16

Schoepp, K., Danaher, M., & Ater Kranov, A. (2018). An effective rubric norming process. *Practical Assessment, Research & Evaluation*, 23, Article 11. https://doi.org/10.7275/erf8-ca22

Tierney, R., & Simon, M. (2004). What's still wrong with rubrics: Focusing on the consistency of performance criteria across scale levels. *Practical Assessment, Research and Evaluation*, 9(1/2). https://doi.org/10.7275/jtvt-wg68

Victorian Department of Education and Training. (2019). *Transition learning and development statements*. www.education.vic.gov.au/childhood/professionals/learning/Pages/transitionstat.aspx

West, S. et al. (2012). *Outcomes and indicators of a positive start to school: Development of framework and tools*. www.education.vic.gov.au/Documents/about/research/outcomesandindicators.pdf

Whitton, D., & Perry, B. (2005). Transition to high school for gifted and mainstream students. *Australasian Journal of Gifted Education*, 14(1), 30–35.

9 Using evaluation to plan future transition to school programs

Sue Dockett and Bob Perry

Introduction

Communicating the findings is a critical step in the evaluation process. So too is utilising these findings to plan and enhance future iterations of the transition to school program. The first section of this chapter explores how and to whom the results of the evaluation could be communicated, noting the importance of reporting in different ways to different audiences, including the different stakeholders who have been involved. In the second section, we consider ways in which the evaluation results can inform future programs. Chapter 9A reiterates the importance of multiple stakeholders in both the evaluation and reporting of evaluation findings. Linking back to discussions in Chapter 3 about what makes a successful transition, and to Chapter 7A which highlights the value of cooperation across ECEC and school settings, Chapter 9A challenges readers to consider the benefits of cooperation and how it could be measured and reported.

Communicating findings

As well as considering who will generate the data that provide evidence for the evaluation, decisions will need to be made about the end product or summative report of the evaluation: What form will it take? How will it be communicated? and With whom is it to be shared? In participatory evaluation, the broad range of stakeholders may be involved in shaping the findings and communicating these. This may involve discussing the results of the data analysis with participants, checking that data have been analysed appropriately, that the conclusions reflect the intended meanings of those participants, and that they have provided permission for these to be shared.

The data-reduction strategies used in analysis can sometimes mean that we create generalisations, such as *parents report this, and educators report something else*. While these are valuable and often tell the story of many participants, checking back with participants helps identify situations where this was not the case and provides opportunities to report differences appropriately. Rather than repeating individual interactions, it may be possible to organise a discussion or focus group to check results. As an example, in one of our national studies, we convened a *search conference*, where participants were invited to engage in a

DOI: 10.4324/9781003055112-16

"large-group task-oriented conversation" (Department of Health and Human Services, Tasmania, n.d., p. 1) in which results were shared, input and interpretation sought, and future directions outlined.

Once determined, two major questions influence the communication of the results of the evaluation:

- With whom are the findings being shared?
- What is the purpose of sharing the findings?

With whom are the findings to be shared?

Another form of this question is "Who is the audience for the results?" The short answer is that there are likely to be multiple audiences. As well as the stakeholders and participants in the evaluation, there are likely to be organisations that supported or encouraged the evaluation, policymakers – both at the immediate local level and maybe at other levels – and any funders or contributors to the program. As well, there may be other people or groups who are interested in the evaluation or who can facilitate the implementation of changes proposed as a result of the evaluation.

Reporting the results of the evaluation to participants is a way of demonstrating value for their input. It is quite possible that not all of them will have participated in the all evaluation activities or data analysis; nevertheless, they will probably be interested in what is being reported and any implications for them.

Identifying the audience/s will help determine how best the results may be shared. Multiple audiences may mean that the evaluation is reported in multiple ways. For example, different forms of reporting could be necessary to share findings with children, families, educators, communities, or professional audiences. These may also be different from a report to a funding organisation or a journal article written for an academic audience.

An evaluation report can take many forms to reflect these different audiences. While a written report of some form is usually produced, it is also possible to share results through formats such as summary documents, oral presentations, and discussions; electronic presentations; web pages; videos; handouts; posters; photographic or other visual displays; and artwork. While these reports may be created by those leading the evaluation, it is also possible that participants share the report with others.

Example: Sharing findings with children

Having sought children's input about what was important information to share with other children about to start school, many schools have produced books designed by the children. Several of these contain both text and images from children, reflecting the information they identified as important (Figure 9.1). In addition, some books include messages from more experienced schoolchildren (Figure 9.2).

Figure 9.1 Important information from first-year-of-school children to children starting school. (Darling Heights State School, 2020; reproduced with permission)

Figure 9.2 Important information from older primary school children to children starting school. (Darling Heights State School, 2020; reproduced with permission)

Using evaluation to plan future programs 197

It is quite possible for children to share some of the findings with others. When reporting their involvement in a buddy program, the schoolchildren in Figure 9.3 chose to make a verbal presentation to a larger group, while another group elected to share a PowerPoint presentation, which included information about what they had done and why they considered it to be important. These data were included as evidence of the importance of the buddy program to these Year 5/6 children as they supported children making the transition to school.

Example: The PowerPoint presentation

We got to know each other on Day 1 by playing some games. It was fun.

We listened to M. talk about leadership and how we need to be good leaders.

[our team leader] helped us to recognise that we are important people in the school and community. We can be good leaders.

We thought about some of the ways the new children might be feeling, but there are also lots of reasons to be happy at school. We can help them. Here is our mind map. We brainstormed some great ideas. We all worked hard as a team. Here is the result of our whole group working together as a team.

We drew maps for our buddies so they won't get lost. We worked really hard on our maps.

We wrote letters to our buddies. We put a lot of effort into our letters.

Our decorated envelopes look great! We decorated the envelopes that our maps and letters will go in. We will give these to our buddies so that they will feel welcome.

Figure 9.3 Reporting about the buddy program.

Figure 9.4 Mind map.

Sharing the findings with families can take many forms. Some family members may wish to access the full evaluation report; others may choose to access a summary, talk about the results, or view a presentation. For many families, access to the results will be facilitated by having information available in relevant languages. Figures 9.5 and 9.6 provide examples.

More formal reports of the evaluation may be required for families or professional audiences and if there has been some funding or external support for the evaluation. The structure of these reports typically includes:

- report summary;
- description of the program being evaluated;
- the purpose of the evaluation;
- the evaluations questions asked;
- description of what data were collected and how and which stakeholder groups contributed;
- summary of key findings;
- discussion of findings;
- implications/recommendations; and
- issues remaining.

Using evaluation to plan future programs 199

Figure 9.5 Information brochures for families available in different languages.

Several examples of formal evaluation reports can be found on the Victorian Department of Education and Training web page entitled *Research about transition to school* (www.education.vic.gov.au/about/research/Pages/transitionresearch.aspx). This site also includes several report summaries – fact sheets – that provide a brief overview of the full report (see, for example, Department of

Figure 9.6 Summary information for parents.

Education and Training (DET), Victoria, 2017; Department of Education and Early Childhood Development (DEECD), 2011a, 2011b). International examples of evaluation reports of transition to school initiatives include McDonnell (2016) and Education Review Office (2015). The Organisation for Economic Cooperation and Development (OECD) (2017) report *Starting Strong V* also includes several country reports related to the evaluation of transition.

The evidence collected throughout the evaluation forms an important element of the report. There are many ways these data can be included and a number of ethical issues to be addressed as decisions are made about this. Some reports include data in the form of stories or case studies. These summarise data and provide readers with an overview of issues, identify possibilities for change, and highlight effective transitions practice. Many are written using strengths-based perspectives (see, for example, Dockett et al., 2011; Mason-White, 2014). Other reports use vignettes, which offer brief, often evocative descriptions of an event or situation.

Example: Excerpt from a case study included in a report

In one of the participating families, a daughter was eligible to start school . . . Her mother was unsure about the daughter's readiness for school and sought advice from the preschool and first-year-of-school teacher. Their advice was contradictory, with the preschool teacher suggesting that the child had some social problems, and the school teacher indicating that she was ready for school. The mother was not certain about the nature of the social problems identified by the preschool teacher. The mother's case worker recommended that the daughter start school, as a strategy to alleviate some of the mother's ongoing depression. However, the mother was concerned that sending her daughter to school was something she was doing for herself, rather than for her daughter. She was concerned that her daughter would be placed in a difficult position coping with school – something she had experienced with her older children.

(Dockett et al., 2011, p. 19)

Both case studies and vignettes can be powerful ways of sharing people's stories. However, they can also provide the sort of detail that means those involved can be identified and confidentiality breached, potentially causing distress. This was evident in the words of an Aboriginal community worker who reported:

I once told a student the story of how I was taken away from my family as a child and the effects it still has on me today. I was shocked and devastated to walk into the school library a few months later and see my story on display. That student had no right to show that in public without my permission.

(Board of Studies, NSW, 2008, p. 26)

One strategy to share powerful stories (with appropriate permissions) and to retain anonymity is to create composite cases or vignettes (Spalding & Phillips, 2007), where information contributed by several people is combined to reflect a specific category or theme from the data. In this way, information from no one person is represented in the vignette or case. Rather, a picture is built up from multiple sources: the issues and themes are highlighted rather than the personal.

One of the cornerstones of both effective transition to school programs and credible evaluation is the building of trusting and respectful relationships. These relationships need to be continued and affirmed through the ways the evaluation is reported. In practical terms, this involves taking care and being respectful in how we report things: focusing on strengths rather than perceived deficits. For example, where some participants may be experiencing vulnerability or marginalisation, it is important not to add to this by highlighting negative, disparaging, or stereotyped images of them and their experiences. Liamputtong (2007, p. 184) reminds us that "the choices we make about how we write about participants, about ourselves and about the cultural context . . . will lead to how these are perceived and reacted to by readers, policy-makers and the service providers".

This does not mean that reports should only include positive findings and ignore potentially negative outcomes or challenges. Rather, it implies that when reporting negative findings, it is important to consider who will be impacted by these, both intentionally and unintentionally. Perhaps the same results can be presented in more positive ways? For example, instead of opening a report with the statement that (say) 10% of children experienced challenges during the transition to school, it is possible to indicate that (say) 90% had positive transition experiences. Discussions of those positive and challenging experiences can follow. When reporting negative findings, it is critical to be clear about what is negative – for example, is it a system, policy, or practice? – and to check that the representation is accurate. Just as important is to report positive findings and to identify what it is that is working, for whom, and why. Both negative and positive findings should be supported by relevant evidence.

When communicating the results of an evaluation, issues of confidentiality and anonymity come to the fore. In some instances, settings and participants choose to be identified in reports. In others, the opposite is the case. In some instances, the setting is identified but the respondents are provided with pseudonyms. Decisions about how data are reported and participants (de)identified will often depend on the commitments required by ethics boards or those approving the study. Even when real names are not used in the report, it may well be possible to identify the source of information. For example, in a school with only one first-year-of-school teacher or an ECEC setting with one director, replacing names with positions is unlikely to provide anonymity.

Similar issues arise with the use of images. While people may give permission for an image to be used in a written report that has limited circulation, they may not give permission for that same image to become the poster image for a campaign, the key feature on an electronic presentation, or a major element of a web page. Similarly, including images of specific settings opens up the possibility of identifying those involved in the evaluation.

Regardless of the ways in which the results of the evaluation are reported and to whom, there are several ethical issues to be addressed. These include questions such as:

- Who owns the report?
- Who will share the findings?

- Who has authority to circulate the report?
- How broadly will it be circulated?

These questions are best addressed in the initial stages of the evaluation rather than at the end. While some changes may occur as the evaluation progresses and the findings and the implications of these emerge, it is important for all to know who holds ownership of the report – in whatever format/s – and who has permission to share it. Answers to the last two of the questions listed relate to the purpose of sharing the results of the evaluation.

What is the purpose of sharing the findings?

There can be multiple purposes for sharing the findings of an evaluation. Foremost among these is to show that participants' perspectives have been listened to and have contributed to the evaluation and that as a result, program improvements can be made. Other purposes include:

- building support for the continuation or development of the transition program among stakeholders;
- accessing additional stakeholders;
- identifying possible changes to the program;
- accessing appropriate resources;
- seeking funding for the program;
- contributing to policy and decision making;
- sharing key issues to be addressed that may be bigger than the transition program itself;
- promoting the sustainability of the program;
- establishing comparative data between this and other programs or for this program over time;
- identifying and responding to community needs;
- identifying professional learning opportunities;
- building communities of practice around transition opportunities; and
- advocacy for evidence-informed transitions practice.

These purposes reflect the broader purposes of informing decision making, learning about and understanding the program, and strategic or political purposes (Smart, 2020). At the local level, learning about the program, how it works, and for whom contributes to decisions relating to the continuation of the program, what practices are included or excluded, how it operates, and who is involved. Learning about the program can also change the ways people think about it. For example, learning that some participants see the transition program as a readiness program could change the way people advertise, talk about, or promote the program, as well as what practices are included and how these are implemented. Learning that parents find the transition program unhelpful in supporting them as their children make the move to school also is likely to result in changes to the program and how it operates.

Sharing the evaluation findings can also be important for strategic or political purposes. If we consider politics in its broadest sense of "the relationships within a group or organisation that allow particular people to have power over others" (Cambridge Dictionary, n.d.), sharing evaluation findings can be a political act as people advocate for the program or for those who access or should access it, for those who implement it, and those who support it. Sharing evaluation findings can also be a strategic act to confirm and/or expand the existing program and position it as a legitimate and worthwhile program deserving of recognition and resources. For example, one of the consequences of sharing the evaluation in a school context can be to raise awareness among all staff about the value and importance of transition and the impact it has not only on the first-year of school but also across the years.

In a strategic sense, sharing evaluation findings can contribute to building a culture of evaluation and evidence-informed practice (Owen, 2003). For those involved in the evaluation, particularly when it has been framed as participatory evaluation, there can be a range of benefits including the development of additional skills; increased opportunities for collaboration and learning from others; opportunities for learning about the program, its aims, and its consequences; building consensus about the transition program and its preferred direction; and promoting critical thinking and reflexivity about the program and its effectiveness. These potential benefits can contribute to a climate characterised by efforts to seek evidence to support practice and inform decision making as well as promote opportunities for ongoing learning. Weiss (1998, p. 25) has referred to these effects as the *enlightenment function* of evaluation, where

> people learn more about what happens in the program and afterwards. They gain a better idea of program strengths, fault lines, opportunities for improvement. Old myths are punctured, issues previously unrecognized come to the fore. As a result, people think differently . . .

A climate that supports critical thinking and reflexivity provides an ideal space for listening to and respecting multiple perspectives, including those of children. One of the consequences of engaging with children about their transition expectations and experiences can be increased regard for their competence in matters that affect their lives and the confidence to share these.

Using findings to inform future programs

One of the key reasons for evaluating transition programs is to inform future programs. Many of the issues discussed earlier in the consideration of the purposes of sharing the findings will impact on the future programs.

One of the key drivers for informing future programs will be the recommendations, suggestions, or options for action that are drawn from the evaluation (Grob, 2015). These can be written in a range of ways and directed towards a range of people or organisations.

Example: Recommendations from a national evaluation report

In their national review of how well early childhood services and schools supported children through the transition to school in New Zealand, the Education Review Office (2015, p. 3) recommended:

> that early childhood services and schools:
>
> - review the extent to which their curriculum and associated assessment practices support all children to experience a successful transition to school
> - establish relationships with local schools and services to promote community-wide understanding and sharing of good practice.
>
> . . . [and] that the Ministry of Education:
>
> - consider . . . ways of supporting school and early childhood teachers to work together as they better understand each other's curriculum, promoting continuity of learning for children.

Example: Options from a state wide evaluation report

The state wide practice review reported in Chapter 4A presented options for consideration rather than recommendations. The first of these (Nolan et al., 2017, p. 8) is:

> Option 1
>
> Formal networks are established, or existing networks built upon, that have the scope to collaborate around transition to school processes and practices for children and families experiencing vulnerability.

Another report of a state-based evaluation utilised project stories to summarise findings and link these to project learnings that suggest future directions for programs.

Example: Stories from a state wide evaluation report

> Project Story 3: Building relationships
>
> Project story: the project provided time and space for settings to come together to reflect on and talk about transition to school promising practices which included discussions of curriculum, routines, working conditions and questions about education and the needs of children and families. These broad ranging discussions enabled members of the sites to hear each other's perspectives and to begin developing relationships.
>
> Project learning: Building strong relationships across sectors supports positive transitions and ongoing connections.
>
> (Smith et al., 2011, p. 59)

Example: Recommendations from a locally based evaluation report

The evaluation of one school's transition program (Dockett, Perry, & Højslet Schürer, 2020) included quite specific recommendations, including that:

- [the school] recognises and celebrates its many achievements in the areas of transition to primary school and uses this recognition to highlight the importance of transition throughout the school;
- the number of gatherings of preschool and school educators aimed at planning, implementing, and evaluating the transition to primary school program be increased to encourage a consistent and collaborative approach to transition for all children starting school;
- the number of visits to [first-year-of-school] classrooms and teachers be increased beyond the current two and that the nature of these visits be revisited.

These examples offer different ways of responding to the evaluation findings. They aim both to identify what was working well and offer suggestions for changes based on the evidence generated and analysed. The recommendations, suggestions or options provide a measure against which future actions can be assessed. For example, as future programs are planned, specific questions can be asked about how actions support the building of relationships between ECEC and school educators or about how additional school visits have been incorporated. One of the reasons for sharing the evaluation findings could well involve advocacy for the program or for those involved, as well as for the provision of resources to implement the recommendations and continue to evaluate the program.

Changes to transition programs

Whatever the format, many evaluation reports spark interest and initial commitment but then end up occupying space on the shelf when the excitement has died down and other priorities have emerged. One of the factors influencing this can be the timing of the evaluation and the sharing of the report. One of the things the evaluation team will need to consider is when the report will have the most impact. It may be, for example, that sharing an evaluation report after the next transition program has started may not have the impact it could have had if it had been shared when the program was being planned.

Nevertheless, changes are possible and the incorporation of findings into future planning can improve the program. The following examples are drawn from Perry and Dockett (2008) and report changes to transition programs across three different settings as a result of incorporating children's perspectives into the evaluation.

Example: Changes in practice

The project has highlighted the importance of buddies in transition – and the school intends to continue and to build on the existing buddy program.

... The [first-year-of-school] students' visit to the preschools was "like a school reunion for them, a one-year school reunion". The importance of this return visit for network and relationships building among children was highlighted and plans discussed to provide ongoing opportunities for the children from both preschool and school to meet. (p. 26)

There has been strong recognition of the importance of collaboration between prior-to-school settings and the school, and particularly the opportunities for children to interact and for teachers to co-operate in the delivery of transition programs and experiences.

... Children's perspectives were already taken seriously across the settings. However, this project has provided opportunities to document and share children's perspectives in different ways. Having the books made by the children in prior-to-school settings at the school, and the books from school at the prior-to-school settings made some very tangible connections. (p. 34)

Changes . . .

- Enhanced visits from the [first-year-of-school] teacher and students to the prior-to-school settings;
- Enhanced visits from the prior-to-school staff and children to the school;
- The introduction of the PowerPoint slide show and providing opportunities for preschool children to ask questions about school;
- Incorporation of the children's suggestions into the transition program; . . .
- Incorporation of suggestions from the parents:
  - We will continue with a parent mentoring system and have an informal morning tea and chat for new parents on the first day . . .
  - During the play sessions, parents will be asked to provide suggestions about what they would like to know about school before their children start school the following year. These suggestions will form a major part of the Parent Information sessions held in term 4. (p. 43)

Conclusion

A great deal of work goes into the planning and implementation of evaluation of transition to school programs. Preparing and sharing the findings of the evaluation process is a critical further step that can influence the impact of the evaluation and guide the future development of programs. Chapter 9A picks up the discussion of multiple stakeholders and multiple perspectives by highlighting the importance of cooperation across ECEC and school contexts and considering how this might be implemented, assessed, and reported. It provides an interesting example of cooperation between ECEC and primary school professionals and some of the potential tensions that may occur.

There are many ways to communicate the evaluation findings and many audiences who will be interested in accessing these. There may also be audiences – such as policy makers or decision makers – who can impact the future of the program, if only they know about it. Sharing evaluation findings is both an ethical commitment to those who have participated and those who are likely to be affected by the program and a strategic exercise in accessing the necessary support, time, and resources to implement the changes recommended in the report, or to maintain practice and programs that have demonstrated the desired impact.

Regardless of the form of the evaluation report, its construction and the evidence included must be accurate and must address some complex ethical issues, including those of confidentiality and privacy, respect for participants and the information they share, and the principle of *doing no harm* in the way participants are represented.

9A Challenges of and strategies within interprofessional cooperation between ECEC institutions and primary schools

Mirja Kekeritz

Introduction

Entering the formal school system is an important step in a child's development – on a personal, academic, and individual level. The extent to which this transition from institutions of early childhood education and care (ECEC) to primary school is successfully mastered depends on a number of factors. However, there is general agreement in international research that cooperation between prior-to-school institutions and schools is crucial in shaping this transition (Ahtola et al., 2011; Fabian & Dunlop, 2002; Hanke, Backhaus, & Bogatz, 2013; LoCasale-Crouch et al., 2008).

The underlying assumption in this chapter is that the "competence of the social system" (Griebel & Niesel, 2004, p. 132) and thus also the cooperation between ECEC and primary school – that is, the interactions between teachers and other participants of both institutions – along with other mutually influencing components of the socio-cultural macro-system (Nickel, 1990), are important bases for the successful management of the transition by the child. Cooperation within transitions plays a key role for individual and social development processes.

What does cooperation mean in the context of ECEC institutions and primary schools? Are there different quality levels or standards within the framework for this cooperation? What does successful cooperation require? Which general conditions prove to be beneficial for cooperative activities?

Initially, I will define interprofessional cooperation in transition and provide key points for the evaluation of cooperation. Based on my study about the weekly routine of cooperation between a German ECEC institution (*kindergarten*) and primary school, I will also present findings about the interrelationships between the *form of cooperation*, the *climate of cooperation*, and *general conditions*. Then I identify, in line with the ecosystem approach, conditions on the level of professionals for successful cooperation between ECEC and primary schools.

Levels of cooperation

What does successful cooperation look like, and how can we *measure* the performance and outcome of cooperation within transition? Cooperation seems to be particularly difficult to grasp as an object of evaluation, because the range of understandings of cooperation goes from a brief exchange of information about a child between ECEC and primary school professionals to extensive cooperation activities including collaborative planning, implementation, and follow-up. As a multidimensional interdependent process, cooperation is more than the mere sum of cooperation partners and their activities but rather an interactive process of mutual work, which is dynamic in its structure. Levels of communication and contact within cooperation differ with regard to the willingness and capacity of the different participants to cooperate with others (Kienig & Margetts, 2013).

Three levels of cooperation can be considered: (Gräsel, Fußangel, & Pröbstel, 2006, p. 208):

1) level of exchange

At this basic level is a mutual exchange of information and materials; activities happen independently of each other, no shared targets are defined, but participants might agree on dates for example for language assessments or just exchange information on the child's developmental status.

2) level of distributed responsibilities

Work-sharing cooperation is a distribution of tasks between professionals taking into account the strengths of the different participants through shared planning processes and through an efficient allocation of tasks among all actors.

3) level of co-construction

On this level the actors work together over longer periods of time, share and expand their knowledge as well as interact with each other. In this process, joint strategies, tasks and solutions, plans and concepts are developed in a shared working process. This most sophisticated form of cooperation can lead, for instance, to shared didactic models or compatible pedagogical concepts between ECEC institutions and primary schools.

What factors influence the level of cooperation?

Expanding this level model, which primarily distinguishes between the intensity of interactions and the degree of common objectives, cooperation can be assessed on the basis of three quality dimensions (Charlesworth et al., 1993; Tietze, Rossbach, & Grenner, 2005):

a) *Process quality:* quality of interactions, experiences, and stimulations (among the different actors of the transition)
b) *Quality of the general pedagogical framework*
c) *Quality of pedagogical attitudes and beliefs* towards cooperation (mental climate)

Cooperation is primarily supported by the teachers, who put into the cooperation their personalities, their attitudes, and values to their work, their motivation, and beliefs about the benefits of the cooperation, their understanding of their responsibilities, and their commitment and expertise. The individual teacher with her/his individual preconditions for cooperation and the prevailing cooperation culture in the specific institutions form the foundation for any further cooperation processes and thus the dimensions of cooperation (Figure 9A.1).

Six dimensions which can be utilised to evaluate interprofessional cooperation have also been suggested by Rathmer (2012). These dimensions can be gathered together into the approach illustrated in Figure 9A.2.

The *general conditions* with cooperation partners and professionals, their institutional background, individual experiences, degrees and qualifications, as well as the *framework conditions* (pedagogical orientation, support, work structure, information channels, etc.), provide information about the structure and

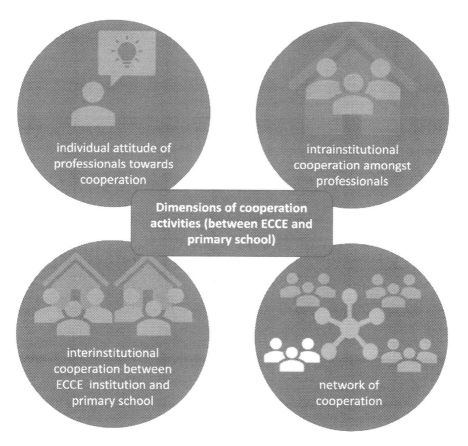

Figure 9A.1 Dimensions of cooperation (after Rathmer, 2012).

212 *Mirja Kekeritz*

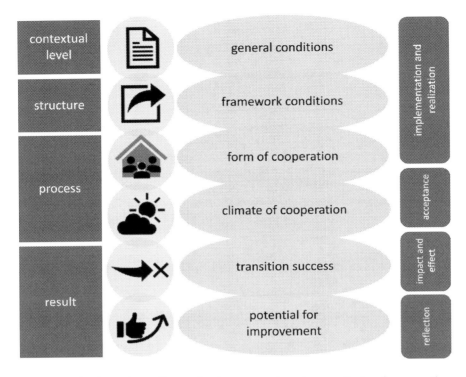

Figure 9A.2 Dimensions of an evaluative approach to interprofessional cooperation (after Rathmer, 2012).

implementation of the cooperation. Process characteristics are considered by examining the *form of cooperation* (exchange/distributed responsibilities/co-construction) and the *climate of cooperation* (motivation of the professionals and other individuals involved, communication and trust among each other), where quality is expressed through the acceptance of the practiced cooperation. *The success of transition* and *potential for improvement* consider the results of the cooperation in terms of expected results and the constructive reflection of possibilities for the further development of the cooperation.

In the study described in what follows, emphasis is given to the evaluation of the climate of cooperation between ECEC institutions and primary schools and the importance of this dimension.

Case study about a co-constructional cooperation

In the following case study, cooperation between an ECEC institution (*kindergarten*) and a primary school in Lower Saxony, Germany, was investigated ethnographically for more than half a year. While a large number of ECEC institutions and primary schools in Germany cooperate at the level of exchange, the investigated institutions cooperated at the level of co-construction (Gräsel et al., 2006). The two institutions had set up a joint room in the primary school based on a concept called *Lernwerkstatt* [Open Inquiry Learning Workshop] (Puddu, Keller, & Lembens, 2012), where preschool children and first graders met together once a week. The main focus was on early scientific experiments and exploration, where ECEC teachers and primary school teachers prepared the activities and environment in mixed teams.

By starting with a circle time of all children and professionals from both institutions, in which ideas for new experiments on a quarterly main topic such as magnets or earth were given, the children were released into an open experiment phase. Different materials which were prepared by the teachers beforehand were displayed on tables. In this phase, the two to four teachers from both institutions acted as facilitators and interactively supported the children in their explorative activities. Finally, the children documented their findings in drawings or by writing in a research booklet and discussed their findings in the final circle time.

The study examined *how* cooperation took place on a day-to-day basis in the *intermediate space* between the primary school and the ECEC institution, which was shared by both professions (ECEC and primary school teachers). In addition to observation protocols, field notes and videos of the cooperative learning workshop sessions, the professionals were also interviewed about their experiences in the cooperative work.

These data were the basis to reconstruct how intensive cooperation *affects* the professionals who deal with the transition between institutions in a cooperative space themselves and provides opportunities for them to change from passive to more active players within the transition.

Challenges and strategies of interprofessional cooperation

Curricular orientation

All the interviewed professionals describe differences between the professions. For example, primary school teachers are more focused on thematic issues and are closely oriented to their curriculum, while early childhood educators are more playful in their interaction with children. The professionals describe it as a challenge to form the common field of cooperation:

> That we just look very closely then here and here and here. And then we aim over to the ECEC *orientation plan* and the teachers often have their curriculum in their mind. [. . .] And there you just see that there are simply these differences again, that there can be also very, very strong tensions.
>
> (Interview ECEC-Veber: 42)

First of all, different curricular and thus also educational orientations create a field of tension. The traditional separation of early childhood and primary education in Germany reflects in the two different curriculum traditions. The professionals describe the tensions and the collaborative search for solutions, strategies, and possibilities for both institutional orientations. The idea of a *middle way* is taken up by most professionals.

> Throughout this cooperation you can see that there are big differences between primary school and ECEC in the general pedagogical approach, in the way the children are addressed //Okay.// (.) and there have been disagreements from time to time, "How do we come together?"
> (Interview-ECEC-Neibel: 42)

> And there's just, there's just this friction in between. Then you have to look, uh, I think you have to find the middle way.
> (Interview-Primary School (PS)-Dräger: 41)

Overall, it can be concluded that the cooperative setting does not follow a clear curricular orientation, and thus the cooperation work is also characterised by the degree to which common points of orientation still need to be negotiated and the extent to which the educators can embrace a cross-professional pedagogical attitude.

Didactic approach

Just as the two professions bring different perspectives into the cooperation on the curricular level, there are also differences between the two professions on the methodological-didactical level. Primary school teachers describe their own approaches as being more oriented towards subject-specific learning goals, which, among other things, set limits to the playful (supposedly aimless) explorations of children, such as playful activities with water (instead of planned experiments with the element of water).

> ... that you can guide a little bit. I think the [primary school] teacher has to direct if you want to reach your goals.
> (Interview-PS-Jakobi: 20)

Other statements in the interviews with the primary school teachers make it clear that they themselves implement their own orientation towards (subject-related) goals through a *guiding* instructive form of interaction with the children. Also, the ECEC teachers are attributing a more ambitious standard to the didactic style of the teachers. In addition to the orientation towards subject-specific goals, this standard is also defined by "sometimes wanting the children to perform even higher" (Interview-ECEC-Noldorf: 8).

What is interesting here is that all professionals state that they have to adapt their didactic approach to the other institution in order to address successfully *all children* in the cooperative setting. Accordingly, *primary school–related* didactic styles of interaction on the side of the ECEC teachers and *ECEC-related* styles of interaction on the side of the primary-school teachers are required in the setting.

Negotiations of a cooperative pedagogy

An ECEC teacher describes a situation in which a primary school teacher accuses her of constantly repeating the children's statements during circle time:

> Well, one thing was, we hadn't really realised it. When we now support the child language-wise in kindergarten, we like to repeat what the child has said. Now if the child has a wrong syntax somehow, you don't say that: "You have to do it this way and that way. That's the right word. You have to say it like that!" Instead, one simply repeats the sentence again in the correct form so that the child hears it again correctly. Without correcting it. At the beginning I probably did this quite often during circle time. Whereupon a primary school teacher told me: Oh, this *teacher echo*, we absolutely refuse to repeat what a child has said! //Mmh.// Because the children should learn to listen to what the others say. //Yes.// And don't rely on the teacher automatically repeating it again. This was one of those points that I now remember, so well . . . . //Yes.//. Where we have to see . . . well, how do we bring it together? Because I still think that our kindergarten children are benefiting from it, because I notice that they are not as concentrated as the school children. When I repeat it again or simply correct it language-wise.
>
> (Interview-ECEC-Neibel: 44)

The educator considers the verbal repetition (*recast* or *parallel speaking* [Albers, 2009]) to be essential for accompanying the younger children in order to act as a language role model and also to maintain the children's concentration. On the contrary, the primary school teacher argues that she wants to encourage active listening, and here, the ECEC teacher notes that both specific ways of interaction must be "brought together".

Based on this, the professionals outline the cooperative setting as a diverse field, in which different professions with individual pedagogical approaches and interactional styles try to meet the specific needs of the children. According to the interviewees, neither completely ECEC nor primary school–based pedagogies are appropriate as the cross-institutional field of cooperation requires its own forms of pedagogy.

Successful transition in cooperative settings

This brief insight into the voices of the professionals shows that intensive cooperation on the level of co-construction especially requires and promotes intensive discussion and exchange in order to establish a culture of cooperation that values differences and recognises commonalities. Summing up, the following four points are essential for fruitful and sustainable cooperation between ECEC institutions and primary schools.

Shared aims of the cooperation partners (integration)

In order for individuals to consider cooperation to be useful, they must establish a positive interconnection between their aims and the aims of the other cooperation partners. The shared, transparent, and clearly worded aims and related activities are important for effective cooperation.

Reciprocal interactions between the cooperation partners (interprofessional interaction)

Dialogues and honest exchange between individuals are the basis for successful cooperative action. On the one hand, this requires opportunities (in terms of time, staff, and space) for exchange and interaction and, on the other hand – especially in the initial phase – support from facilitators or mentors who encourage the communication process between the different institutions and persons.

Confidence among the cooperation partners (cooperation climate)

An essential factor for cooperation is that the stakeholders and partners trust and feel confident in each other. Sharing a common understanding of the rationale for cooperation and thus highlighting the common interest towards each individual child can be key factors in achieving this respect.

Autonomy of the cooperation partners (differentiation)

Autonomy is an ambivalent factor here, because too much autonomy for the participants can impede collaboration, and too little autonomy can have a negative effect on the motivation of individuals (Gräsel et al., 2006; Steinert et al., 2006). The cooperation format, such as the open-inquiry learning workshop described in this chapter, should offer space for the interests and ideas of all professionals and, in addition, encourage them to work in small multi-professional teams in order to implement innovative ideas.

References

Ahtola, A., Poikonen, P.-L., Kontoniemi, M., Niemi, P., & Nurmi, J.-E. (2011). Successful handling of entrance to formal schooling: Transition practices as a local innovation. *International Journal of Transitions in Childhood*, 5, 3–21. https://education.unimelb.edu.au/__data/assets/pdf_file/0007/3549877/journal5_Annarilla-Ahtola,-Pirjo-Liisa-Poikonen,-Marita-Kontoniemi,-Pekka-Niemi,-and-Jari-Erik-Nurmi.pdf

References – Chapters 9 and 9A

Albers, T. (2009). *Sprache und Interaktion im Kindergarten – eine quantitativ-qualitative Analyse der sprachlichen und kommunikativen Kompetenzen von drei- bis sechsjährigen Kindern.* [Language and interaction in kindergarten – A quantitative-qualitative analysis of the language and communication skills of three to six year old children]. Bad Heilbrunn: Klinkhardt Verlag.

Board of Studies, NSW. (2008). *Working with Aboriginal communities. A guide to community consultation and protocols.* Sydney: Author. https://ab-ed.nesa.nsw.edu.au/files/working-with-aboriginal-communities.pdf

Cambridge Dictionary. (n.d.). *Politics.* https://dictionary.cambridge.org/dictionary/english/politics

Charlesworth, R., Hart, C. H., Burts, D. C., Thomasson, R. H., Mosley, J., & Fleege, P. O. (1993). Measuring the developmental appropriateness of kindergarten teachers' beliefs and practices. *Early Childhood Research Quarterly, 8*(3), 255–276. https://doi.org/10.1016/S0885-2006(05)80067-5

Darling Heights State School (Eds.). (2020). *Welcome to Darling Heights State School.* Toowoomba: Darling Heights State School.

Department of Education and Early Childhood Development (DEECD). (2011a). *2011 Follow-up evaluation. Transition: A positive start to school.* www.education.vic.gov.au/Documents/about/research/transeval2011keyfindings.pdf

Department of Education and Early Childhood Development (DEECD). (2011b). *Research into practices to support a positive start to school. Report summary.* www.education.vic.gov.au/Documents/about/research/pospracsummary.pdf

Department of Education and Training (DET), Victoria. (2017). *Transition to school: Supporting children and families at risk of experiencing vulnerability.* www.education.vic.gov.au/Documents/childhood/professionals/learning/Fact%20Sheet%20Transition%20to%20School%20Supporting%20Vulnerable%20Families.pdf

Department of Health and Human Services, Tasmania. (n.d.). *Search conference.* https://health.tas.gov.au/__data/assets/pdf_file/0003/89409/Search_Conference.pdf

Dockett, S., Perry, B., Hampshire, A., Mason, J., & Schmied, V. (2011). *Facilitating children's transition to school from families with complex support needs.* www.csu.edu.au/__data/assets/pdf_file/0004/517036/Facilitating-Childrens-Trans-School.pdf

Dockett, S., Perry, B., & Højslet Schürer, M. (2020). *Expectations and experiences of starting primary school.* Unpublished evaluation report.

Education Review Office. (2015). *Continuity of learning: Transitions from early childhood services to schools.* www.ero.govt.nz/assets/Uploads/ERO-Continuity-of-Learning-FINAL.pdf

Fabian, H., & Dunlop, A.-W. (2002). *Transitions in the early years: Debating continuity and progression for young children in early education.* London: Taylor & Francis.

Gräsel, C., Fußangel, K., & Pröbstel, C. (2006). Lehrkräfte zur Kooperation anregen – eine Aufgabe für Sisyphos? [Encouraging teachers to cooperate – A task for Sisyphus?] *Zeitschrift für Pädagogik, 52*(2), 205–219. www.pedocs.de/volltexte/2011/4453/pdf/ZfPaed_2006_2_Graesel_Fussangel_Proebstel_Lehrkraefte_Kooperation_anregen_D_a.pdf

Griebel, W., & Niesel, R. (2004). *Transitionen. Fähigkeit von Kindern in Tageseinrichtungen fördern, Veränderungen erfolgreich zu bewältigen* [Transitions. Promote the ability of children in day care centers to successfully cope with change]. Weinheim: Beltz.

Grob, G. (2015). Providing recommendations, suggestions, and options for improvement. In K. Newcomer, H. Hatry, & J. Wholey (Eds.), *Handbook of practical program evaluation* (4th ed., pp. 725–738). Hoboken, NJ: Jossey-Bass. https://doi.org/10.1002/9781119171386.ch27

Hanke, P., Backhaus, J., & Bogatz, A. (2013). *Den Übergang gemeinsam gestalten: Kooperation und Bildungsdokumentation im Übergang von der Kindertageseinrichtung in die Grundschule* [Shaping the transition together: cooperation and educational documentation in the transition from daycare to primary school]. Münster: Waxmann Verlag.

Kienig, A., & Margetts, K. (2013). Beliefs, policy and practice: Challenges. In K. Margetts & A. Kienig (Eds.), *International perspectives on transition to school: Reconceptualising beliefs, policy and practice* (pp. 149–154). New York: Routledge.

Liamputtong, P. (2007). *Researching the vulnerable*. London: SAGE.

LoCasale-Crouch, J., Mashburn, A. J., Downer, J. T., & Pianta, R. C. (2008). Pre-kindergarten teachers' use of transition practices and children's adjustment to kindergarten. *Early Childhood Research Quarterly, 23*, 124–139. https://doi.org/10.1016/j.ecresq.2007.06.001

Mason-White, H. (2014). *The journey to big school. Supporting Aboriginal and Torres Strait Islander children's transition to primary school*. Melbourne: SNAICC. www.snaicc.org.au/wp-content/uploads/2016/01/03316.pdf

McDonnell, L. (2016). *Developing culturally sensitive evaluation and assessment tools for early childhood programs*. https://uakn.org/wp-content/uploads/2015/05/WRC-Final-Report_Developing-Culturally-Sensitive-Evaluation-and-Assessment-Tools-for-Early-Childhood-Programs_2015-2016.pdf

Nickel, H. (1990). Das Problem der Einschulung aus ökologisch-systemischer Perspektive [The problem of school enrolment from an ecological-systemic perspective]. *Psychologie in Erziehung und Unterricht, 37*, 217–227.

Nolan, A., Kilderry, A., Beahan, J., Lanting, C., & Speldewinde, C. (2017). *Early years transitions. Support for children and families at risk of experiencing vulnerability: Practice review report*. Melbourne: Department of Education and Training, Victoria. www.education.vic.gov.au/Documents/childhood/professionals/learning/Transition%20to%20School%20Vulnerability%20Project%20Practice%20Review.pdf

Organisation for Economic Cooperation and Development (OECD). (2017). *Starting strong V. Transitions from early childhood education and care to primary education*. Paris: OECD Publishing. https://doi.org/10.1787/9789264276253-en

Owen, J. (2003). Evaluation culture: A definition and analysis of its development within organisations. *Evaluation Journal of Australasia, 3*(1), 43–47. https://doi.org/10.1177/1035719X0300300107

Perry, B., & Dockett, S. (2008). *Voices of children in starting school*. www.transitiontoschool.net/uploads/2/9/6/5/29654941/voices_of_children_in_starting_school_-_bob_perry_and_sue_dockett.pdf

Puddu, S., Keller, E., & Lembens, A. (2012). Potentials of Lernwerkstatt (Open Inquiry) for preservice teachers' professional development. In C. Bruguière, A. Tiberghien, & P. Clement (Eds.), *ESERA conference 2011* (pp. 153–159). Lyon, France: European Science Education Research Association.

Rathmer, B. A. (2012). *Kita und Grundschule: Kooperation und Übergangsgestaltung. Konzeptionen – empirische Bestandsaufnahme – Perspektiven* [Kita and elementary school: cooperation and transition planning. Concepts – empirical inventory – perspectives]. Münster: Waxmann Verlag.

Smart, J. (2020). *Making the most out of evaluation*. https://aifs.gov.au/cfca/expert-panel-project/making-most-out-evaluation

Smith, K., Kotsanas, C., Farrelly, A., & Alexander, K. (2011). *Research into practices to support a positive start to school*. www.education.vic.gov.au/Documents/about/research/pospracmelbuni.pdf

Spalding, N. J., & Phillips, T. (2007). Exploring the use of vignettes: From validity to trustworthiness. *Qualitative Health Research*, 17(7), 954–962. https://doi.org/10.1177/1049732307306187

Steinert, B., Klieme, E., Maag Merki, K., Döbrich, P., Halbheer, U., & Kunz, A. (2006). Lehrerkooperation in der Schule: Konzeption, Erfassung, Ergebnisse [Teacher cooperation in schools: Conception, recording, results]. *Zeitschrift für Pädagogik*, 52(2), 185–204. www.pedocs.de/volltexte/2011/4452/pdf/ZfPaed_2006_2_Steinert_Klieme_MaagMerki_Doebrich_Lehrerkooperation_Schule_D_A.pdf

Tietze, W., Rossbach, G., & Grenner, K. (2005). *Kinder von 4 bis 8 Jahren: Zur Qualität der Erziehung und Bildung in Kindergarten, Grundschule und Familie* [Children from 4 to 8 years: On the quality of upbringing and education in kindergarten, elementary school and family]. Weinheim, Basel: Beltz.

Weiss, C. H. (1998). Have we learned anything new about the use of evaluation? *American Journal of Evaluation*, 19(1), 21–33. https://doi.org/10.1177/109821409801900103

10 Looking forward

Sue Dockett and Bob Perry

Introduction

Despite the challenges of the pandemic, or perhaps even because of these, we have had the opportunity to collaborate with colleagues around the world and to continue our conversations about transition to school and the importance of evaluation in guiding future directions. For this, we are most grateful.

In each of our countries and throughout the pandemic, educators, families, children, and communities have faced major educational challenges. In some contexts, schools were closed, yet early childhood (ECEC) settings remained open; in others, both schools and ECEC settings were expected to operate *as normal*, albeit sometimes with adults required to wear masks and sanitise equipment several times a day. Across many contexts, transition programs were curtailed or adapted as visits and other contact between ECEC settings and schools were prohibited both for educators and children. Parents and family members were required to drop their children at the school gate and collect them at the same place, with no visitors allowed on school grounds. Some schools even had systems in which educators greeted children at the car door each morning and returned them to the car door at the end of the school day (Hopps, personal communication). Many parents were expected to support children's learning at home as well as managing their other work and family commitments; many educators were expected to develop online learning resources and supports in a short space of time; and many children were expected to manage vertical transitions – from ECEC or home to school – as well as horizontal transitions – from home to school to learning from home and back to school. In most contexts, the usual pattern of engagement among children and families and educators was disrupted.

In these extreme circumstances, it would be easy to say that transition to school programs do not matter; that children and their families will *manage* even if they do not get to visit the school, meet their peers or their educators; families do not get to meet educators; and educators do not have opportunities to cooperate. However, these difficult circumstances have indicated the exact opposite; these are the times when working together, feeling supported, recognising challenges, and working to overcome them are critical and when just

DOI: 10.4324/9781003055112-18

managing in an educational sense is not sufficient to promote ongoing positive engagement with school or to build the transitions capital (Dunlop, 2014) that helps children and families manage successive transitions. These are times when children and families may be confronted with significant stress, possibly exacerbated by concerns about entering new school contexts, being separated from family, and engaging with new people. Yet these are also times when there are opportunities to question and reflect on what has been taken for granted and adapt or adopt practices that promote the building of the trusting and respectful relationships that form the basis of effective transitions. Around the world, there have been many educators across ECEC settings and schools who, despite experiencing high levels of stress themselves, have continued to work on building effective early years practice and to support children, families, and communities (Atiles et al., 2021; Dayal & Tiko, 2020; Park et al., 2020; Pascal & Bertram, 2021; Pramling Samuelsson, Wagner, & Ødegaard, 2020). We hope that some of the positive changes and innovations that have been documented around transition to school during this time can be sustained.

Reflection and reflexivity have central places in many approaches to evaluation. As we have engaged with this manuscript, we have had many interesting and challenging conversations about the nature of transition to school, strategies for evaluation, and the possible impacts of evaluation. While these reflections have resulted in the affirmation of many of our beliefs and values, they have also provoked the continued questioning of others and recognition of the importance of constantly challenging what we do, how we do it, and the impact this has on others. We share some of our thoughts about these issues in the following discussion.

Evaluation and transition to school programs

The focus of this book is transition programs – the schedule of practices and activities that together aim to promote positive transition to school experiences for all involved. It is important to note that we characterise transitions as times of continuity and change, with changes most evident in the roles, identity, and status of individuals. While organised and structured transition programs have the potential to support the processes of continuity and change, the processes of transition involve more than the program itself. As outlined in Chapter 2, essential elements of transition include the internal changes in the ways people see and think about themselves and the social changes in the ways other people regard and interact with them.

Invisible transitions

Much of this book has focused on building supportive, collaborative, and professional relationships among those involved in transition and the ways in which these provide resources to support and respond to both continuity and change. Relationships between ECEC and school educators have featured strongly in this discussion. One of the assumptions that could be made from this discussion is that all children will attend some form of ECEC setting before they start school and/or participate in a transition to school program. This is the expected path for many children around the world (Lago, 2017). However, as ECEC is not compulsory in Australia and in other countries, there will always be some children who do not attend ECEC or transition programs or who arrive as unexpected school enrolments. There are many possible reasons why this may occur, including families having recently arrived in the area being unable to access ECEC or encountering geographical, social, or cultural barriers to accessing ECEC.

In recent years, we have been asking what happens to support the transition of these children and their families (Dockett & Perry, 2021). We refer to their experiences as *invisible transitions*, as they are often not included in transition planning, and this, in turn, can contribute to a sense of social invisibility for those involved (Clifford, 1963). Transition planning that incorporates provision for these children and families recognises that transition neither starts with participation in a transition program nor finishes the day children start school. Rather, these transition to school processes and programs continue at least throughout the first year of school and are responsive to individual children, families, and circumstances. They acknowledge that building a sense of belonging, while strongly integrated with the social context and the people involved, also involves individual change that occurs over different periods of time for different people. One immediate implication to be drawn from this is that there is value in reconceptualising how we define and consider transition to school programs: How do we build programs that make provision for children and families that we don't know about? When does a transition program start and finish? Who determines this and on what basis? What would a whole-school or whole-community approach to transition look like?

The consideration of invisible transition does not mean that professional relationships among ECEC and school educators can be neglected. Indeed, the opposite is the case. In contexts in which there are strong, trusting, and reciprocal relationships between ECEC and school educators and other community professionals, there also tend to be good connections with the broader community and collective awareness of families and children eligible to start school as well as some of the most appropriate ways to reach out to them.

The importance of program theory

Effective evaluations don't *just happen*. They need to be planned and thought through – just as effective transition to school programs need to be well planned and implemented. Chapter 4 defined evaluation as focusing on both the worth and merit of programs. Evaluation of transition to school programs needs to reflect both these elements – the ways in which a program addresses the identified goals as well as the value of the program. Critical to both the transition program and the evaluation is the *program theory* – the underlying model of how the program is expected to work or how change is expected to occur. Identifying the possible mechanism for change involved in an effective transition to school program can aid in both designing the program and focusing the evaluation. It leads to starting with what we expect to happen and then planning activities and practices to match that rather than starting with activities and seeking some way to justify these.

While identifying the program theory could look like a simple step to start the processes involved with implementing and evaluating programs, the chapters in this book remind us that there can be very different views of what constitutes a transition program, its purpose, how it should operate, whom it should serve, and how its effectiveness can be judged (see, for example, Chapter 8A). The chapters also highlight the importance of collaboration among stakeholders and the benefits of clarifying the purposes of the transition program and how the evaluation might address those purposes (see, for example, Chapters 4A, 9A). These processes can take time and present major challenges (for some examples of challenges and how they have been overcome, see Dockett & Perry, 2014). However, working through these to establish some taken-as-shared principles and ideas is central to effective evaluation. Working without consensus or at cross purposes means that mixed messages and confusion may take the place of a coherent program or evaluation strategy.

Building evaluation into program design and implementation

Typically, evaluation has been positioned as something that occurs at the end of a program. This form of summative evaluation (Chapter 4) is most often associated with establishing the outcomes or impact of a program. Large-scale external evaluations often draw on summative approaches to determine whether programs should be supported, maintained, or scaled up for further implementation. These evaluations are valuable and contribute much to the corpus of studies identifying effective programs. However, formative evaluation approaches and process evaluations (Chapter 4) may be more accessible to those involved in locally based evaluations and offer a range of evidence not only about program outcomes but also about implementation choices during the program that are responsive to people and place. Whatever the form of evaluation to be undertaken, it is most likely to be effective if it forms part of the planning process.

Planning the evaluation provides opportunities to consider what data might be generated, as well as the people and resources involved. It also sets up evaluation as part of the ongoing cycle of program design, development, implementation, and evaluation. In doing so, evaluation planning can contribute to building a culture that supports evidence-informed practice by valuing critical thinking and reflexivity and creating spaces for listening to and respecting multiple perspectives, including those of children (Chapters 6, 6A, and 9).

However, planning should not stop once the evaluation has been completed. It is important to build in time to reflect on the results and the ways in which this information will be used to inform future programs or practices. If no noticeable change or no explanation comes from the evaluation, participants are likely to feel that their efforts have gone unheeded and that future engagement in evaluating transition is pointless.

Involving a range of stakeholders

Just as collaboration can support effective evaluation strategies, participation underpins many evaluations of transition to school programs. Transition programs and evaluation strategies afford opportunities for the involvement of a range of stakeholders, including children, families, educators, other professionals, and community members. Apart from the value of including multiple perspectives of transition, the involvement of multiple stakeholders spreads the workload, often making the evaluation more manageable and responsive than if it were the responsibility of an individual or very small group.

In recent years, increased attention has been paid to considering children's perspectives, recognising that they are active participants in their transition and have the right to be consulted about their experiences and expectations (Dockett, Einarsdóttir, & Perry, 2019). However, the involvement of families as transition and evaluation partners has received less attention, despite acknowledgements that educators and families working together can be beneficial for all concerned (Dockett, Griebel, & Perry, 2017). Even less attention has been paid to involving other professionals and/or school personnel as transition and evaluation partners, despite some impressive collaborations involving multi-disciplinary teams (Iverson et al., 2006; Nolan, Kilderry, & Chu, 2019; Sarja, Poikonen, & Nilsson, 2012), supporting Indigenous children, families, and communities (Barblett et al., 2020; Mason-White, 2013, 2014), and children and families experiencing disadvantage and/or disability (Curle et al., 2017; Davis, Ravenscroft, & Bizas, 2015; Krakouer et al., 2017; Smart et al., 2008; Wilder & Lillvist, 2017). These examples affirm the view that "strong and respectful cross-sector relationships generate the space for educators to share their expertise and to negotiate critical understandings of effective and appropriate practice across the transition to school" (Dockett & Einarsdóttir, 2017, p. 146).

One of the benefits and also one of the challenges of collaboration is that it introduces multiple perspectives and multiple understandings of transition. When these different views emerge in contexts in which stakeholders are supported to examine, reflect on, and seek to improve their own practice and interactions, they can be transformative by generating new ways of being and doing as well as challenging practices and approaches that are unintended or unjust (Chapter 7A). However, for this to occur, there is a need for leadership.

Leadership in evaluating transition to school programs

While "little research has been done on the direct effects of leadership on transitions" (Organisation for Economic Co-operation and Development (OECD), 2017, p. 95), there is considerable evidence of the link between effective leadership in ECEC settings and schools and positive educational outcomes (Australian Children's Education and Care Quality Authority, 2017; Fullan, 2006; Siraj-Blatchford & Manni, 2007). The importance of leadership is also highlighted in Chapters 3A, 4A, and 8. Arguing that the leadership of transition initiatives rests largely with school principals and ECEC centre leaders, the OECD advocates for these people to be both highly skilled and responsive to issues around transition.

This position reflects traditional perspectives of leaders and leadership in schools as focused on the attributes of individuals and their actions associated with the performance of their role (principal, assistant principal, executive). The equivalent in ECEC settings may be the director or pedagogical leader. From this perspective, leadership is vested in an individual who occupies a specific position. There is some evidence that a dynamic educational leader is important in achieving the synergies among people that are necessary for successful initiatives (Brooker, 2008; Dockett & Perry, 2007; National Education Goals Panel, 1998). However, the notion that top-down leadership is the most effective way to drive change has been challenged for some time (Hargreaves & Shirley, 2020), particularly in ECEC contexts (Nicholson et al., 2020; Waniganayake et al., 2017). Replacing these have been discussions of distributed leadership (Heikka, Waniganayake, & Hujala, 2012), collective leadership (Gibbs, 2020), and leading from the middle (Hargreaves & Shirley, 2020).

In one of the few studies investigating leadership and transition to school, Boyle and Wilkinson (2018) emphasise the concept of leading as practice. This exploration draws on the theory of practice architectures (Kemmis & Grootenboer, 2008), which emphasises the context-based nature of practices that occur withing specific sites. In describing leading practices for transition to school, Boyle and Wilkinson (2018) argue that this framework provides a productive way to explore the building of shared understandings around policies and practices of transition to school.

There is little doubt that the support of the designated leader, be it the school principal or ECEC director, is central to efforts to optimise transition to school programs. It is also clear that these leaders fill major roles in building understanding of the importance and nature of transition and committing to developing responsive transition programs (see, for example, Hand, 2014; Chapter 8 of this book). However, effective leadership in transitions is likely to rest with a range of people who undertake different roles and engage in different practices at different times. Brooker (2008, p. 154) summarises this in her concluding comment that "in supporting transitions, we all need to be early childhood leaders".

Learning from success and failure

Chapter 4 discussed several possible purposes for evaluating transition to school programs. Underlying each of these is a commitment to improving the program in some way. Often, we look for evidence of what seems to work well and consider improvement to mean that we continue these practices either in their current form or with some minor amendments. However, there will be times when the evidence indicates that a program or practice has unintended consequences, is unfair or unjust, or is not supporting the program theory. It may also be that some practices have become taken for granted, and the original rationale for them has been lost or changed. Evaluation processes undertaken in contexts that support reflexivity may well result in some practices being adapted or omitted from future iterations of the program. Rather than considering this a failure, it can be seen as promoting an evidence-informed approach to transition: it recognises that transition programs need to be flexible and responsive; not everything will work for all participants at all times; and transition programs will change as those involved and their contexts change.

Potential benefits of evaluation

We choose to conclude this book by recognising that evaluating transition to school programs can be challenging but arguing that there are also many potential benefits. There are the possible pitfalls of additional stress in working with others to generate and analyse evidence and in utilising this to inform future programs. Sometimes, there is also the challenge of advocating for the importance of transition programs when there seem to be so many other priorities for children, families, communities, and educators. Despite these, there can be genuine excitement as people share stories of addressing challenges, strategies used to develop engaging and responsive programs, and evidence of effectiveness. There are many benefits when participants feel that they have been listened to and that their input has contributed to change. Strengthening connections with stakeholders and building communities of practice can be linked to the processes of evaluation. When these create climates of trust and respect, there are opportunities for critical thinking and reflexivity to flourish. One of the most powerful benefits is the collective advocacy that comes from groups working together to strengthen transition to school programs for all. Our aim in compiling this book has been to contribute to this process.

References

Atiles, J., Almodóvar, M., Vargas, A. C., Dias, M. J., & Zúñiga León, I. M. (2021). International responses to COVID-19: Challenges faced by early childhood professionals. *European Early Childhood Education Research Journal, 29*(1), 66–78. https://doi.org/10.1080/1350293X.2021.1872674

Australian Children's Education and Care Quality Authority. (2017). *Occasional paper 5: Leadership and management in education and care services.* Sydney: ACECQA. www.acecqa.gov.au/acecqas-occasional-paper-5-quality-area-7

Barblett, L., Barratt-Pugh, C., Knaus, M., & Cooper, T. (2020). Supporting Aboriginal families' and children's developing sense of belonging at KindiLink. *Australasian Journal of Early Childhood, 46*(4), 309–321. https://doi.org/10.1177/1836939120966079

Boyle, T., & Wilkinson, J. (2018). Two worlds, one site: Leading practices and transitions to school. *Journal of Educational Administration and History*, *50*(4), 325–342. https://doi.org/10.1080/00220620.2018.1510384

Brooker, L. (2008). *Supporting transitions in the early years*. Maidenhead, Berkshire: Open University.

Clifford, E. (1963). Social visibility. *Child Development*, *34*, 799–808. https://doi.org/10.2307/1126773

Curle, D., Jamieson, J., Poon, B. T., Buchanan, M., Norman, N., & Zaidman-Zait, A. (2017). Working together: Communication between stakeholders during the transition from early intervention to school for children who are deaf or hard of hearing. *Exceptionality Education International*, *17*(2), 54–71. https://doi.org/10.5206/eei.v27i2.7752

Davis, J., Ravenscroft, J., & Bizas, N. (2015). Transition, inclusion and partnership: Child-, parent- and professional-led approaches in a European research project. *Child Care in Practice*, *21*(1), 33–49. https://doi.org/10.1080/13575279.2014.976543

Dayal, H. C., & Tiko, L. (2020). When are we going to have the real school? A case study of early childhood education and care teachers' experiences surrounding education during the COVID-19 pandemic. *Australasian Journal of Early Childhood*, *45*(5), 336–347. https://doi.org/10.1177/1836939120966085

Dockett, S., & Einarsdóttir, J. (2017). Continuity and change as children start school. In N. Ballam, B. Perry, & A. Garpelin (Eds.), *Pedagogies of educational transitions. European and antipodean research* (pp. 133–150). Dordrecht: Springer. https://doi.org/10.1007/978-3-319-43118-5_9

Dockett, S., Einarsdóttir, J., & Perry, B. (Eds.). (2019). *Listening to children's advice about starting school and school age care*. London: Routledge. https://doi.org/10.4324/9781351139403

Dockett, S., Griebel, W., & Perry, B. (2017). Transition to school: A family affair. In S. Dockett, W. Griebel, & B. Perry (Eds.), *Families and the transition to school* (pp. 1–18). Cham, Switzerland: Springer. https://doi.org/10.1007/978-3-319-58329-7_1

Dockett, S., & Perry, B. (2007). *Transitions to school: Perceptions, expectations and experiences*. Sydney: University of New South Wales Press.

Dockett, S., & Perry, B. (2014). *Continuity of learning: A resource to support effective transition to school and school age care*. Canberra, ACT: Australian Government Department of Education. https://docs.education.gov.au/system/files/doc/other/pdf_with_bookmarking_-_continuity_of_learning-_30_october_2014_1_0.pdf

Dockett, S., & Perry, B. (2021). Invisible transitions: Transitions to school following different paths. *Australasian Journal of Early Childhood*. https://doi.org/10.1177/18369391211009698

Dunlop, A.-W. (2014). Thinking about transitions – One framework or many? Populating the theoretical model over time. In B. Perry, S. Dockett, & A. Petriwskyj (Eds.), *Transitions to school: International research policy and practice* (pp. 31–46). Dordrecht: Springer. https://doi.org/10.1007/978-94-007-7350-9_3

Fullan, M. (2006). *Turnaround leadership*. San Francisco, CA: Jossey-Bass.

Gibbs, L. (2020). "That's your right as a human, isn't it?" The emergence and development of leading as a social-just practice in early childhood education. *Australasian Journal of Early Childhood*, *45*(4), 295–308. https://doi.org/10.1177/1836939120966093

Hand, R. (2014). *Great Start, Great Futures: Engaging local partnerships in a framework for transition.* Paper presented to the 2014 ECA conference, Melbourne: 5–6 September. https://2019.ecaconference.com.au/wp-content/uploads/2014/09/Hand-Rebecca.pdf

Hargreaves, A., & Shirley, D. (2020). Leading from the middle: Its nature, origins and importance. *Journal of Professional Capital and Community, 5*(1), 92–114. https://doi.org/10.1108/JPCC-06-2019-0013

Heikka, J., Waniganayake, M., & Hujala, E. (2012). Contextualising distributed leadership within early childhood education: Current understandings, research evidence and future challenges. *Educational Management Administration and Leadership, 41*(1), 30–44. https://doi.org/10.1177/1741143212462700

Iverson, S., Ellertsen, B., Joacobsen, S., Råheim, M., & Knivsberg, A.-M. (2006). Developing a participatory multidisciplinary team approach to enhance the quality of school start. *Action Research, 4*(3), 271–293. https://doi.org/10.1177/1476750306066802

Kemmis, S., & Grootenboer, P. (2008). Situating praxis in practice: Practice architectures and the cultural, social and material conditions for practice. In S. Kemmis & T. Smith (Eds.), *Enabling praxis: Challenges for education* (pp. 37–62.) Rotterdam: Sense Publishers. https://doi.org/10.1163/9789087903275_004

Krakouer, J., Mitchell, P., Trevitt, J., & Kochanoff, A. (2017). *Early years transitions: Supporting children and families at risk of experiencing vulnerability: Rapid literature review.* Department of Education and Training, Victoria. https://research.acer.edu.au/cgi/viewcontent.cgi?article=1015&context=early_childhood_misc

Lago, L. (2017). Different transitions: Timetable failures in the transition to school. *Children & Society, 31*, 243–252. https://doi.org/10.1111/chso.12176

Mason-White, H. (2013). *Supporting transition to school for Aboriginal and Torres Strait Islander children.* Melbourne: SNAICC. www.snaicc.org.au/wp-content/uploads/2016/01/03193.pdf

Mason-White, H. (2014). *The journey to big school. Supporting Aboriginal and Torres Strait Islander children's transition to primary school.* Melbourne: SNAICC. www.snaicc.org.au/wp-content/uploads/2016/01/03316.pdf

National Education Goals Panel. (1998). *Ready schools.* Washington, DC: Author. http://govinfo.library.unt.edu/negp/reports/readysch.pdf

Nicholson, J., Kuhl, K., Maniates, H., Lin, B., Bonetti, S. (2020). A review of the literature on leadership in early childhood: Examining epistemological foundations and considerations of social justice. *Early Child Development and Care, 190*(2), 91–122. https://doi.org/10.1080/03004430.2018.1455036

Nolan, A., Kilderry, A., & Chu. C. (2019). Cross-sectoral professional relationships and transition to school: An Australian study. *Early Years.* https://doi.org/10.1080/09575146.2019.1617250

Organisation for Economic Cooperation and Development (OECD). (2017). *Starting strong V. Transitions from early childhood education and care to primary education.* Paris: OECD Publishing. https://doi.org/10.1787/9789264276253-en

Park, E., Loghan, H., Zhang, L., Kamigaichi, N., & Kulapcihitr, U. (2020). Responses to coronavirus pandemic in early childhood services across five countries in the Asia-Pacific region: OMEP Policy Forum. *International Journal of Early Childhood, 52*, 249–266. https://doi.org/10.1007/s13158-020-00278-0

Pascal, C., & Bertram, T. (2021). What do young children have to say? Recognising their voices, wisdom, agency and need for companionship during the COVID pandemic. *European Early Childhood Education Research Journal*, 29(1), 21–34. https://doi.org/10.1080/1350293X.2021.1872676

Pramling Samuelsson, I., Wagner, J., & Ødegaard, E. (2020). The coronavirus pandemic and lessons learned in preschools in Norway, Sweden and the United States: OMEP Policy Forum. *International Journal of Early Childhood*, 52, 129–144. https://doi.org/10.1007/s13158-020-00267-3

Sarja, A., Poikonen, P.-L., & Nilsson, M. (2012). Interprofessional collaboration in supporting transition to school. In P. Tynjälä, M.-L. Stenström, & M. Saarnivaara (Eds.), *Transitions and transformations in learning and education* (pp. 87–101). Dordrecht: Springer. https://doi.org/10.1007/978-94-007-2312-2_6

Siraj-Blatchford, I., & Manni, L. (2007). *Effective leadership in the early years sector: The ELEYS study*. London: Institute of Education, University of London.

Smart, D., Sanson, A., Baxter, B., Edwards, B., & Hayes, A. (2008). *Home-to-school transitions for financially disadvantaged children. Final report*. Sydney. The Smith Family and Australian Institute of Family Studies. www.thesmithfamily.com.au/-/media/files/research/reports/home-school-full-2008.pdf?la=en&hash=732D9B6AF03B74A4A20BAED828E09588

Waniganayake, M., Cheeseman, S., Fenech, M., Hadley, F., & Shepherd, W. (2017). *Leadership: Contexts and complexities in early childhood education* (2nd ed.). Oxford: Oxford University Press.

Wilder, J., & Lillvist, A. (2017). Collaboration in transition from preschool. Young children with intellectual disabilities. In N. Ballam, B. Perry, & A. Garpelin (Eds.), *Pedagogies of educational transition: European and antipodean research* (pp. 59–75). Dordrecht: Springer. https://doi.org/10.1007/978-3-319-43118-5_5

Index

Page numbers in *italics* indicate a figure and page numbers in **bold** indicate a table on the corresponding page.

Aboriginal and Torres Strait Islander 24, 73, 85, 171
academic skills 21, 41, 135, 142
Ackesjö, H. 17, 20, 21, 30, 39
action research: participatory 79–81; critical 161
Adams, J. 170
adults' perspectives, program evaluation: consultation 143–146; data generation 147–158; different from children's 112, 127; ethical considerations 131, 158–159; expectations, feeding off 134; participatory evaluation 146–147; stakeholders and their involvement 141–143
Ahtola, A. 2, 20, 21, 53, 209
Albers, T. 215
Alexander, K. 49
Allen, D. 169
Allen, K. 42
Alldred, P. 130
analysis: conceptual frame for 27; criterion-based 52; needs 66–67; of data 95–96. 107, 126–129; sound 181
Anderson, B. 80, 157
anxiety 20, 113, 117
anxious: child 28; feeling 18
Arndt, A. 142
Arndt, P. 53
Arslan, G. 42
aspirations 5, 24, 42, 162, 173, 176, **178**, **180–82**,
Astbury, B. 75, 77, 92
asymmetrical power relations 161

Atiles, J. 221
attitudes: children's 76, 127, 155; pedagogical 210; professional 83, 211; school and learning 41, **55**; societal 22
audio-recording 105, 152, 162
Australian Children's Education and Care Quality Authority 225
Australian Curriculum, Assessment and Reporting Authority 101
Australian Institute of Family Studies 77
Austrian transition practices 2
awareness: adult 8; community 143; educator 86, 204, 222; of belonging 43

Backhaus, J. 209
Ball. S. 27
Barblett, L. 142, 224
Barnett, C. 98, 100, 158
Bassok, D. 21
Baumfield, V. 79, 146
BBPLC *see* Building Bridges Professional Learning Community (BBPLC)
belonging 42; axes of 43, **44**; cartography of 43; cultural 43, **45**; emotional 43, **45**; feeling of 48; legal 43, **47**; as marker, effective transition 42–43; moral/ethical 43, **47**; personal feelings of 43; personal sense of 42; physical 43, **46**; political 43, **47**; sense of 44, 73, 114, 115, 117–118, 118–122; social 43, **45**; spatial 43, **46**; spiritual 43, **47**;

temporal 43, **46**; transition to school 44–48, **45–47**
Bertram, T. 221
Besi, M. 51
Biesta, G. 27
Bigras, N. 20
bioecological systems theory 5, 15, 18, 54, 75, 186
Birch, S. 149
Bizas, N. 224
Board of Studies, NSW 201
Bogatz, A. 209
Bohan-Baker, M. 77
Bortz, J. 53
Bottrell, D. 110
Boyle, T. 18, 19, 21, 23, 39, 160, 163, 64, 225
Bradbury, H. 79, 80
Bradley, B. 44
brokerage role, children 20
Bronfenbrenner, U. 4, 5, 15, 18, 75
Brooker, L. 2, 225
Broström, S. 21, 48, 111
buddy/buddies 23, 24, 77, 111, 113–15, 117, *197*
Building Bridges Professional Learning Community (BBPLC) 160, 161; evidence 161, **162**; key learnings 164; principles 161; changing practices 162, 163; participants 161; questionnaires 162, 163
Büker, P. 20, 52

Camfield, L. 98, 100, 158
Canadian Homelessness Research Network 77
Caribbean children's readiness 133
categorisation, axes of belonging 43
Centre for Community Health 2
Centre for Equity and Innovation in Early Childhood (CEIEC) 39
Chan, W. 142
change 16; families 16; future programs planning 206–207; internal 16–17; parents/parental, roles and identities 16; and people feeling 18; role 16; theory of 74; and transition 15–18
Chard, S. 81
Charlesworth, R. 210
Charlotte Bühler Institut 2
Charmaz, K. 107, 128
Chen, H. 73
Child Family Community Australia Promising Practice Profiles 77

child permission *105*, 129; *see also* informed consent
children: advice about transition 81–82, 111, 113; cognitive skills 133; competence 8, 22, 111–112, 114, 130, 204; and educators 16, 81, 113; experiencing vulnerability 83, 84, 86; future learning 18, 49, 51–53; participation 112–14, 130, 131; preparation for school 53; preparedness 4, 21, 28, 133–35; with special educational needs 29, 53, 156, 187; well-being 41–43, 51, **179**
Chu, C. 224
Clark, H. 77
Clarke, C. 115, 130, 132, 136
Clifford, E. 222
cooperation: climate of 209, 212; co-constructional 212, 213, 215
coding: data 96, 107, **154**; framework 107, 128, 155
Coghlan, A. 78, 143
Cohen, L. 158
Coley, R. 25
collaboration among educators 21, 53, 56, 57, 86, 204, 224
Communication Diary Log *156*
communication: of evaluation results 195; preferred modes of 84, 156; between stakeholders 94, 151, 170, 189; reciprocal 41; strategy **47**, 68, 85, 87, 144,
communicative space 160
communities influence of 17; of practice 20, 69, 203, 226; role within transition programs 22, 49–50, 67, 177–80
preschool class 29
confidentiality 100, 105, 130, 150, 151, 159, 201, 202
confirmability of data 129
consent for participation 98, 104, 130
constructivist grounded theory 107, 128
consultation 112, 143–146
contact log 147–148, 156, **156**
content analysis 96, 154
context, importance of 4, 15, 18, 21–22, 25, 38, 40, 50, 53, 65, 74, 76–77, 94, 111, 183, 225; social and cultural 15, 18, 19, 21, 22, 26
continuity 18–19, 39, 142; and change 19–20, 50, 142, 221; of learning 39, 51, 160, **179**

Convention on the Rights of the Child 5, 111
conversational interviews 94, 105–106, 150–152
conversations 39, 71, 115–118, 143–144, 150, 163
Cook, K. 25
cooperation: among educators 52–58, 209, 213–216; areas 54; climate 216; co-construction 210, 212–213; curricular orientation 213–214; didactic approach 214–215; dimensions *211*; evaluation *212*; form 212; fruitful and sustainable 216; levels 209–210; self-evaluation instrument 52–58
cooperative pedagogy 215
Correia, K. 62, 142
Corsaro, W. 15, 22, 110
Corter, C. 170
Cousins, B. 79
Cousins, J. 79
COVID-19 challenges and evaluation planning 102, 104, 107
Cowan, P. 15, 17
Cox, M. 18, 64
Crane, P. 80
credibility of analysis 129, 158
critical friend 69
critical reflection 129
critical theory 161
Curle, D. 224
curricular orientation 213–214
curriculum 51; alignment, continuity 39, 187, 189, 205

Danish transition practices 2
Darling Downs South West 173–174
Darling Heights State School *196*
data, analysis 95–96; 107, 126–128; generation 65, 94–96, 150
David, M. 130
Davies, J. 155
Davis, J. 224
Dayal, H. 221
de Bono, E. 154
democratisation of knowledge 80
Denzin, N. 128
Department for Education and Child Development, South Australia 147, 169
Department of Education and Early Childhood Development 92, 200

Department of Education and Skills (DES) 186
Department of Education and Training, Victoria 23, 185, 199
Department of Education, Skills and Employment (DESE) 42, 51
Department of Health and Human Services, Tasmania 195
dependability 129
Dickinson, P. 170
Dickson, R. 75
Diem, K. 150
disposition 112, 127, 155, 186–187
diversity: of children's experiences 130–131; of stakeholders 79, 95; respect for 174
documentation/documenting 115, 152, 157, 181, 187; conversations 115; group events 152–154
Dodge, K. 25, 49
Döring, N. 53
Dowling, M. 129
Dufour, R. 161
Dunlop, A.-W. 2, 4, 15, 18–19, 40, 111, 129, 160, 209, 221

Early Years Learning Framework for Australia (EYLF) 42
Ecological and Dynamic Model of Transition 4, 18
ecological model 18, 25
Education Review Office 3, 200, 205
educational environment 127, 155
Educational Transitions and Change (ETC) Research Group 5, 21, 41, 105, 157, 173
Edwards, A. 3, 21
Edwards, R. 130
effective transition 2, 20, 25, 42, 48–51, 54, 74–76, 112, 142, 202, 221, 224
Einarsdóttir, J. 18–20, 25, 39–40, 81–82, 94, 110–111, 113–115, 128, 130, 132, 136, 142, 148, 164, 224,
Elliott, S. 149
Emotional: attachment 42; belonging 43, **45**
engagement levels 112
entitlements 5, 42, 173, 176, **180**, 181
Entwisle, D. 49
equity 2, 20, 22
Erzieher see educators
ethical approaches in evaluation 98, 100, 104, 150, 158–159;

202; challenges 69–70; children's perspectives 130–131; sharing findings 208; valuing diversity 81
evaluation: definitions 64–65; external 65, 69, 72, 100, 102–103; frameworks 73–75; evidence of impact model 75–76, 76; needs analysis 66–67; outcome evaluation 69–73; participatory action research (PAR) 79–81; participatory evaluation 78–79; practitioner inquiry 79; process and outcome 72–73; process evaluation 67–69, 72–73; project approach 81–82; promising practices 76–78; purposes 65–66; transition to school programs 65; types 66
expectations 48, 103, 176, **179**; diversity 3, 16, 131, 163; of primary school 16, 71, 97, 132

Fabian, H. 2, 209
face-to-face interaction 150–151
familiarity with school 74, **75**, 102, 114–115, 117–118, 124
families 20: changes experienced at transition 16–18, 142, 155, 182, *182*; sharing findings 198, *199,* as stakeholders in evaluation 141–147; 224
Faust, G. 53
feedback 3, 49, 67, 107, 150,
feeling/feelings: anxious 18; of belonging 48, 51; comfortable **45**, 107; connected **46**; safe and secure 107; scared 128; suitable 48; supported 220
Fenton, A. 20
Fink, A. 150
Finnish transition practices 2
first day of school 16–17, 19, 26, 112
First Five: A Whole-of-Government Strategy for Babies, Young Children and their Families 2019–2028 190
Flick, U. 163
Flottman, R. 174
focus groups 84–85, 152, 194
formative evaluations 67, 69, 223
formative self-evaluation 53–54
former kindergarten child 17
Fournier, D. 64
frameworks: for action 74; coding 107, 155; *Evidence of Impact Model* 75, 76; for evaluating cooperation 211, *211*;
for evaluating effective transitions 40–42, 73–74, **172**, 174; interpretive 114; for promising practices 77; for promoting participatory evaluation 79
frequency count 149–150
Friedman, D. 142
friends/friendship 42, 107, 113, 127, 135, **172, 179**, 189
Fullan, M. 225
functional linkages 160
Fußangel, K. 53, 210

Garvis, S. 77
Giallo, R. 70
Gibbs, L. 225
Gill, S. 142
global knowledge assessments 30
Goodenow, C. 42
Goonellabah Transition Program 93–94
Gorrell, J. 142
Government of Ireland 190
Grady, K. 42
Graham, A. 74, 93, 129
Gräsel, C. 53, 54, 210, 213, 216
Graue, E. 22
Great Start Great Futures Early Years Transition Project 173
Grenner, K. 210
Gresham, F. 149
Griebel, W. 5, 16, 18, 20, 40, 53, 54, 142, 209, 224
Grieshaber, S. 18, 39, 163, 164
Grob, G. 204
Grootenboer, P. 225
Groundwater-Smith, S. 110, 115, 163
Guba, E. 128, 158
Gubrium, A. 128
Guidelines for Effective Transition to School Programs 7, 40, 91, 148
Guijt, I. 78

Habermas, J. 160, 161
Hall, E. 79, 146
Hammarström-Lewenhagen, B. 28
Hand, R. 173, 225
Hanke, P. 209
Hard, N. 158
Hargreaves, A. 225
Harlacher, J. 150
Harms, A. 66
Harper, K. 128
Harper, L. 75
Harris-Mortley, S. 132, 133

Harrison, L. 115
Harvey, H. 142
Heikka, J. 225
Heim, D. 54
high-intensity practices 25
high-quality evaluation 65
Hinton, S. 143
Hirst, M. 39
Højslet Schürer, M. 206
Höke, J. 20, 52, 53, 55
Holly, P. 52
Hopps(-Wallis), K. 3, 20, 21, 156, 185
horizontal transitions 18, 220
Howard, P. 170
Huberman, A. 154
Huf, C. 20
Hujala, E. 225
Human Research Ethics Committee 98, 103
Huser, C. 53
Hustedt, J. 142, 143

identity: changing 2, 16, 38, 119; construction 16–17, 19; school 16, 51
impact assessment 69
Index of Community Socioeducational Advantage (ICSEA) 101
Indicators of Progress ECEC 148, 171–172, **172**, 176
informed consent 104–105, 130, 158
initial teacher education (ITE) 86, 190
intensity of contact 25, 210
intensive cooperation 55–56, 213, 215
internal changes 16–17
interpreter 50, 85, 94, 98, 141–142, 159
interprofessional interaction 216
interviews 94, 143–144, 147, 150–152
invisible transitions 221–222
Iverson, S. 224

Jadue-Roa, D. 20, 115
James, A. 5, 15
Jenks, C. 5, 15
Jensen, D. 129
Joerdens, S. 43, 110
Johansson, E. 42, 43
joint meetings **56**, 108; pedagogy 58; professional learning **24**, 77, 189; strategies 210
Juutinen, J. 42

Kagan, S. 2
Karila, K. 3, 21
Katz, I. 72, 73
Katz, L. 81
Kearney, E. 2
Keller, E. 213
Kemmis, S. 80, 160, 161, 225
KidsMatter 147, 169
Kienig, A. 2, 210
Kilderry, A. 224
Kinkead-Clark, Z. 132, 133
Kipp, K. 53
Kirk-Downey, T. 143
knowledge 18, 21, 79, 127, 155, 186; democratisation 81; efficiency 30
Kogen, Y. 81
Kraft-Sayre, M. 23, 25, 147, 148
Krakouer, J. 224
Kratzmann, J. 53
Kumpulainen, K. 115, 132, 136,
Kvale, S. 163

Ladd, G. 149
Lago, L. 20, 37, 222
Lansdown, G. 111, 112, 143, 146
Lanzi, R. 41
Latham, S. 21
Laurin, I. 20
Lauter, L. 23
Lawrence, F. 142
leadership 224–225, role of schools 174
leading as practice 225
learning 22; children's 3, 41; continuity of 18–19, 39, 51, 160; impact of transition 49, 51; professional **24**, 72, 86, 146, 203–204
Lee, N. 29
Lee, P. 158
legal belonging 43, **47**
Lehrer (teacher) 53
Lehrer, J. 20
Lembens, A. 213
Leo-Rhynie, E. 133
Lernwerkstatt (Open Inquiry Learning Workshop) 213
liaison officers 141–142
Liamputtong, P. 202
Lillejord, S. 2, 19, 20, 21
Lillvist, A. 20, 224
Lin, H. 142
Lincoln, Y. 128, 158
Linking Schools and Early Years project 72

literacy 4, 21, 150, 163
Little, M. 26
Little, P. 77
Lloyd, J. 38
LoCasale-Crouch, J. 20, 26, 49, 209
logic model 38, 74, 78, 92
Luluquisen, M. 78
Lundy, L. 112, 131

Maden, M. 75
Malone, P. 25, 49
Manion, L. 158
Manni, L. 225
Margetts, K. 2, 26, 142, 210
Marques-Pinto, A. 40, 142
Mashburn, A. 49
Mason, T. 171
Mason-White, H. 24, 201, 224
Mathison, S. 67
maturational theory 21–22
maturity 132, 134; school 28–29
McAteer, M. 81
McDonnell, L. 200
McKernan, A. 174
McLeod, N. 80, 157
McTaggart, R. 80, 161
mechanism for change 38, 74, 75, 115, 148, 223
Meisels, S. 2, 22
mentor 69, 80, 143
Mertens, D. 64
Miles, M. 154
Miller, K. 20, 142, 151
Ministry for Children and Social Affairs 2
Ministry of Education and Culture, Finland 2
Ministry of Education and Research 2
Minott, C. 133
Mirkhil, M. 39, 132
Mitchell, S. 81
Mo Scéal 185, 189, 190
Mockler, N. 163
Molinari, L. 110
moral/ethical belonging 43, 47
Morris, P. 5, 15, 18, 75
Morrison, J. 66
Morrison, K. 158
Moss, P. 21, 22, 39
Murphy, R. 3, 25, 186
Murray, E. 115
mutual professional appreciation 56
mutual trust and respect 81, 143

narrative data 127; analysis 98, 107, 128, 154
National Council for Curriculum and Assessment (NCCA) 186; transition initiative 187–190
National Education Goals Panel 225
National Health and Medical Research Council 98
NCCA *see* National Council for Curriculum and Assessment (NCCA)
needs analysis 66–67, 93–94, 110, 143
Nergaard, K. 42, 43
nervousness 128
New South Wales Education Standards Authority 163
Newell, S. 74, 93
Nicholson, J. 225
Nickel, H. 209
Nicolson, D. 170
Niesel, R. 16, 40, 54, 142, 209
Nilsson, M. 224
Nixon, R. 80, 161
Nolan, A. 147, 205, 224
non-academic skills 142–143
Norwegian Directorate for Education and Training 2
NSW Department of Education 147, 169, 185
numeracy skills 4, 21, 163

O'Kane, M. 2, 3, 25, 186
O'Regan, M. 80
O'Sullivan, C. 133
observation 44, 68, 124, 157
Ødegaard, E. 221
Ohle, K. 142
Ólafsdóttir, S. 81, 82, 113
older children 82, 105–107, 111, 115, 129, *196*
one-size-fits-all approach 40, 76, 111
Open University's Children's Research Centre 114
opportunities 42, 102, 131, 143, **172**, 174, 176, **177**, 204, 207, 223, 224, 226
optimal transitions 39–40
Organisation for Economic Co-operation and Development (OECD) 2, 19, 26, 38, 64, 200, 224, 225
organisational adjustment/change 78, 126–127

orientation: curricular 213–214; pedagogical 211; programs 5, 22, 40, 67, 101, 147, 213
outcome evaluation 69–72; children's expectations and experiences 71; families survey 71; parent program 70; process and 72–73
Owen, J. 204

Packer, R. 39
Paderborner Qualitätsstern (PQ³) 53, 57; pedagogical activities with children 55; quality levels 54; roles of collaboration 57; roles of heads of educational institutions 56; structures within individual institutions 55–56; working in cooperation networks 56
Pálsdóttir, K. 20
Papadopoulou, M. 42
parent/parental: categories of response 126–127, 127; changes in roles and identities 16; consultation with 144; effective transition for 45–47; enhanced engagement 51; ethical considerations 158–159; information sessions 50, 68, 94; interactions with children 16; involvement, children's preparedness 133; notions of adjustment 127; of a school child 142; parent-initiated questionnaire 147; reporting to 200
Park, E. 221
participation choices 114, 130, 158
participation rights: adults, 112; children, 5, 111, 114
participatory action research (PAR) 79–81; critical 161
participatory evaluation 78–79, 81, 112–113, 143, 146–147, 194, 204
Pascal, C. 221
Patton, M. 96
Pawson, R. 74
Pears, K. 49
pedagogical-didactic aims 55, 55
pedagogical/pedagogy: alignment between preschool and school 187, 210; play-based 21, 189; traditions 52–53
performativity, axis of belonging 43
performing (obligated) pupil 30
performing school pupil 29
Peridot Education Transition Reflection Instrument 170–184, 177–180;
constructs 176; documenting progress 181–183, *182*; school profiles *184*; use 183–185, *184*
personal contact 25
personal reflections 96
personal sense of belonging 42, 44
personal sympathy 56
Persson, S. 21, 20, 39
Peters, S. 2, 20, 110,
Petriwskyj, A. 2, 3, 15, 21, 22, 39, 160, 164, 173
phases of transition 17, *17*
Phatudi, N. 142
Phillips, T. 201
photo elicitation 151
physical: belonging 43, **46**; category of response 127, 155; contexts 128, 163
Pianta, R. 4, 18, 22, 23, 25, 37, 50, 64, 147, 148, 149
planning evaluation: activities 94–95; data analysis 95–96, 107; data-generation phases 105–106; ethical considerations 98–100, 104–105; experiences of participants 107–108; focus 93–94, 103–104; information booklet for children 99; purpose 92–93, 101–103; reporting results *97*, 97–98, 107; synthesis 95–96
playful child 30
Poikonen, P.-L. 224
political belonging 43, **47**
Ponizovsky-Bergelson, Y. 133
positive transition 39; as a predictor 186
Powell, M. 129
power 204; imbalances 84, 161; in transition 17, 22; relationships 79, 98, 100, 130, 158
PQ³ *see* Paderborner Qualitätsstern (PQ³)
practice architectures 161, 225
practice review 83–87
practitioner inquiry 79, 146–147
Pramling Samuelsson, I. 221
preference for involvement 94, 104–105
preschool class (Sweden) 29
privacy, ethical principles 100, 130, 208
problematic child 27, 30
Pröbstel, C. 53, 210
process evaluation 67–69, 104, 106, 223
processes of inquiry 65
program theory 39, 73–74, 77–78, 92, 148, 222–223

project approach 81
promising practices 76–77, 86, 205
Prout, A. 5, 15
Puddu, S. 213
Puroila, A.-M. 42
Purtell, K. 39

Queensland Department of Education 5, 147, 169, 174, **175**, 185
Queensland, developments in: *Great Start Great Futures Early Years Transition Project* 173; *School Decision-Making* matrix 174, **175**, 176; *Successful Transitions: School Decision-Making Tool* 174
questionnaires 71–73, 94, 147–150, 158, 188
Qvortrup, J. 130

Ramey, C. 41
Ramey, S. 41
Rantavuori, L. 3, 21
Rathmer, B. *211, 212*
rating scale *126,* 148–149
Ravenscroft, J. 224
readiness: ready children 23, 135; ready families 23; ready schools 23, 26, 174; ready communities 23; transition and 21–22; 53, 80, 203
realist evaluation 74–75
Reason, P. 80
reciprocal: relationships 174, **175**, 222; visits 74, 94
reflection 110, 119–123, *123–126,* 221
reflexivity 129, 204, 221, 226
Reid, A. 79, 146
Reineke, J. 22
reliability 158
Renner, M. 155
resistance and desire, axis of belonging 43
responsiveness 76, 100
rights: of children 15, 42, 111–112
rights-based practice 114, 173
Rimm-Kaufman, S. E. 4, 18, 22, 37, 50
Rinaldi, C. 112
Rogers, S. 174
Rogoff, B. 15, 38
role changes 16
Rorem, A. 21
Rosier, K. 80
Rossbach, G. 210

rubrics: definition 169; norming process 170; *Peridot Education Transition Reflection Instrument* 170–173, 176–185; strengths and weaknesses 170
rules 127; children's responses 107, 112, 127
Ryan, T. 42

Sagor, R. 79
Sakellariou, M. 51
Salmi, S. 115, 132, 136
Sandberg, G. 110
Sandseter, E. 43
Sarja, A. 224
Savaya, R. 38, 74
Schoepp, K. 170
School Decision-Making matrix 174, **175**, 176
School Decision-Making Tool 174
school visits: brainstorming sessions 116, *116, 152–153,* 154; children's perspectives of 114–118; what happens 74, 82
school-(im)mature child 28
schoolarisation 29–30, 39
schoolification 21, 39
Schulting, A. 25, 49
Schultz, T. 3
Scott, D. 98
Scull, J. 77
seamless transition 18, 39
Seland, M. 43
self-evaluation instrument *see* Paderborner Qualitätsstern (PQ[3])
self-initiated processes 113–114, 146
Semann and/& Slattery 68, 77, 92
Sharp, C. 110
Sharpe, P. 132, 136
Shirley, D. 225
siblings, contributors to transition programs 42, 48, 111, 189
Simon, M. 169, 170
Simpson, S. 128
Siraj-Blatchford, I. 225
Smart, D. 2, 224
Smart, J. 203
Smith, D. 132, 133
Smith, K. 77, 92, 205
Smithson, J. 152
smooth transition 20, 23, 28, 39, 48, 70
SNAICC 24, 73
Snow, K. 64

social belonging 43, **45**
social rejection and exclusion 43
Social Skills Rating System 149
social-emotional skills 23, 142
socio-cultural theories 22, 209
Soriano, G. 77
Southern Cross University's Centre for Children and Young People 114
Southworth, G. 52
Spalding, N. 201
spatial belonging 43, **46**
spiritual belonging 43, **47**
Stake, R. 164
stakeholders in transition 22, 44, 147: involvement in evaluation of transition programs 64–68; 78–79, 84; 94, 103, 141–143
Starting School Research Project 170–172
Steinberg, D. 38
Steinert, B. 216
Stratigos, T. 44
strengths-based 20, 22, 114, 201
Student-Teacher Relationship Scale 149
subjectification 27
successful transition 37–42, 49, 51, 212, 215
Successful Transitions: School Decision-Making Tool 174
SuccessWorks 92, 148
summative evaluation 69, 223
Sumsion, J. 7, 43, 44, **45–47**, 124
surveys and questionnaires 143–144, 150
Swedish state policy documents 27–29

Tanner, K. 169
Tarrant, K. 2
Tatalović Vorkapić, S. 39
Tatlow-Golden, M. 118
Tayler, C. 2, 174
Taylor-Powell, E. 155
Teacher Rating Scale for School Adjustment 149
telephone interviews 85, 104–105
temporal belonging 43, **46**
theory of change 73–74
Thorpe, K. 2
Tierney, R. 169, 170
Tietze, W. 210
Tiko, L. 221
Tilley, N. 74

timing: of transition practices 25, 144; of evaluation 106, 159, 206
Toronto First Duty Project 170
Tracey, D. 96, 170
transferability 128–129, 158
Transition to School: Position Statement 41–42, *106*, *157*, 173
Transition: A Positive Start to School Initiative 23, 68, 92
transition networks 3, 23, 44, **45**, 53, 56, 69, 73, 76, 86, 94, 146–147
transition to school statements 3; Australia 25, 92, 145–146; Ireland 185
transitions capital 18, 111, 129, 221
translated information 98, 142
Truscott, J. 129
trustworthiness 65, 128–129
Turunen, T. 20

UN *Convention on the Rights of the Child* 5, 111
United Nations 5, 15, 111
Urbina-Garcia, A. 39

valentine, K. 72, 73
validity 158
van Gennep, A. 15, 17, *17*
vertical transition 18, 220
Victorian Auditor-General 5
Victorian Department of Education and Training 23, 185, 199
Victorian Government 84
visual: data 107, 128; plans 74
Vitiello, V. 39
Vogt, F. 54
Voices of Children Expo 130
voluntary participation 98, 150, 158
vulnerability/vulnerable 83–87; 100, 202

Wagner, J. 221
Wall, K. 79, 146
Waniganayake, M. 225
Waters, L. 43
Watson, J. 77
Waysman, M. 38, 74
Weaver, L. 79
Wehner, F. 53
Weiss, C. 204
well-being 42, 43, 49, 51
Wenger, E. 20
West, S. 5, 169
Westhorp, G. 74

White, G. 110
Whitehead, J. 81
Whitmore, E. 79
Whitton, D. 171
Wilder, J. 20, 224
Wildgruber, A. 53
Wilhelm-Chapin, M. 38
Wilkinson, J. 160, 161, 225
Winters, D. 142
Wise, S. 77
Wong, M. 111

Wong, S. 7, 43, 44, **45–47**, 124
Woo. M. 23
Wood, L. 81

Yeboah, D. 39
Yeo, L. 115, 130
Yuval-Davis, N. 43

Zittoun, T. 15, 19
Zukoski, A. 78
Zumwald, B. 54

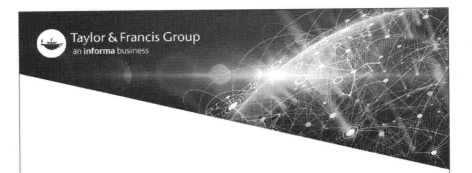